CANOECRAFT

CANOECRAFT
AN ILLUSTRATED GUIDE TO FINE WOODSTRIP CONSTRUCTION

TED MOORES

Photography by Jennifer Moores and Ted Moores
Illustrations by Ian Grainge
Lines and offsets by Steve Killing

FIREFLY BOOKS

A FIREFLY BOOK

Published by Firefly Books Ltd., 2000

Fourth Printing, 2006

National Library of Canada Cataloguing in Publication Data

Moores, Ted
          Canoecraft : an illustrated guide to fine woodstrip construction
Rev. & expanded ed.
ISBN-13: 978-1-55209-342-9   ISBN-10: 1-55209-342-5
1. Canoes and canoeing. 2. Boatbuilding, I. Simonds, Merilyn, 1946 – II: Title
VM353.M66 2000   623.8'29   C99-932437-3

Publisher Cataloging-in-Publication Data (U.S.)
(Library of Congress Standards)

Moores, Ted.
Canoecraft : an illustrated guide to fine woodstrip construction / Ted Moores and Merilyn Simonds; photography by Jennifer Moores and Ted Moores ; illustrations by Ian Grainge
Rev. & expanded ed.
[208] p. : ill. ; cm.
Includes bibliographical references and index.
Summary : Step-by-step illustrated guide to building a woodstrip canoe, including plans.
ISBN-13: 978-1-55209-342-9   ISBN-10: 1-55209-342-5
1. Canoes and canoeing. 2. Canoes and canoeing—Construction. I. Simonds, Merilyn   II. Moores, Jennifer.   III. Title.
623.8/ 12 —dc21   2000 CIP

Published in Canada by
Firefly Books Ltd.
66 Leek Cresent
Richmond Hill, Ontario L4B 1H1

Published in the United States by
Firefly Books (U.S.) Inc.
P.O. Box 1338, Ellicott Station
Buffalo, New York 14205

Produced by
Bookmakers Press Inc.
12 Pine Street
Kingston, Ontario K7K 1W1
(613) 549-4347
tread@sympatico.ca

Design by
Ulrike Bender, Studio Eye

Cover: A contemporary woodstrip/epoxy canoe (background) mirrors the lines of its turn-of-the-century forerunner. Photograph © Jim Merrithew.

Printed and bound in Canada by Friesens, Altona, Manitoba

Printed on acid-free paper

The Publisher acknowledges the financial support of the Government of Canada through the Book Publishing Industry Development Program for its publishing activities.

This book is dedicated to Jim Barrett, whose understanding and support made the development of the Bear Mountain Boat Shop possible.

CONTENTS

I SAW MY FIRST WOODSTRIP CANOE IN 1971, almost 30 years ago. I was working as a freelance commercial artist in downtown Toronto, Ontario, and was looking for a way out of the city and out of the job. Every weekend, I would drive north, up Highway 11, and as I drove through the little village of Trout Creek, I'd see a couple of beautiful wooden canoes stretched out on the lawn of a fellow I eventually came to know, Ross Ellery. Ross had started out building strip-planked/polyester-resin/fiberglass-reinforced marathon canoes for his own use, and before he knew it, he was in the canoe business.

Being a dreamer, I didn't find it hard to visualize a peaceful life in cottage country, building beautiful boats for people who would line up at the door, with money in hand, begging for one of my swift little craft. It pays to be naive: a person can do a lot when he doesn't know any better.

I began building boats in 1972 in Gravenhurst, Ontario, but after only two years of life at Sundance Canoes, where I discovered the hard reality of operating a laborintensive craft business on my own, I sold the business to Greavette Boats and escaped

even farther from the big city to a hilltop, known as Bear Mountain, on the northern edge of Algonquin Park.

When I sold Sundance, I was already having worries about the instability of the polyester-resin system I was using, but I hadn't lost the boatbuilding dream. Perhaps it was the blood of seafaring ancestors in my veins. It certainly wasn't my upbringing: I was a city boy who had worked every summer since the age of 9, missing out on the usual Canadian boy's introduction to canoes at summer camp.

After learning about the epoxy resins being developed by the Gougeon Brothers and reading in John Wilson's *Woodenboat Magazine* about the wooden-boat revival in the eastern United States, I decided to give boatbuilding another try. My partner Joan Barrett and I were still looking for a way to earn a satisfying living in the country working for ourselves. We built a stone house with a workshop attached and named the business the Bear Mountain Boat Shop, a name that has stuck through half a dozen moves, first to Bancroft, then south to Peterborough, the heartland of Canada's historic canoebuilders.

I started as a builder of canoes

and added boat restoration as I became more and more interested in the history of the craft. Now I spend my time building 30-foot racing canoes, producing plans for amateur builders, preparing books, teaching wooden-boat building and helping out at the Canadian Canoe Museum. Over the years, I have met a lot of amateur builders, both those who have bought *Canoecraft* and those who have signed up to build a boat with me.

When I think about it, the faces of so many of these people come back to me: the airline pilot who was scheduled for a second triple bypass and wanted to leave something of himself to each of his five daughters; the administrator of a juvenile correctional institution who started building a boat in his

office to relieve the stress and, before long, was approached by his rebellious clients, who crowded into his office, asking questions, offering to help; the family that came, three generations at once, to build a boat together. I've taught people as young as 11 and as old as 87, and if I've learned anything, it's that anyone with the proper attention span can do it.

Most of these builders are motivated, at least in part, by a dream. Many have been harboring the urge to build something beautiful for decades, while they raised children and pursued careers, and only now, at retirement age, are they in the position to do something for themselves.

I am always amazed at the number of people who find the decision to build a small boat a pivotal point in their lives. Maybe this is because building a good boat has all the components of a life under control. Working through the building, step by step, from thoughtful preparation and careful execution to the reward of a finished boat is a pattern of living that makes sense. Learning to respond to and to work in harmony with materials can tell us something about getting along with ourselves and others. Finding a fair curve requires looking at a line from many different perspectives before making up your mind —not a bad life lesson either, when you think about it.

Because of the attention to detail I recommend in these pages, a reader might be inclined to take me for a perfectionist. But the truth is that after more than 27 years of building wooden boats, I have yet to build one that wouldn't be different next time. Perfection is a journey. The point for me— and I hope for you—is to take pleasure in where you are today, believing that it will be somewhere else tomorrow.

Looking back over the years, I can see that my initial inexperience has in many ways proved an asset. I started building boats with a technique that was still in the experimental stage. I had no woodworking or boatbuilding experience, which meant that the learning curve was slow and frustratingly steep at times; but the solutions I eventually worked out for myself were ones that produced good results in the shortest time, using common sense and simple tools. Had I been a boatbuilder by trade, or an engineer, the system I developed would not have been as accessible to amateur builders like myself.

The rightness of my approach lies in this book, which has been continuously in print for more than 15 years. It was ahead of its time when I first wrote it with my friend and northern neighbor Merilyn Mohr. When *Canoecraft* was published in 1983, little information was available on building woodstrip/epoxy canoes. The book quickly became the most used and most respected text on this method of canoe construction, accepted internationally as "the Bible of canoebuilding." It sold more than 100,000 copies in North America and in 1996 was translated into German.

Although it was updated regularly with each reprinting (the first edition went through 10 reprints), I eventually felt the need to update the text with new materials and tools and the techniques that I have learned over the years. I know a lot more about the craft of canoebuilding now than I did in 1983, and after a decade of teaching workshops, I have learned a few things myself.

Casual boatbuilders are better educated and more sophisticated than they used to be. Teaching kayak- and canoebuilding to about 100 students every year has given me a better idea of the skill level of the typical builder. A growing number of potential builders are about 50 years old, with the majority of these being professionals who need to occupy their time as their careers wind down. These people want concise information presented in a language they can understand. Even though their standards are high and they expect a lot of themselves, this is a vulnerable period in their lives. Instructions, I've discovered, must be complete enough that the boat they build will be of professional quality the first time.

In preparing this second edition, I have tried to offer something for the second-time builder too. I have included a larger variety of plans, many of them different from those in the first edition.

To avoid confusion, plans are now presented as a traditional table of offsets. I have added a series of builder's tips—tricks of the trade that those familiar with basic woodworking will especially appreciate. I have also included some new techniques—such as building a stapleless boat—and a whole new chapter on carving a paddle, the perfect accompaniment to your handmade canoe. Fans of the original *Canoecraft* will also notice that the book has been redesigned for easier reading and that the photographs have been reshot and now follow a single boat—a 16-foot Redbird—through every stage of construction.

I started building canoes with the assumption that a person can get professional results if good materials are used and simple steps are performed with care in the proper order. My techniques have evolved, as have the materials, but that basic assumption has always served me well— and, as you begin to build your boat from these pages, it will serve you well too.

—*Ted Moores*

CHAPTER 1

THE POOR MAN'S YACHT

Craftsmanship & Common Sense

IT IS NOT POSSIBLE TO PUT TOO MUCH QUALITY INTO A PLEASURE CRAFT, OR INDEED INTO ANY CRAFT THAT FLOATS.

—Walter Dean

He looked more like an exile from a MuchMusic video than a habitué of the dusty interior of a carpentry shop, and by all appearances, his fingers would be more familiar with joysticks than with random orbital sanders and circular saws. Among his possessions, the youth had but a single woodworking tool: a rubber-handled Canadian Tire hammer.

Little wonder, then, when barely suppressed guffaws greeted his announcement that as a summer project, he intended to convert the ruddy stack of wood strips piled behind his parent's garage into a canoe. The proposed vessel, he claimed, would not merely float but would comfortably handle the meanest rapids. What's more, this thoroughly functional watercraft would inspire praise normally reserved for a piece of handcrafted furniture.

With blissful disregard for naysayers, the youth removed the family car to a place under the trees, where it became subject to the whims of passing thunder-heads and pigeons. He called in outstanding favors with the next-door neighbors to augment his tool collection. And by the time the first hints of red appeared on the maples, he was enjoying leisurely paddles in his own woodstrip/ epoxy canoe. In place of the earlier cries of derision, he was now greeted with, "That belongs in the living room, lad, not on the lake."

What makes this youth's story heartening for anyone contemplating building a woodstrip/ epoxy canoe is that he is far from being the least likely would-be boatbuilder to have transformed pipe dreams, eagerness and a healthy dollop of sheer naïveté into a canoe whose classic lines and warm-hued natural wood finish make it as much a work of art as a boat.

During the same three months the youth spent bent over the emerging form of his canoe in his parents' Ontario garage, a doctor from Saskatchewan, a septuage-narian in California and a New York State man who was legally blind all proved that anyone who has a dozen spare weekends, about $1,000 for materials and the requisite patience can create his or her own woodstrip master-piece. This has been borne out by dozens of backyard builders who, like the youth, doctor, septuage-narian and New York State man, constructed woodstrip canoes from kits they purchased from the Bear Mountain Boat Shop.

Over the past two decades, Bear Mountain has earned an interna-tional reputation for the quality of its woodstrip canoes, one of which was a wedding gift to His Royal Highness Prince Charles and Princess Diana from Canadian Prime Minister Pierre Trudeau. But such quality does not come cheaply. So, as the price of a finished Bear Mountain canoe climbed to $2,500, the company decided to sell kits to paddlers whose lack of affluence was over-come by their ambition. Those kits contained an instruction manual that became refined and aug-mented as users contacted Bear Mountain with their questions and suggestions.

The result is this book, which,

because of its hands-on origins, has gradually evolved to fit the needs of everyone from the confused amateur looking for a quality canoe at discount-store prices to the experienced woodworker seeking a personal challenge. Each phase of the building instructions begins by outlining sound, basic techniques, then proceeds to include increasingly interesting and intricate variations that add character and style to the finished canoe.

But the foundation of all so-called "stripper" canoes, exotic and plain, rests on a substance familiar to the first native practitioners of the canoebuilder's art: wood, which is unexcelled for its stiffness, strength, buoyancy and striking appearance. Slender strips of cedar, 1/4 inch thick and less than an inch wide, are glued together on forms that are fixed at regular intervals on a secure, level base. This provides shape and support for the hull, which is sanded, planed and then sheathed inside and out with fiberglass cloth and epoxy resin. The last step is to trim the hull with gunwales, seats and decks.

As well as containing basic step-by-step how-to information, this guide also provides detailed illustrations and photographs that show how to make professionally perfect molds, how to create a clear, tough epoxy sheath and how to protect it all with a final, flawless coat of varnish.

Woodstrip/epoxy construction is not only feasible but also well within the reach of anyone who is the least bit handy with tools. When launching day arrives, the builder will be able to christen a craft which can ride out the heavy seas that pound the Magdalen Islands or confidently challenge the Class IV rapids in the main channel of the Ottawa River. And do it with class.

Because a quality wooden boat begins with fine lines, this guide also includes a primer on canoe design that explains, in simple terms, the interplay between a canoe's form and function. Each curve of a canoe, from keel to sheer, from bow to stern, profoundly affects performance. Understanding these characteristics and how they interact will enable the backyard boatman to construct a vessel that will be as satisfying to paddle as it was to build.

To this end, plans for eight canoes are included here. Some, like the Peterborough and the Prospector, are original, historic designs. Others are modern and incorporate up-to-date hydrodynamics with time-tested styles. Together, these plans reflect the most popular canoe sizes and shapes and include designs suitable for virtually any waters.

Practical Elegance

Regardless of whether the backyard builder opts for a historic design or a modern adaptation, he participates in a tradition born in the middle years of the 19th century, long before the advent of aluminum and plastic construction, when Canada's classic canoebuilders employed ingenuity and artistry to transform native designs into cedarstrip classics. Nurtured in an obscure river valley in eastern Ontario, the skills of 19th-century innovators like John Stephenson, Thomas Gordon and Daniel Herald became known from remote African jungles to the tundra of the high Arctic, making "Canadian" and "Peterborough" synonymous with "canoe."

One reason for this widespread acclaim was that these vessels combined the practical joys of a small, affordable boat with the materials and attention to detail of a sailing sloop appointed with gleaming teak and brass. "A canoe is a poor man's yacht," wrote the well-known paddler George Washington Sears in 1885. "In common with nine-tenths of my fellow citizens, I am poor—and the canoe is my yacht, as it would be were I a millionaire."

Regrettably, these artisans have been denied their rightful place in Canadian and boating history. Their beautiful canoes were all but supplanted by products whose form followed not function but the dictates of marketing experts and cost accountants. By the late 1960s, the rich tradition of Canada's master canoebuilders was carried on by one elderly man toiling in the obscurity of a marina in Lakefield, Ontario.

But the past few decades have seen a renaissance in canoecraft, sparked by a handful of commercial shops like Bear Mountain and by thousands of inspired amateurs spurred on by the belief that there is still a place for quality and aesthetics in watercraft. The modern woodstrip/epoxy method they developed is a direct offspring of the cedarstrip construction made popular during canoeing's heyday.

The new technique retains the unquestionable beauty of wooden boats while eliminating many drawbacks of that material: dry rot, excessive weight and constant maintenance. Best of all, from the standpoint of nonprofessional woodworkers, woodstrip/epoxy construction eliminates the need for an elaborate form and for fastening the canoe's planking to ribs. This, for the first time, places cedarstrip construction within the limited skills and resources of backyard boatbuilders.

Perhaps more important, however, is that woodstrip/epoxy construction is enjoyable. And, although few beginners will be able to produce the sort of artistry that earns a berth in a royal boathouse, anyone who follows the steps outlined in this guide will receive a thrill that had at one time all but disappeared from marine pursuits: the pleasure of skimming over the water in a masterpiece that is so intimately one's own.

CHAPTER 2

THE WELL-BRED CANOE

Canada's Cedarstrip Tradition

WHEN A MAN IS PART OF HIS CANOE, HE IS PART OF ALL THAT CANOES HAVE EVER KNOWN.

—Sigurd F. Olson

To the untrained eye, it is nothing more than a blackened skeletal form, the salvaged remains of a boat that has been rotting in some beaver swamp since Queen Victoria's Diamond Jubilee. The setting does nothing to dispel this gloomy impression: a dim little garage with greasy windows, a bare concrete floor and sagging racks of milled cedar overhead.

Ancient tools clutter a messy workbench, beneath which are piled cans of varnish and paint, dusty and partially buried in waves of saw-dust. What appears to be the relic of a 30-foot-long war canoe dominates the flotsam of what is unmistakably an old man's workshop.

Resting beside the century-old boat forms, however, is a gleaming new double-ended rowing skiff that belies the frail, useless appearance of the vintage mold from which it has risen.

The skiff's hull is formed of long, tightly joined, gracefully tapered and curving strips of western red cedar, sparkling with the heads of hundreds of copper nails arranged in dead-even rows along its entire length. Inside, it is held together by a row of delicate half-round oak ribs running the length of the boat from stem to stern at even, 2-inch intervals and punctu-ated by four wide seats fashioned of clear-grained Ontario white cedar. The seats are supported by sculpted mahogany brackets; gun-wales of white ash and oak merge smoothly at each end into elegant pointed decks of rich butternut. Finished but for a final coat of varnish, the skiff is stunningly beautiful in the middle of the dingy shop, glittering like a dia-mond in a coal mine. Obviously, this is not an ordinary boat shop, and this is not an ordinary boat.

The overseer of this place is Walter Walker, a small man with a gentle demeanor, sparkling eyes and precious little to say to the casual visitor. The man is painfully understated, but his hands—big, rough hands for a person of his slight frame—do the talking. They are callused and scarred from 65 years of steady boatbuilding, but the breathtaking skiff is evi-dence that their movements re-main as light and alive as the hands of a young virtuoso. They are the hands of a master crafts-man, one who long ago surpassed his teachers and all rivals. They build what many consider to be the finest canoes and skiffs known today—works of art. When these hands are finally folded, there will be none to replace them.

At the age of 91, although officially retired, Walker can be found on most workdays in his crowded little basement near a marina in the village of Lakefield, Ontario, which, together with neighboring Peterborough, has long been noted as the home of Canada's—and the world's—top canoebuilders. Here, in the val-ley of the Otonabee River, hun-dreds of craftsmen were once employed to turn out the unique cedarstrip canoes that were celebrated throughout North America, Europe and the inter-national boating world for their beauty, workmanship and grace in the water.

Anyone now who would build a woodstrip canoe cannot help gaining inspiration from the legacy of the Peterborough and Lakefield canoes that are the unmistakable forebears of all lightweight canoes today. Their builders, early Canadian craftsmen in a backwater valley in eastern Ontario, can be credited with starting what can best be described as the Golden Age of the Canoe at the turn of the 20th century. As a floating vessel of luxury, the finely finished cedarstrip canoe—the "poor man's yacht"—was leagues ahead of any competition, perfectly suited to the leisurely ways of quiet lakes and rivers, especially those in central and eastern Ontario, which had recently been transformed into affluent cottage country.

Water courtship became an institution, with the word "canoe" serving as a staple rhyme for "you" in the lexicon of Tin Pan Alley. One contemporary pundit, speculating as to why so many proposals took place in canoes, thought that a woman reclining in the bow of a canoe presented the image of maximum desirability and the fact of minimum accessibility, which momentarily flummoxed the suitor.

One 1920s cedarstrip canoe recently restored by Walker bears witness to the extent the craft became refined in its romantic role. It contains a specially molded seat in the stern for the paddling swain, with a long deck in the bow partially enveloping a virtual throne in which the passenger sat facing the stern while coyly trailing one hand in the rippling water. Cabinets are built beneath the deck on either side of the foremost seat, one apparently intended for liquid refreshment and the other equipped with a complicated sliding door that opens to reveal a built-in Victrola.

In crafting a woodstrip canoe today, one takes full advantage of the most modern resins, fibers and finishes that high technology can provide, but at the same time, one must stop and ponder the fact that this design can be easily traced to indigenous Canadians. In the short century and a half that trace the white man's influence on the light canoe, evolution has made it faster, lighter and far more durable but has left intact the fundamental elegance of the basic design.

The White Man's Canoe

The history of North American plank canoes begins in a dog-eared edition of the *Katchewanooka Herald* dated 1857—a handwritten news sheet circulated among the settlers in the colonial Upper Canada clearing known as Lakefield—in which the lead editorial waxed effusive about an upcoming canoe race: "We trust the numerous young men of the clearing will show themselves as invincible at the regatta as they would be no doubt in the case of an invasion."

North America's first recorded canoe regatta had taken place 11 years earlier at nearby Rice Lake, but informal races date from precolonial times in Canada. Native canoeists often tested their paddling speed and skills against one another, and the settlers soon followed suit, staging social gatherings around race days.

The 1857 regatta was the first of what was to become an annual event. Although this was a white man's race, the canoes being used were all fundamentally Indian: dugouts and birchbark canoes. Before the regatta was over, two observers had hatched an idea for a new kind of canoe, a white man's canoe made of basswood planks rather than a hollowed-out trunk or bark. This was the beginning of the Otonabee canoe industry.

By 1857, the dugout canoe had evolved into a surprisingly sophisticated craft in the Otonabee Valley. The aboriginal dugouts were made by slowly burning out the inside of a tree trunk, controlling the fire with wet mud and scraping away char until a canoe hull appeared. It was then stretched into a flared shape and fixed permanently with thwarts by filling it with water warmed by hot stones.

Such canoes could be bought cheaply from local Indians, but many settlers preferred to fashion their own and quickly became skilled. In the early 19th century, Major Sam Strickland, a brother of Catharine Parr Traill and Susanna Moodie, reported that his first attempt at a dugout "looked more like a hog trough than a boat."

But by 1857, his son George had perfected a new method of making dugouts and constructed his *Shooting Star* within five days to compete in the regatta. It was dramatically lighter and better-shaped than its predecessors. There is a dugout canoe probably very much like the *Shooting Star* hanging in the Peterborough Centennial Museum today. With sophisticated lines and a hull planed to an even ½-inch thickness, it defies visions of mud-wielding char scrapers. Indeed, it shows all the stylish touches that would later become known as quintessentially "Peterborough."

The time of the first regatta marked a turning point in the history of the Otonabee Valley. Now dammed and placid, the river seems typical of the many small streams that wind through the settled eastern Ontario countryside. But in the early 19th century, when the sisters Traill and Moodie wrote of their arduous lives in the "clearings" of the Otonabee Valley, the river was strewn with rapids and flanked by virgin stands of butternut, basswood and cedar. Peterborough and Lakefield were rough-and-tumble mill towns, and the river was constantly choked with logs driven down from the north country. In the minds of

The Indians' birchbark construction was adopted with few alterations by explorers and traders who crossed the continent.

enthusiastic British readers of both Moodie and Traill, this was the Canadian wilderness.

But by 1857, the settlement had been completed, the land was clear, and the logging business was slowly starting to give way to the manufacturing industries that would permeate Ontario by the turn of the century. And the canoes that had always been part of daily life in the workaday world of the original settlers were being put to new, less utilitarian uses.

By contrast, the Indian birchbark canoe survived the white man's use remarkably unaltered. Even the legendary fur traders, who depended almost exclusively on bark canoes, adopted native construction methods wholesale, content merely to substitute metal for stone and bone tools and to standardize the sizes they built.

In part, this was due to the genius of its design and construction, which had been refined over centuries to adapt perfectly to the varied conditions of wilderness travel. Like the log cabin, however, the birchbark canoe played a much smaller role in the lives of the pioneers than our mythology supposes. It was not nearly sturdy enough for the tough life of the clearings; only the pretentious favored it over the dugout.

At the Katchewanooka regatta of 1857, the two types of canoe competed side by side. George Strickland took all honors in the singles "log" division, but even his elegant *Shooting Star* seemed cumbersome and awkward alongside the light, finely shaped birchbark canoes. Among the shorebound spectators, there were two young men with a vivid appreciation of that fact: John Stephenson, 27, co-owner of a planing mill across the river from Peterborough, and Thomas Gordon, a Lakefield man three years his junior. As hunting companions and canoeists, as well as skilled woodworkers, they were attuned to any possible improvements in either the heavy dugout or the frail bark canoe.

Watching the regatta, one, or perhaps both, of these young men had an idea. Why not combine the best features of the refined dugout with the principles of lightweight Indian canoe construction? Instead of hollowing out the basswood trunk for a dugout, why not mill the wood, then use an existing dugout as a mold around which to bend those boards? Not only would such a boat approach the featherweight quality of a birchbark hull, but the process would be repeatable, again and again.

We will probably never know

who built the first white man's canoe. But it is probable that it was made by bending square ribs over an overturned dugout and then nailing three wide basswood planks on each side, joining them at either end with rough-sawn stems and sealing the seams between the planks with square battens on the inside—a crude but historic craft.

We do know, however, that Gordon was the first to exploit the invention commercially, quickly establishing the world's first wooden-canoe building shop in 1858. He was not only an entrepreneur; he was also a craftsman, an exacting perfectionist with an eye to both beauty and utility. The degree to which the new wooden canoe simultaneously fulfilled both requirements eventually proved to be its greatest legacy, a legacy first intimated as early as 1866, when Gordon won the Prince of Wales medal for craftsmanship at the British Empire Exhibition in London.

Stephenson remained a loner, building canoes freelance, with only his son to help, and later selling his patents and business to a firm that became the Peterborough Canoe Company.

Combining as they did the best qualities of Indian design and fine European carpentry, the new canoes flourished with a kind of hybrid vigor. The wide-board, ribbed basswood canoe proved as capable an ally in a

The Lakefield Canoe Building and Manufacturing Company, circa 1910, one of the early eastern Ontario canoe factories.

summer of hunting and fishing as the dugout had been in the clearings, and within a few years, two other men had joined in the business of making them. They were William English of Peterborough and Daniel Herald of Gore's Landing, on the south shore of Rice Lake. Among them, these four men pushed the refinement of their craft at a remarkable pace, and within 25 years, most of them were offering what would later be perceived as their crowning glory —the cedarstrip canoe.

The first step was the development of solid molds to replace the overturned dugouts on which those first hulls were formed. Like the canoes themselves, these molds are unique in boatbuilding history. Built solidly to shape the thin planks and withstand years of hammering, their service to generations of canoe-makers helped preserve the characteristic lines of the Peterborough canoe.

With the molds in place, two other factors combined to push the wide-board basswood canoe in the direction of the cedarstrip. One was the difficulty of bending the wide planks to conform with the compound lines of the mold. To prevent splitting, and because good-quality wide lumber quickly became scarce, the builders were soon using up to four planks per side. Each plank had to be carefully shaped to follow the narrowing girth of the hull toward its ends, and this was accomplished by the use of patterns that determined the taper of each board as it was sawn to shape.

According to Walker, even the best builders of the day botched two or three canoes before they managed to produce accurate patterns for a new mold. Their patience paid off, though, and the use of more planks and ribs and more skillful pattern-making combined to make the cedarstrip possible. Even though the number of planks quadrupled, the new canoes could be built efficiently, because all were preshaped on a single pattern.

The challenge of sealing the seams between the butt-joined planks was another crucial factor in the development of the cedarstrip. The first wooden canoes were sealed with raised battens that were fitted over the seams between planks.

This awkward arrangement soon gave way to a system of flush battens running along the entire length of each seam. They were installed first by rabbeting (notching) the inside edge of each plank to half its original thickness. Joining the planks together produced a long, shallow channel centered over each seam. But before they were joined, the planks were fitted with wooden battens that filled the channel and rose flush to the inside of the planking, producing a watertight seal. Flush-batten construction was used by Walker as long as he built war canoes.

This system, in turn, led to the metallic flush batten, a canoe-long "staple" of zinc or brass pressed into cuts sliced on each side of a seam. Although they probably cut weight and production time, metallic flush battens did not provide the strength of hardwood battens, so the builders responded by moving the ribs closer together. This new "close-rib" design and the practice of rabbeting the edges of the planks eventually became essential features of the cedarstrip.

Some spectacular innovations were born within this natural evolution, most notably Herald's "Patent Cedar" canoe and Stephenson's "Patent Cedar Rib" canoe. Both builders aimed to eliminate the ridged interior of the ribbed canoe.

Herald succeeded with an extraordinary craft built with one interior layer of planking, butt-joined and running from gunwale to gunwale, and another longitudinal layer on the outside. Between them was sandwiched a sheet of waterproof canvas.

Stephenson's boat was even more awkward to build. It consisted of a single layer of narrow tongue-and-groove planks running from gunwale to gunwale like ribs, with only a few longitudinal battens inside the hull for support.

"A beautiful job but too expensive to build," commented Gilbert Gordon (son of Thomas). "It was built on a special mold, and it had adjusting screws on the ends that fitted on the planking. They put it in a dry kiln. Every day, they took it out and tightened up the screws."

Walker remembers builders having to assemble Cedar Rib canoes on special molds, completely dismantling them to get them off the molds and then putting them back together again in a special jig. "It was quite a job," he says. Another contemporary observer was more emphatic: "Some of the mildest-mannered people turned into fiends if they were told they had to build a Cedar Rib."

The development of the Cedar Rib gives evidence of the unadulterated ingenuity of the Otonabee builders and the pace with which they strove to perfect the white man's canoe. The almost incredible amount of handwork involved in making these canoes made them impractical for large-scale production. Nevertheless, the master builders of the Peterborough Canoe Company remained skillful enough to build a Cedar Rib for Princess Elizabeth on the occasion of her wedding.

While the cedarstrip was evolving from the native dugout along the banks of an obscure colonial river, the canoe was undergoing a metamorphosis across the Atlantic—started by an English philanthropist named John MacGregor, who had been inspired by the bark-and-skin canoes and kayaks he had seen during his travels in Siberia and Canada.

PLEASURE CRAFT

In 1865, six years after MacGregor's return to England, he designed what he took to be a facsimile of the native watercraft for his own use. The "Rob Roy" was 15 feet long, clinker-built with overlapping strakes as in a rowing skiff, topped with long kayaklike decks enclosing a small central cockpit.

Sitting on the bottom and propelling himself with a double-bladed paddle, MacGregor set out across Europe on a three-month journey in this strange craft. With him went armloads of religious tracts and a little Union Jack fluttering on the foredeck. Shortly after his return that fall of 1865, he published *A Thousand Miles in the Rob Roy Canoe on Twenty Rivers and Lakes of Europe*, and in the eyes of the world—if not the Otonabee Valley—the modern sport of canoeing was born.

MacGregor's book and its sequels were a tremendous success. The public responded not only by buying them but also by forming canoe clubs of their own and building more decked boats in the style of the Rob Roy. Not everyone was impressed with these craft, however. "It is necessity, not choice or pleasure, which justifies recourse to such an imperfect, unscientific, uncomfortable imitation of the true boat," one anonymous cynic fumed. Even so, MacGregor promoted canoeing aggressively and successfully.

Ironically, MacGregor had his greatest influence in the United States, where genuine native canoes had become rarities and the populace found itself suddenly peaceful, prosperous and suffused with a romantic disposition born of the writings of Whitman and Thoreau. Although they experimented with many novel forms of construction, the Americans essentially adopted MacGregor's method for their boats, clinching narrow, overlapping planks on sectional forms and then inserting ribs for stiffness and shape.

Among American builders, the most famous was J. Henry Rushton of upper New York State, who refined the lapstrake construction method by feathering each narrow plank to reduce the amount it overlapped its neighbor, a technique he borrowed from the builders of the famous Adirondack guide boat. Although Rushton's early boats were still entirely distinct from the wooden canoes of the Otonabee builders, their example quite possibly influenced the final stages of the evolution of the Peterborough cedarstrip.

The evidence for this specula-

tion rests in a mammoth exhibition in Philadelphia, where the Republic was celebrating its centennial in 1876. Somewhere on the 236-acre site, among 60,000 other exhibitors strung out along 72 miles of aisles, were three canoebuilders from the Otonabee Valley: English, Gordon and Herald. Rushton was also there, represented by a display of lapstrake rowboats as well as his first canoes, two Rob Roy canoes that had been paddled to Philadelphia from Louisville, Kentucky.

BIRTH OF THE CEDARSTRIP

Before the exhibition was over, Gordon had added another gold medal to his growing collection. Soon after, according to his son Gilbert, he built his first longitudinal-strip canoe. Is it possible that he found Rushton amid the overwhelming jumble and admired his unusual lapstrake canoes? Their feather-edge lap would have been unfamiliar, but their rib style and placement were identical to his own close-rib metallic-batten canoes. But Rushton's ribs supported 2-inch planks, which seemingly solved a primary drawback plaguing the wide-board canoe—the inevitable shrinkage and splitting that occurred after exposure to repeated cycles of wet and dry.

The first hard evidence of such a narrow plank appears in the original catalog of the Ontario Canoe Company of 1883, which grew from Stephenson's cottage

industry and eventually became the Peterborough Canoe Company. It refers to a "longitudinal-rib" canoe, cousin of the notorious tongue-and-groove Cedar Rib.

"These canoes have not been much tried," admitted the catalog, "but we are confident that we can recommend them to the public."

This particular model quickly disappeared, but soon, all the Otonabee builders were offering longitudinal-strip models. The difference lay in the method of sealing the seams. The edges of the strips in the new canoes were rabbeted like the planks of the flush-batten canoes, except that the milling was done on opposite sides of each adjoining strip. When joined together, instead of forming a channel to receive a batten, they interlocked, enclosing a shiplap joint. This was the cedarstrip canoe, built the same way as the canoes that Walker builds today.

By the time the wooden canoe had been perfected as the cedarstrip, the Otonabee Valley had completely lost its frontier atmosphere. Peterborough had embarked on its own industrial revolution, which, by the turn of the century, had altered it from a sleepy Mariposa into a hustling dynamo. Railways were being flung across the countryside, and industrial development was the standard of progress. Any town that had a rail connection and an able workforce happily plunged into the tumultuous foray.

It was only fitting that canoe-building should begin to take place in factories which were governed not by builders but by aggressive entrepreneurs. In 1892, the Ontario Canoe Company suffered a fortuitous (some say deliberate) fire that enabled it to expand into a larger, more automated plant and to pursue export sales.

Meanwhile, in Lakefield, Gordon had taken on a partner with the same aim. Soon his factory was exporting 600 canoes a year to England alone. They were shipped overseas partially disassembled and nested one inside the other. In this manner, as many as seven canoes could be packed into one crate, which was itself built on a canoe mold and shaped accordingly.

In Europe and the United States, where decked Rob Roy-style racing and sailing canoes remained current coin, the new "Canadian" open canoes made an immediate impression. In 1880, Tom Wallace of Gore's Landing served notice of the invasion by winning the one-mile race at the first annual American Canoe Association (ACA) regatta using a single-blade paddle in an open canoe "while nonchalantly smoking his pipe and pausing to scoop up a drink of water."

The Otonabee canoes continued to surpass the performance of their Rob Roy cousins, while American devotees of the decked

Despite their utilitarian roots, canoes became a symbol of leisure, and canoe-golf one of the more ludicrous crazes of the '20s.

craft concentrated on perfecting highly specialized sailing canoes. By 1900, an ACA historian would comment that "those who follow any other branch of the sport but [sail] racing do so in the open Canadian canoe."

The Peterborough canoes were successful partly because of their versatility. They were fast and agile in racing competition, yet equally at home on extended wilderness journeys or afternoon fishing jaunts. What really set them apart, though, were their smooth, sleek cedarstrip hulls and the sophisticated shapes they inherited from their Indian forebears.

One gauge of the impact of these Canadian boats was the speed with which Rushton developed his own version of the "smooth-skin" hull in order to compete with the Otonabee canoes. Not long after, he introduced open canoes to his catalog, and these are the boats for which he is best remembered today.

Despite their popularity as purely recreational craft, the Otonabee canoes never completely abandoned their true roots as working boats for the bush. In

1893, two 18-foot Peterborough cedarstrips were taken by the Tyrrell brothers on what remains one of the greatest canoe trips ever attempted. Heading north out of Edmonton, the Tyrrells covered thousands of miles in the Barren Lands to the west of Hudson Bay, exploring territory never before traveled by white men.

"Just after reaching the Athabaska River," reports C.E.S. Franks in *The Canoe and White Water*, "they amazed some Indians by paddling their Peterboroughs in circles around the natives' birch-bark canoes. This was a measure of the improvement caused by western craftsmanship."

For many years, the Hudson's Bay Company was the largest purchaser of Peterborough freight canoes. These were shipped out of Ontario in the dead of winter and left in caches at the ends of the western rail lines until they could be picked up during the spring runoff. By 1898, the success of these large canoes had prompted the Peterborough company to create a serious oversupply that threatened its already precarious financial stability. The problem was cleverly solved by the company's banker, who loaded the entire inventory onto a westbound freight train and personally sold the lot in Seattle to willing Klondike-bound sourdoughs.

William Ogilvy, Dominion Land Surveyor and first Governor of the Yukon, used a Peterborough canoe

THE WELL-BRED CANOE

in his travels to the northern Pacific Coast, as did both the American and Canadian engineers on the Alaska Boundary Survey. But perhaps the most exotic journey ever undertaken in a Peterborough canoe took place in South America, when Peterborough's own David Hatton and two anonymous companions motored up the Amazon River in a canoe specially designed to accommodate an inboard motor.

In 1904, the future of recreational small craft was altered irrevocably when Ole Evinrude created his first sputtering outboard motor. By this time, Herald was dead, and Stephenson and English had retired. Of the pioneers, only Gordon remained an active physical presence in his boat shop. In the United States, the canoe boom had already completely succumbed to the bicycle craze of the 1890s. In Canada, there was no abrupt decline in canoebuilding as there had been in the United States. Nevertheless, over the first half of the new century, the production of the Otonabee canoe factories was increasingly given over to outboard runabouts.

Actually, as early as the turn of the century, the role of the cedarstrip as a working boat had begun to be undercut by the development of the canvas-covered wood canoe. It was rugged, much easier to build, just as efficient and half the price of a cedarstrip. The painstaking hand labor and high level

Walter Walker, shown above at 75 in the mid-1980s, could be found most days at work in his Lakefield shop.

of skill required to build a cedar-strip simply carried too high a price, and as the market for recreational canoes slowly dwindled, so did the production of the Otonabee canoe factories. By the end of World War II, they were producing more runabouts, water skis, paddles and even lawn chairs than canoes. And with the advent of the maintenance-free aluminum and fiberglass boats in the 1950s, the factories' history was completed.

Walker once had two helpers in his Lakefield shop, but when business tailed off, they found other jobs. Now he is retired, and when he dies, a unique century-old tradition of wooden-boat building will die with him.

However, an offspring will survive in the form of the modern woodstrip canoe. Just as racing stimulated the first board canoes, it was racing that rescued the cedarstrip from oblivion and stimulated a return to good design and innovative construction.

As the Otonabee factories were folding, competition paddlers in the American Midwest were rediscovering the fine lines of vee-bottom Peterborough cedarstrips. They tried to reproduce the shape, but instead of a solid mold, they used a strongback with sectional forms—one in the center and two others equidistant from the stems. After the canoe was planked, the hull was inverted with the forms still in it. Ribs were steamed and nailed between the forms, which were finally removed to insert the last ribs. The difficulties in achieving true lines must have been considerable with such widely spaced forms, but the move was significant—the solid mold, appropriate for mass production, was successfully replaced with sectional forms more accessible to the amateur boatbuilder.

From the late 1930s through the early 1950s, racing paddlers tried to eliminate ribs to reduce weight in the cedarstrip, but it was postwar technology in the form of waterproof glues and fiber-reinforced resins that facilitated the transition from cedarstrip to ribless woodstrip canoes.

No longer were the innovations limited to a narrow river valley and a handful of builders who devoted their lives to canoes. The woodstrip/resin canoe emerged simultaneously across the continent, in Minnesota, Quebec and California, with commercial and backyard builders all contributing to its improvement. When magazine articles and how-to books began to appear, the posterity of the cedarstrip offspring was assured.

At the hands of literally thousands of serious amateur canoe-makers, these new woodstrip/resin canoes have, since the early 1960s, moved slowly toward the method described in this book. The sectional forms have been improved and moved closer together to reproduce lines more accurately. The strongest and lightest combinations of wood, glue, resin and cloth are being discovered after years of experimentation. And most important, builders have learned the hard way that modern technology cannot replace time-honored boat-building basics.

The great boat shops of a century ago are now gone; most of the precious molds have been taken to the closest dump, broken up and burned. All we have left are the canoes themselves, which continue to surface through the wooden-boat revival of recent years. A grown-up third generation is lifting grandmother's cedarstrip down from the boathouse rafters and rediscovering the joys of a beautiful, well-built boat.

What cannot be resurrected are the proud men in dusty overalls who put something of themselves into each boat they built, doing their best with the materials and tools at hand, always working toward that elusive perfection in form and function. However the techniques evolve, the spirit of those builders will be preserved wherever boats are built with integrity and respect.

CHAPTER 3

ANATOMY OF A CANOE

Essentials of Good Design

IT IS DOUBTFUL WHETHER ANY FIRST-CLASS CANOE IS THE RESULT OF ANY ONE PERSON'S STUDY. THE BUILDER'S SHOP IS THE MILL, HE IS THE MILLER. THE IDEAS OF OTHERS ARE GRISTS.

—J.H. Rushton

One does not have to be a naval architect to understand the basic principles of canoe design. They are relatively simple, yet vitally important—especially to the builder.

The curves of a well-designed canoe are its calling card—a proclamation of the kind of paddling it does best. At one time, the lines of the slender, double-ended craft were directly traceable to a particular locale or people. The curious profile of a Newfoundland Beothuk canoe was a far cry aesthetically, functionally and geographically from the sturgeon-nosed craft of British Columbia's Kootenay people.

Within the limits of materials and technology, both native canoes and those built by the early whites were traditionally shaped to conform to the kind of water they plied and to the job they had to do. But with the advent of mass production, that connection was broken. In the post-World War II era, canoes were more often designed to conform to the demands of new materials than to function in a specific environment. Efficiency in the water took a backseat to efficiency in the factory.

Commercial designs have vastly improved in the past 15 years or so, as the emphasis has shifted back toward performance. Even so, by building your own canoe, you gain unique control; with the design and construction decisions you make, you can reestablish that perfect harmony among canoe, paddler and water.

There is no point in expending energy to build a craft that is going to paddle like a barge. At the same time, every builder, designer and paddler has his own version of the perfect canoe. The following section bares our personal biases; you can find others by referring to the books listed in Sources.

The key to sorting through the maze of designs is to determine what you expect of your canoe. Where will you most often paddle, for how long and with what gear? Most paddlers face a range of circumstances. The challenge is to select a design that meets most needs most of the time.

If your experience in canoes is limited, go to the water to test these principles where they really count. Examine hull contours and paddle different canoes to discover what suits your style best. Your woodstrip canoe will be a thing of aesthetic beauty, but understanding design will assure that it is satisfyingly functional as well.

A CANOE IN PERSPECTIVE

When a canoe is taken out of its watery element and projected onto a drawing board, it can be reduced to three views—profile, body plan and plan view.

The *profile view* (illustrated on page 29) shows a canoe from one side, as if it were cut in half lengthwise. This perspective describes the accurate length and depth of the boat, its sheer-line (curve of the gunwale, or top edge), its keel-line (curve of the hull, or bottom edge), the shape of its bow and stern and its waterline length (hull length that is wetted when the canoe is in the water).

The *body plan* (illustrated on page 30) shows a canoe from the end, as if it were sliced crosswise at regular intervals, or stations, the shape and dimensions of which are each represented by a single line. Each cross section shows the accurate width and depth of the canoe at that point, as well as the shape of the hull bottom and the shape of the sides. A centerline drawn perpendicular to the waterline splits the cross section in two, but since each half is identical, only one half is shown in the body plan.

The *plan view* (illustrated on page 31) shows a fish-eye perspective of the canoe from directly underneath the boat, as if it were sliced end to end at regular waterlines. Each lengthwise section shows the true length and width at that level, as well as the contour from its maximum width to the point at each end. This describes the path the water must take at various levels as it moves from the entry line at the bow to the exit line at the stern. When the slices are superimposed over a common centerline, the plan view also indicates whether the canoe is symmetrical (bow and stern halves are the same shape) or asymmetrical.

THE ELEMENTS OF PERFORMANCE

Each of the many physical elements illustrated by the three views has a profound effect on a canoe's performance. Although they are discussed separately below, none of them acts

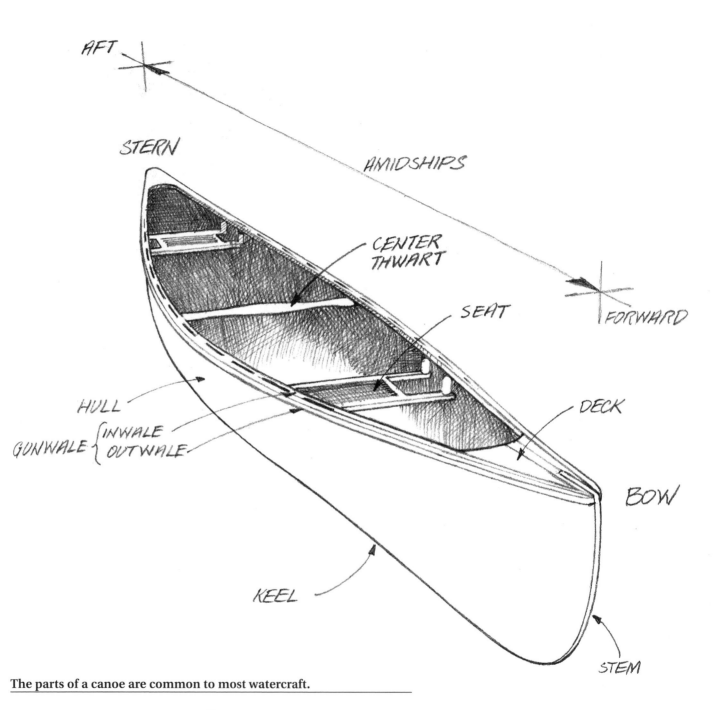

The parts of a canoe are common to most watercraft.

The *profile view* shows a canoe from the side, sliced in half lengthwise, illustrating the top and bottom curves as well as the length and depth of the canoe.

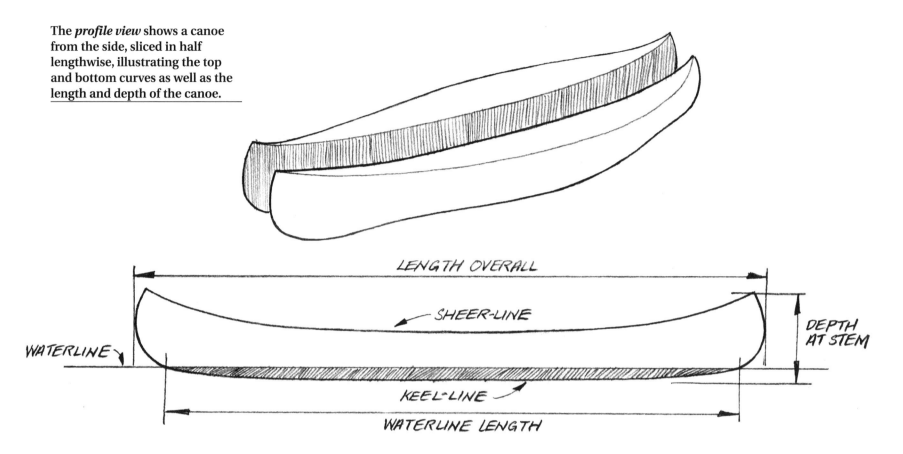

in isolation. Each affects the others to some extent; in a well-designed canoe, they function in delicate balance.

LENGTH

On average, the center half of a well-designed hull provides 75 percent of its stability and carrying capacity, while the end quarters function primarily to part the waters at the bow and bring them back together at the stern. Obviously, a longer hull will carry more weight, but length also affects speed.

Generally, the greater the waterline length and the higher the ratio of length to width, the faster the canoe and the easier it is to paddle. This is partly due to the physics of waves and partly to the fact that, in comparison to a short, wide hull, a long, narrow hull rides higher, with less wetted surface, and thus generates less friction against the water. A long hull will also track (hold its course) better than a short one will, but it will not turn as easily.

BEAM

This is the maximum width of a canoe. With a narrow beam, less effort is required to push the water aside, and less friction is created by the hull surface. But, although a wide canoe generally paddles slower than a narrow one does, it has greater carrying capacity and is more stable when loaded to its design capacity.

Beam may be the same throughout the depth of the hull, in which case, its sides are *plumb* (see page 32). But if the maximum beam occurs at the gunwales, the hull is *flared*. Most often found on narrow hulls, flared sides afford good "final stability." The hull becomes more stable when it is loaded down, because it becomes wider the lower it sits in the water. Flared sides also deflect waves.

When the gunwale beam is nar-

The **body plan** is an end view of the canoe, sliced crosswise at regular intervals, bow to stern, with the contours superimposed in sequence over a common centerline. It illustrates the canoe's depth and width.

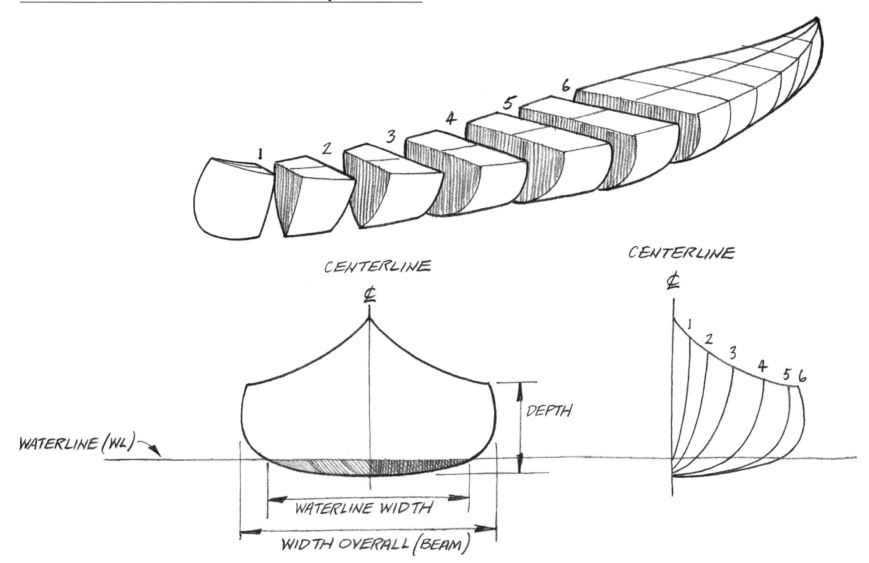

CENTERLINE

CENTERLINE

DEPTH

WATERLINE (WL)

WATERLINE WIDTH

WIDTH OVERALL (BEAM)

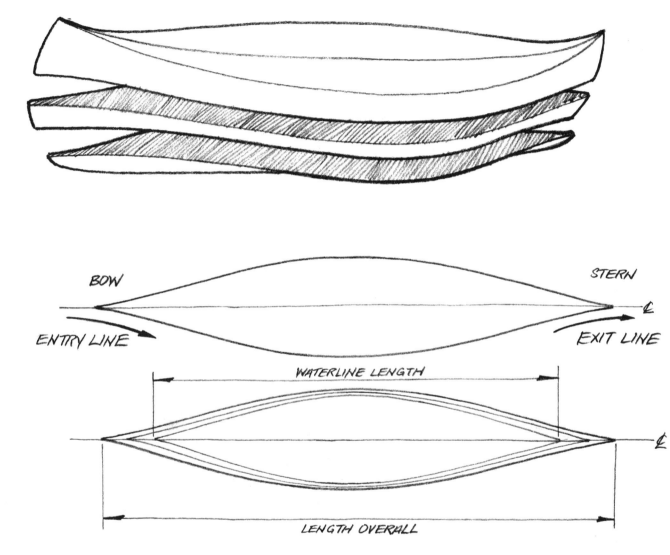

BOW

STERN

ENTRY LINE

EXIT LINE

WATERLINE LENGTH

LENGTH OVERALL

The *plan view* shows the hull from below, sliced lengthwise at regular waterlines. It illustrates the hull shape and the canoe's width and length.

rower than the maximum beam, the sides are *tumblehome* (they "tumble home"). Tumblehome is usually found on wider hulls: the reduced gunwale width allows the paddler to reach over the side easily without sacrificing good carrying capacity. The arcing sides also help stiffen the hull. Although tumblehome does not affect initial stability, it can result in very poor final stability when too extreme, especially in combination with a wide, flat bottom.

DEPTH

The depth of a canoe is measured amidships from the gunwales to the bottom of the hull. This can range from 10 inches in a little solo canoe to more than 24 inches in a freighter. Depth is also measured at the bow and stern, from the top of the stem to the lowest point of the keel-line.

Freeboard, another measurement of depth, is the distance from the water to the gunwales. Freeboard affects the seaworthiness of a canoe: high sides will make it susceptible to wind, reducing speed and controllability, whereas low sides will render it susceptible to swamping in whitewater and waves.

Predicting the freeboard of a design when the canoe is fully loaded can be done several ways. When "capacity" is listed in canoe specifications, it usually refers to the weight that can be loaded into the canoe while retaining

Anatomy of a Canoe

6 inches of freeboard. "Design displacement" refers to the weight that will lower the canoe to its design waterline.

As you study different plans, watch for figures that indicate pounds per inch of immersion. Ultimately, this is more meaningful than capacity is and will give you perspective on how a particular hull will handle loading.

HULL CONTOUR

More important than depth, beam or length is the way these measurements are drawn together to form the hull contour. How this shape moves through the water is the key to canoe performance.

A canoe has a displacement hull. It is basically a moving trough, dividing water at the bow and replacing it at the stern. Its efficiency depends on the amount of friction created by the hull surface meeting the water and the smoothness with which the water is displaced around its form.

A semicircular, or *round-bottom*, hull produces the least wetted surface, but its tippiness makes it practical only for flat-water racing shells.

A *flat-bottom* hull has the greatest wetted surface and is capable of carrying large loads. It can also turn quickly in every direction, making it appropriate for whitewater, where high maneuverability is a priority. This skidding action, however, means tracking can be difficult in any-

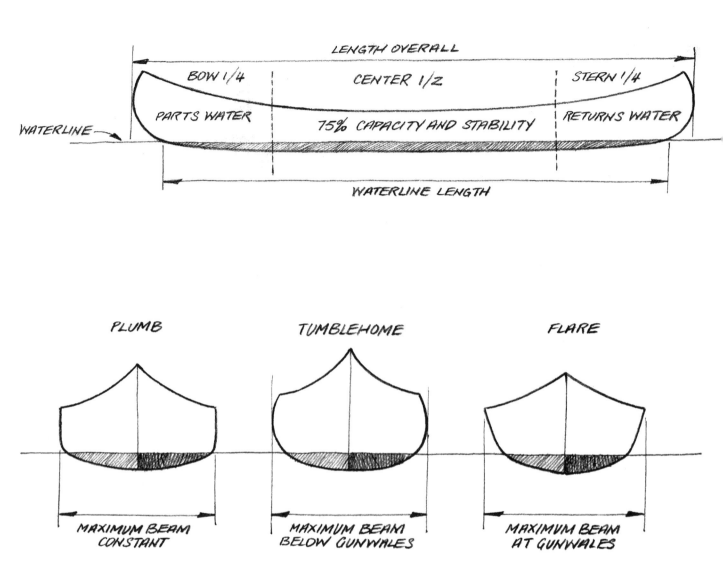

Top: Up to half of the length of a well-designed canoe is devoted primarily to parting the water at the bow and returning it at the stern. The longer the canoe, the faster it is. **Above:** The placement of maximum beam on the side of the hull determines the shape of the sides and the canoe's stability, speed and carrying capacity.

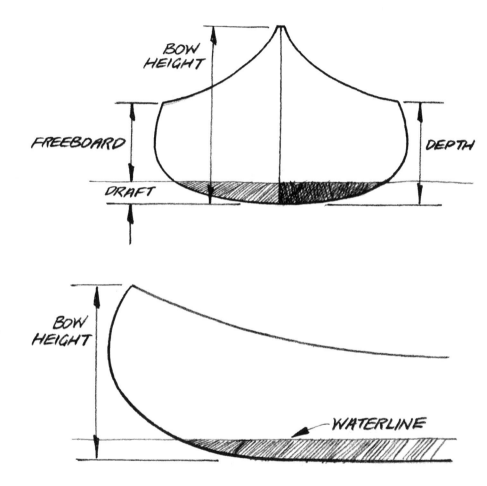

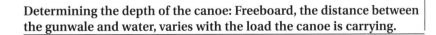

Determining the depth of the canoe: Freeboard, the distance between the gunwale and water, varies with the load the canoe is carrying.

thing less than glassy waters, and even then, flat-bottom hulls are slowed by high friction.

Since it is buoyant over a large surface, a flat-bottom hull feels the most stable when you first climb in but remains so only in calm water. In rough water, the flat, buoyant hull follows the profile of the waves and can turn turtle suddenly when tipped past the sharp turn of its bilge. A flat bottom may be justified in freight canoes but is unsafe in recreational craft on anything but flat water.

The *shallow-arch*, or semi-elliptical, hull contour is a good compromise between the round and flat bottoms. Its domed shape helps stiffen the hull, which is especially important with lightweight construction techniques, and reduces instability in the bilge area. In addition, waves tend to slide under the boat.

This hull feels "canoey," with good initial and final stability. Because such hulls take less abuse from heavy waters, naval architects often characterize them as "sea kindly." A shallow-arch hull will also track better than will a flat hull. Because of its seaworthiness and average tracking and turning ability, this contour is the starting point for most general-purpose touring or cruising canoes.

A *shallow-vee* contour takes the hull deeper and sharper into the water and produces slightly more wetted surface. Like the shallow-arch hull, the shallow vee affords a high degree of final stability. But it tracks better, since the vee shape functions like a keel, keeping the canoe on course. It is less responsive in turning, however. Because the shallow vee cuts cleanly through waves, with little pounding or skidding, it is especially appropriate for sailing and lake canoes.

Most hulls employ a combination of these forms. For instance, a cruiser might have a deep-vee bow to part the waters efficiently, opening gradually to a shallow vee, then a shallow arch to pass the waves cleanly along the hull, then narrowing back into a deep vee at the stern. Such a design would combine seaworthiness and directional stability with good maneuverability. It would also offer *reserve buoyancy*—extra width at the vee sections when the canoe sits deeper in the water.

Separate keels are the subject of some controversy in canoe design. They do add a measure of stiffness and protection to the hull bottom and will be much appreciated when paddling through a crosswind on a lake, but that same keel will be roundly cursed when you try to maneuver through rockstrewn rapids.

As a general rule, a shoe keel (a keel generally ⅜ inch deep by 2 to 3 inches wide) is a good idea for protection on a river boat, while a deeper keel is appropriate on a lake canoe, where maneuverability is less important than

33

tracking ability. Keels should be avoided on whitewater canoes, since they get hung up on obstructions and inhibit the sideways movement critical to dodging through rapids.

The *keel-line* of a canoe also affects maneuverability and directional stability. A straight keel-line from stem to stem produces a fast, easy-paddling canoe that tracks exceedingly well but turns poorly.

A keel-line that curves upward from the middle toward each end of the canoe is said to have *rocker*. Essentially, rocker allows the canoe to pivot on its midpoint. The more rocker on the keel-line, the shorter the canoe's waterline length and the easier it turns and rises over waves. Too much rocker forces the center of the canoe to support most of its weight, driving it deeper into the water, increasing displacement and friction and decreasing speed.

Rocker can range from moderate lift in a cruiser to the banana-like profile of a competition slalom canoe. Poorly made or old canoes sometimes develop reverse rocker, or *hogged* keel-lines, which inhibits performance.

Rather than a fully rockered keel-line, a canoe can have a slight *uplift* just at the stems. In a loaded boat, this allows enough of the hull to ride in the water for good tracking, but with the bow and stern riding slightly above the waterline, maneuverability and reserve buoyancy are improved.

The profile of the bow affects performance as well as the line of the hull body. Some bows rise vertically or on a slight incline, yielding a fairly straight sheer-line and maximum waterline length. This inclined, or *plumb*, bow forces the sides of the canoe to flare. The greater the incline, the more the sides must flare.

Most traditional canoe bows, however, rise up out of the water and curve back slightly toward the paddler. This *recurve*, a logical extension of the rockered keel-line, reduces the area exposed to the wind for a given waterline length. But as the bow curves, it puts tumblehome into the sides, reducing reserve buoyancy.

To compensate for this, extra height is often added at the stems. Extreme recurve, with a sharply rising sheer-line, makes the canoe more susceptible to wind and adds some unnecessary weight, but the trade-off may be worth the beautiful sweeping lines.

The *entry line* of a canoe— the shape of the forward point of the bow that cuts the water —plays a large part in its efficiency. The smoothness with which water is displaced around the hull affects both speed and the amount of effort required to attain it.

A canoe that carries its fullness well into the ends must quickly push aside a large volume of water, which tends to slow down as it moves along the hull. Thus

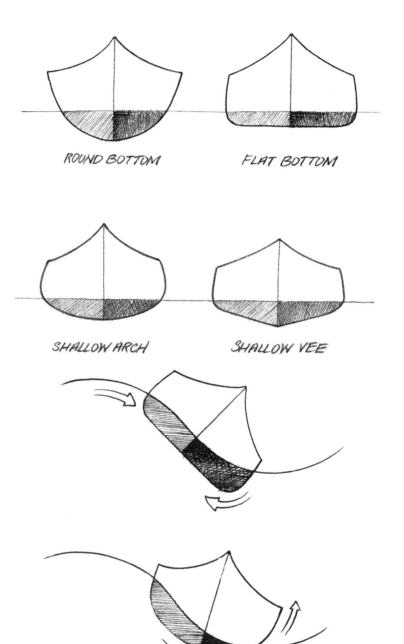

ROUND BOTTOM FLAT BOTTOM

SHALLOW ARCH SHALLOW VEE

The contour of the hull below the waterline determines the efficiency of the canoe as well as its stability in rough water.

34

Even without a keel, the profile of a hull bottom strongly affects performance and the way the canoe rides out rough waters. Keel-lines range from the razor's edge of a racing cruiser to the extreme rocker of a slalom canoe. Recreational canoes fall somewhere between.

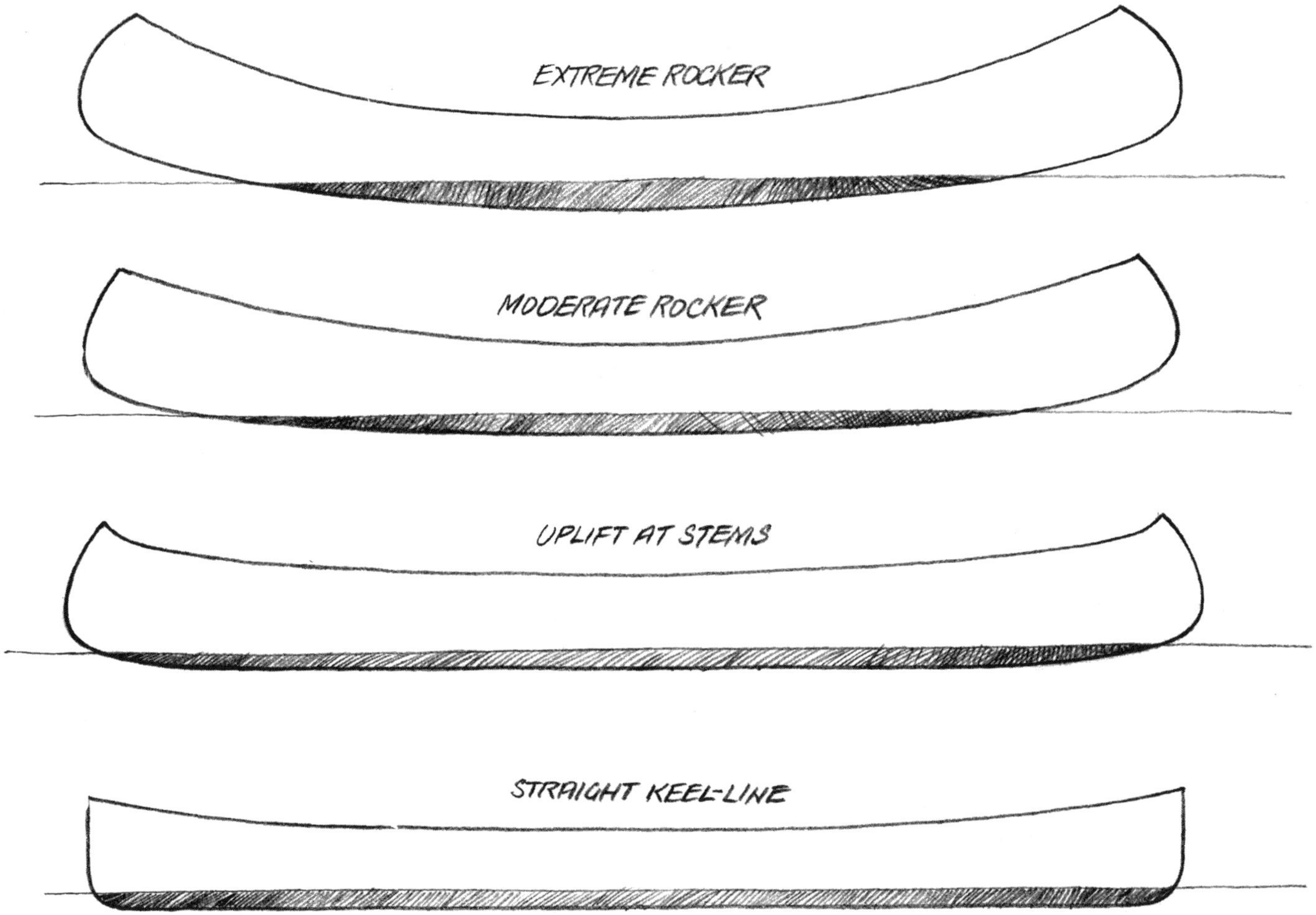

EXTREME ROCKER

MODERATE ROCKER

UPLIFT AT STEMS

STRAIGHT KEEL-LINE

the canoe tends to plow through the water.

On the other hand, a hull with a fine entry line moves the water aside more slowly. Because the displaced fluid has more time to get out of the way, the paddler exerts less of his own force to move it. The fine lines part the water neatly, producing little spray and a small set of waves that accelerate naturally along the hull.

Fine entry lines are desirable under all conditions, albeit in varying degrees. A flatwater cruiser should have the finest entry, whereas a whitewater canoe must have its fullness carried as far forward as possible, without disturbing the fine entry.

Although traditional canoes are generally symmetrical in shape, some modern designers have abandoned that principle. In an *asymmetrical* design, the beam is placed slightly aft of center, creating a longer bow. Paddling and tracking become easier because of the fine entry of the long bow and the extra buoyancy in the stern quarter.

COMPROMISES AND CONUNDRUMS

Between the extremes of the blunt-nose, flat-bottom freighter and the stiletto racer, infinite variations in canoe design are available. At the same time, however, there is no ideal form. Each of the principles discussed above can be manipulated for specific

ANATOMY OF A CANOE

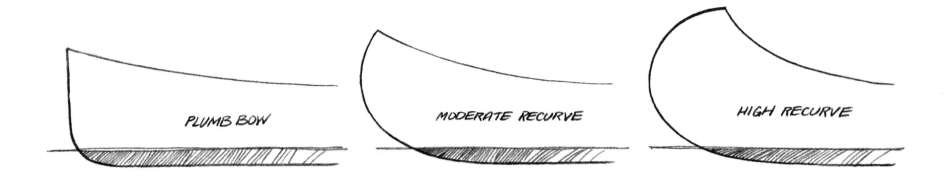

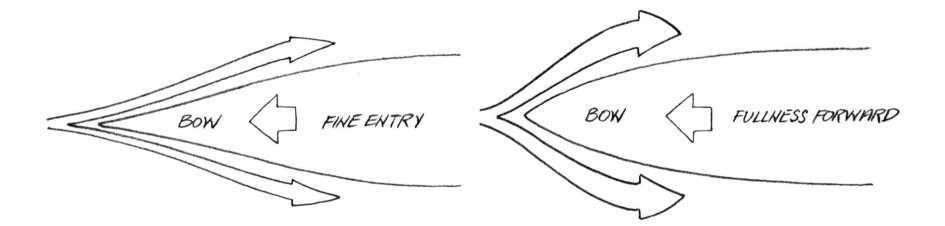

Top: A plumb bow forces the canoe's sides to flare, while traditional re-curved bows result in tumblehome sides. High recurve is traditionally attractive but can make the canoe susceptible to wind. *Above:* Fine entry lines part the waves more smoothly than a blunt-nosed bow that plows the water. The result is greater speed with less paddling effort.

results, but the gain of one advantage inevitably entails the loss of another. If you opt for tracking, you will sacrifice maneuverability, while the extreme rocker that offers optimal maneuverability will rob your canoe of tracking ability.

Even within each design variable, there are no absolutes. Final stability is a prime concern if you are out for a paddle with the kids, but it is a low priority if you delight in the solo canoe "ballet" of Bill Mason. And finally, no matter how functional a well-designed canoe may be, it must also be visually pleasing, balancing practicality with beauty of line.

The flexibility of canoe design, however, is its own reward. All these disparate elements can be orchestrated in several different ways to produce a variety of canoe prototypes well suited to different requirements. If there is no such thing as the perfect all-purpose canoe, there are individual types that do specific jobs very well.

A *cruising*, light-tripping or general-purpose, canoe should have a keel or vee end sections, a fairly straight keel-line and a fine entry line for good tracking and efficient paddling. It should have a shallow-arch or shallow-vee hull with low stem profiles. Asymmetrical designs are appropriate. Overall length can range between 14 and 18.5 feet, with at least a 12-inch depth and a beam between 30 and 34 inches.

A *wilderness*, or tripping, canoe must meet all the challenges of extended bush travel—large lakes, shallow streams, whitewater and portages—and still be able to carry sufficient gear. The hull should be as full as possible toward the bow and stern without disturbing the fine entry, with a slight uplift or rockered keel-line for maneuverability in rough water and a shallow-arch contour. A bit of tumblehome in the sides is ideal. The hull should be keelless or shoe-keeled, and weight is a definite consideration. Competent wilderness canoes are at least 16 feet and as much as 18.5 feet long, with a 12-to-14-inch depth and 34-to-36-inch beam.

A *whitewater*, or downriver, canoe should have a shallow-arch to flat-bottom hull, well rockered for easy turning and with a good lift at the ends so that it can ride through heavy rapids without taking water. Moving the bow seat back somewhat will improve this ability. Keels are undesirable, unless a shoe keel is considered necessary for protection. In any case, a whitewater canoe has to be strong enough to withstand inevitable encounters with rocks. Decks should be long and gunwales wide enough to shed water, with tumblehome sides to accommodate the beam. The consideration of weight has to be balanced against durability. Dimensions are similar to those for a wilderness canoe, although depth should be about 14 inches.

The design of a *solo* canoe depends on the individual canoeist's paddling technique. A traditional Canadian-style solo canoe, paddled heeled over, is 14 to 15 feet, with a symmetrical shallow-arch hull. Widths range between 25 and 34 inches, with a slight tumblehome to the sides.

The traditional American Rushton-style solo canoe, on the other hand, is paddled flat with a double blade. It is typically narrower (24 to 30 inches) and shorter (10 to 14 feet), with a shallow-arch/shallow-vee hull. The paddler sits on the hull bottom, supported by a backrest.

The contemporary Gault-style solo canoe, a new design now fashionable in the United States, is paddled well heeled over. It is also narrow (24 to 30 inches), with shallow, flared sides and an asymmetrical hull 13 to 16 feet long, with a rounded-vee bottom and soft bilges.

After digesting this chapter, you may not be ready for the world of custom design, but you should be able to set your own personal performance priorities. As one builder exclaimed after mastering the mysteries of canoe design: "I'm not trained, but now I certainly can tell an ugly canoe when I see one, and I have a pretty good idea about how poorly it must handle." In the next chapter, you will find plans for a range of canoes that are as sweet in the water as they are on the shelf.

CHAPTER 4

PIPE DREAMS TO PAPER

Choosing the Right Plan

THE ONE GREAT PRINCIPLE, FAR TOO OFTEN FORGOTTEN—
THAT A COMFORTABLE BOAT, LIKE A SHOE OR A COAT, MUST BE
BUILT FOR THE WEARER AND NOT WORN DOWN TO HIS SHAPE.

—John MacGregor

"There is no more perfection in canoes than in wives," Professor Edwin Fowler of the Knickerbocker Canoe Club of New York City observed in 1883. "There are only convenient compromises.

"An ideal canoe is a bundle of compromises," he continued, "yielding something of her paddling speed to be able to sail fairly, sacrificing a portion of her sailing lines to secure reasonable lightness and sharpness, losing somewhat of her steadying weight and momentum for the sake of portability, and being less portable because she must be strong and stiff. . . .

"A canoe must be equally at home with wings for the breezes and with paddles for the water, yet be able to move on the legs of her master over dry land."

With all due respect to Professor Fowler, the perfect canoe (and no doubt the perfect wife) does exist. There are hundreds, even thousands, of them—a perfect canoe for each discriminating paddler. Unfortunately, though, what is perfect for one canoeist is not necessarily right for another, since everyone has his own tastes and needs. Even the legendary canoebuilder J. Henry Rushton advertised his boats with this caveat:

"It will be impossible—even if it were desirable—to have any one model, any one mode of construction or any one builder please all. It depends very much upon the individual canoeist, as well as the waters upon which he will use his canoe, as to what model will suit him best."

THE EVOLUTION OF A PLAN

Many of the designs included at the end of this chapter are based on traditional canoes, but they are not, strictly speaking, reproductions of the original. Take our Prospector, for instance. We are often asked whether it is the Chestnut Prospector, but the answer is not a simple yes or no.

If a designer could take the lines off the original mold in its original condition, he would have the definitive shape of the original Prospector mold but not necessarily the shape of the Prospector canoe itself. This is because, after a traditional cedarstrip canoe came off its mold, the tension in the ribs and planking would adjust itself to reach an equilibrium. In other words, a flat bottom would try to become round. As a case in point, we took the lines for our Bob's Special from two canoes that had, in all probability, been built on the same mold, yet one had a very flat bottom and the other a shallow arch.

In the case of the Prospector, our design comes via the late Bill Mason, a remarkable Canadian paddler, naturalist and filmmaker. The Prospector was one of his favorite canoes. Mason generously supplied us with bristol-board templates that he had taken from the inside of the planking on his original Chestnut Prospector, using 24-inch centers.

From Mason's information, we decided on an appropriate rocker for the hull, added on the thickness of the original planking, lofted the canoe full size, then deducted the ¼-inch thickness

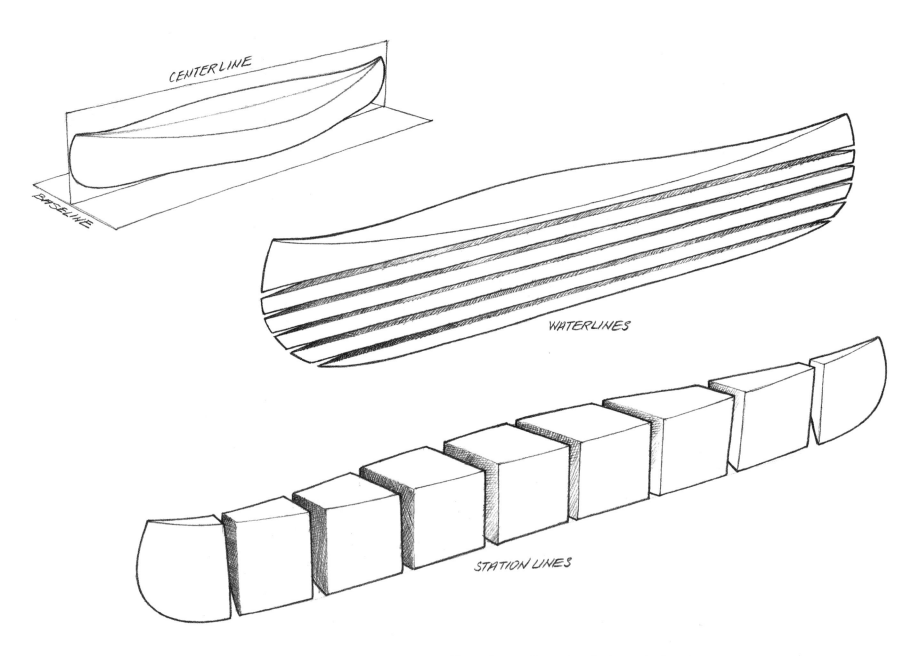

CENTERLINE

BASELINE

WATERLINES

STATION LINES

From the top: Canoe in relation to its baseline and centerline; divided by various waterlines; and segmented at its stations.

of the strip planking and divided the length of the boat into 12-inch sections to produce Bear Mountain's version of Bill Mason's Prospector. In 1998, yacht designer Steve Killing refaired the lines and made further adjustments for ease of strip planking.

The result is a very successful design. People who have paddled many different Prospectors, both originals and re-creations, tell us that they prefer the Bear Mountain model. The difference appears to be in a slightly narrowed beam and slightly increased rocker. In the end, we seem to have struck a good balance among load-carrying capacity, directional stability and maneuverability.

So is this a reproduction of the original Prospector? Not really. Even though the lines were taken from an original canoe, with great attention to accuracy, what we have at best is a good representation of the originally intended lines. In the end, after lofting and fairing, the design for this new canoe is just one person's interpretation of a moment in the lifetime of an individual heritage boat.

DECIDING WHAT TO BUILD

Building your own boat gives you the opportunity to choose a canoe that is right for you. The previous chapter outlined the basic design components of a canoe and the sort of conditions each is suited for. Now is the time to give deep thought to what you

really want in a canoe. Then you'll be able to choose a design to fill those needs and desires.

Make your choice first on function, then try to satisfy your eye. If you are a person who harbors a strong image of what a canoe should look like, choosing a design can be an emotional undertaking. But don't let the profile of a canoe seduce you into building something unsuitable, either the wrong size for a growing family or the wrong shape for the waters you are likely to paddle.

If you are already an experienced canoeist, you'll no doubt have some preferences when it comes to size and style in a canoe. If you are relatively inexperienced, try to paddle as many different canoes as possible before coming to a decision about what you'll build.

Consider who will be paddling the canoe and under what conditions. Will you be paddling a lake or a river or both? Do you want the boat for general use around the cottage, or do you envision annual three-week excursions into the wilderness? Are you bent on speed, or are you a person who prefers a quiet, contemplative paddle? Knowing yourself and your needs thoroughly will ensure that you choose a plan for a boat that you'll be happy with for a long, long time.

In selecting the plans to include in the second edition of this book, we've tried to keep in mind how

individual a person's tastes in canoe design and performance can be. On the following pages are the lines and offsets for eight canoes that have been developed by the Bear Mountain Boat Shop. They reflect some of the most familiar and desirable traditional canoe designs and range in size and purpose from an ultralight 13-foot solo canoe to a 17½-foot two-paddler canoe for serious wilderness tripping.

These eight represent just a sample of the plans on the market, available from Bear Mountain and similar companies that offer both traditional and contemporary designs to suit most paddling styles and preferences. If none of the plans included in this chapter match your own design priorities, check Sources, page 200, for a list of mail-order companies that sell plans.

When you purchase a plan, you will receive the full-size lines of the boat, taken at specific intervals, which you then simply have to trace to produce the section molds. Space limitations make it impossible for us to include full-size lines here.

Instead, we have included a table of offsets expressed in the traditional format of feet/inches/ eighths of an inch. With these numbers, it is possible to make full-size drawings using a process known as *lofting*. Because of the complexity of the subject, however, it is beyond the scope of

this book to provide accurate and thorough instructions on this fascinating aspect of boatbuilding. If you want to loft these plans yourself, consult the references listed in Sources, page 203. For your first boat, however, we recommend buying plans from one of the sources listed.

READING PLANS

The full-size plans you buy will usually have the lines for all the station molds as well as the lines for the bow and stern molds all on one sheet of paper. Seeing the lines all together will help you make better sense of the shape of the canoe and the relationship between the mold and the strongback than if each mold were reproduced separately. However, this can make plans a little confusing to read at first.

Professionally prepared plans will have full-size drawings that correspond to the three views that illustrate each of the canoes in this chapter: a side, or profile, view; the plan view, a fish-eye perspective from the bottom; and the body plan, a head-on view that looks like superimposed cross sections of one half of the canoe. (For further explanation of these views, see Anatomy of a Canoe, page 27.)

These three drawings have two reference lines in common: the *baseline*, a horizontal bow-to-stern plane upon which the hypothetical canoe sits, and the *center-*

line, which runs from bow to stern (perpendicular to the baseline) and divides the canoe in half neatly down the center.

Because each of the three views has both of these reference lines in common, you can pick any point of the canoe at random, and by relating its position to the baseline and the centerline on one perspective, you can readily find exactly the same point on the other two views. With this information, you will be able to create a three-dimensional mold of the canoe.

Turn to page 30, and examine the body plan at the bottom right of the page. Now imagine that you are looking at a canoe head-on. If it is a *symmetrical* design, the first thing you will notice is that the left side of the hull is missing. That is because the left side is a mirror image of the right and can be reproduced by simply flopping the view over. An *asymmetrical* design will have the bow on the right side of the centerline and the stern on the left.

The second thing you will notice is that there are numbered lines curving out at different distances from the centerline. Each of these lines represents one station of the canoe and shows the exact shape of the canoe hull at that specific spot. As we already mentioned, the stations for these plans are measured at 12-inch intervals.

If the design is symmetrical, the station lines will be on one side of the centerline only. The center station will be "0," and numbering will continue to the bow/stern. To produce a full mold, you will make two copies of each numbered station. If the canoe is asymmetrical, there will be station lines on both sides of the centerline. Each of these will be numbered, bow to stern. To produce the mold for an asymmetrical canoe, you will make only one copy of each numbered station.

If you build a full-size mold of each station shape (complete with a matching left-hand side) and attach them at the correct height to a foundation (a strongback) in correct sequence and properly spaced, you will have a perfect skeletal replica of the canoe.

Accompanying the plan drawings in this chapter is a three-dimensional sketch of how each finished canoe will look, a short description of its background and performance capabilities and a list of specifications.

A table of offsets is also provided. The offsets for the plans in this book are expressed in the traditional format of feet/inches/eighths and are given to the outside of the planking. If plans are being drawn from these offsets, the ¼-inch plank thickness will be deducted from the body plan or half-breadths after lofting the waterlines full size.

Professionally prepared plans that you buy will include a sheet of line drawings to scale, showing the body plan, the profile, waterlines

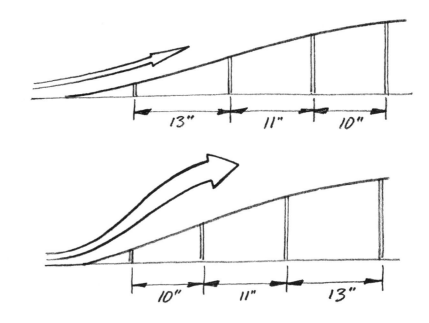

By altering the distances between stations, the shape of the canoe can be changed significantly, affecting the way it cuts through water.

and technical specifications, such as length, depth, gunwale width, et cetera. There should also be specifications for displacement and seat placement.

MODIFYING EXISTING DESIGNS

Canoes have been around almost as long as the human race; there has been ample opportunity to try different hull shapes and understand how each contributes to a specific function. Because form is a product of function (the interaction of hull shape and water), shape and proportion can always be combined in new ways to fulfill new objectives.

With the aid of yacht-design software, contemporary canoe designers have instant access to massive amounts of data that allow them to fine-tune shape for a specific purpose. While this may suggest that the canoes are computer-designed, in reality, the computer is just a machine that helps the designer translate experience into three dimensions.

Even with computers, however, most casual builders will not be designing their own canoes. Still, it is feasible to "customize" a canoe by modifying an existing design to suit personal needs and desires more perfectly. If you find a plan that meets most but not all of your criteria, it is fairly simple to adjust some of the design variables, such as length, rocker and entry line. But unless you have had considerable paddling experience, it is better to build a professional design than to risk disappointment on launching day.

Should you decide to modify an existing design, cut out the molds according to the directions on page 93. It is then relatively simple to vary the canoe length by manipulating the distance between stations and to adjust the height of stations above the strongback.

Master builders like Rushton often used one mold for two or three different lengths of canoes. Ideally, stations should be spaced 12 inches apart, but that interval can be stretched to 14 inches without sacrificing the essential quality of the shape. Over a total of 15 stations, this adjustment will extend a design by more than 2 feet. Conversely, a design can be shortened by shrinking the distance between stations, or if you have a symmetrical design that is both too long and too beamy, you can produce a shorter, slimmer canoe by omitting the center mold.

When the stations remain equidistant, most basic design characteristics of the canoe stay the same despite the altered length. Because the waterline length and length-width ratios are changed, however, the way the canoe handles will also change.

When the distance between stations is varied unequally, the shape of the waterline (the prismatic coefficient) is changed fundamentally. For a longer entry line, the stations can be moved progressively farther apart toward the bow. For increased fullness in the bow, the stations can be moved progressively closer together toward the bow.

You can also alter the profile of the keel-line by modifying the height of the molds. A flat keel-line can be adjusted to a 1-inch rocker by first raising the center mold 1 inch, then tacking a batten along the centerline from stem to stem and raising the other molds to the design.

The practice of tacking temporary battens along the hull at regular intervals to check for fairness and to avoid surprises during planking is recommended for any of these modifications. More complex modifications are best done by lofting the plans full size first. It will save you time and confusion in the long run.

However you have procured them—by buying or by lofting one of the models in this chapter—you now have the full-size body plan of your canoe hull on a single sheet of paper. Before you can translate that into a boat, you need to assemble your materials and tools and clear a space you can call your boat shop.

THE PLANS

The eight designs on the following pages were chosen to span the most desirable and beautiful shapes in canoes. Each plan includes perspective line drawings, a traditional table of offsets and construction specifications, as well as a short description of the background and primary functions of that particular model.

For information about ordering plans from Bear Mountain Boat Shop for the boats featured here, please turn to page 200. Also, please note that the designs of these boats are the intellectual property of the designers and are protected by international copyright. If you purchase plans, they are for your personal use for the construction of one boat. Use of the plans for any commercial purposes, sale of or transfer to any third party is expressly prohibited without the permission of the designers.

ROB ROY: A CLASSIC DOUBLE-PADDLE SOLO CANOE

Truly the poor man's yacht, the Rob Roy originated in England in the mid-1800s. John MacGregor, after seeing our native birchbark canoes and the Eskimo kayak, designed his idea of an efficient cruising canoe, calling it the Rob Roy. This style of solo canoe, often rigged for sail, was typically 12 to 15 feet in length and was propelled with a double-blade paddle used from a sitting position.

Early canoebuilders, such as J. Henry Rushton and W.P. Stephens, were influenced by the style, which dominated American recreational canoeing until the 1900s. The hull design has been built in many versions, from a simple lightweight, fast-cruising canoe to a fully trimmed boat with bookmatched walnut veneer decks, sliding seat, footrest, floorboards and a hand-rubbed varnish finish.

TABLE OF HEIGHTS Dimensions are in feet-inches-eighths

Station	12	11	10	9	8	7	6	5	4	3	2
Sheer	0-06-4+	0-07-1	0-07-4+	0-07-6	0-07-6+	0-07-6	0-07-4	0-07-0+	0-06-2+	0-05-2+	0-03-6
Butt 2"	1-03-3+	1-05-0	1-05-4	1-05-6	1-05-7+	1-05-7	1-05-5+	1-05-2+	1-04-6	1-03-5+	1-01-1+
Butt 4"	0-11-5	1-04-0	1-05-1	1-05-4+	1-05-6+	1-05-6+	1-05-4+	1-05-1	1-04-2	1-02-4	0-09-2+
Butt 6"		1-02-0	1-04-3	1-05-1+	1-05-4+	1-05-4+	1-05-2+	1-04-5+	1-03-3	1-00-2	
Butt 8"		0-08-5+	1-02-7+	1-04-4	1-05-0+	1-05-1+	1-04-6+	1-03-7	1-01-5+	0-07-4+	
Butt 10"			0-10-7+	1-03-0	1-04-1	1-04-2+	1-03-7	1-02-2	0-09-5+		
Butt 12"				0-09-7	1-01-7	1-02-4	1-01-4+	0-09-1+			
profile	1-05-0	1-05-3+	1-05-5+	1-05-7	1-06-0	1-06-0	1-05-6	1-05-3+	1-05-0	1-04-2+	1-03-1+

TABLE OF HALF-BREADTHS

Station	12	11	10	9	8	7	6	5	4	3	2
Sheer	0-05-2+	0-08-2+	0-10-5	1-00-1+	1-01-1	1-01-4	1-01-2	1-00-3	0-10-6+	0-08-4+	0-05-4
WL 4"											0-05-3+
WL 6"										0-08-3+	0-05-0
WL 8"	0-05-0	0-08-1	0-10-4+	1-00-1+	1-01-1	1-01-3+	1-01-1+	1-00-1+	0-10-3+	0-07-6+	0-04-3+
WL 10"	0-04-4	0-07-5	0-10-1+	1-00-0	1-01-0	1-01-2+	1-01-0	0-11-6+	0-09-7	0-07-1	0-03-5+
WL 12"	0-03-6+	0-07-0	0-09-5	0-11-4+	1-00-5+	1-01-0+	1-00-4+	0-11-2	0-09-0+	0-06-1	0-02-6
WL 14"	0-02-7+	0-06-0	0-08-5+	0-10-5+	0-11-7+	1-00-2+	0-11-6	0-10-1+	0-07-6	0-04-4+	0-01-3
WL 16"	0-01-4	0-04-0	0-06-5+	0-08-7	0-10-1+	0-10-4+	0-09-6+	0-07-6+	0-04-6	0-01-2+	

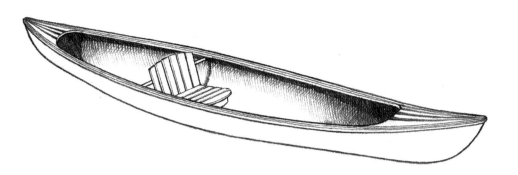

Distance from Station 1 to forward edge of inside bow stem:

WL	2"	1-04-1+
WL	4"	1-03-4
WL	6"	1-02-5
WL	8"	1-01-3+
WL	10"	1-11-6+
WL	12"	1-09-4+
WL	14"	0-05-2

Distance from Station 13 to aft edge of inside stern stem:

WL	6"	1-03-7+
WL	8"	1-03-0+
WL	10"	1-01-7
WL	12"	1-00-3+
WL	14"	0-10-3+
WL	16"	0-06-2+

Rob Roy Specifications

Length: 12' 11"
Beam: 27"
Beam WL: 24½"
Depth: 10' ¼"
Draft: 4"
Weight: 30 to 40 lbs.

Design © Ted Moores/Steve Killing

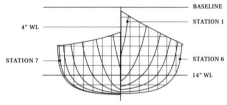

Stern Stations   Bow Stations

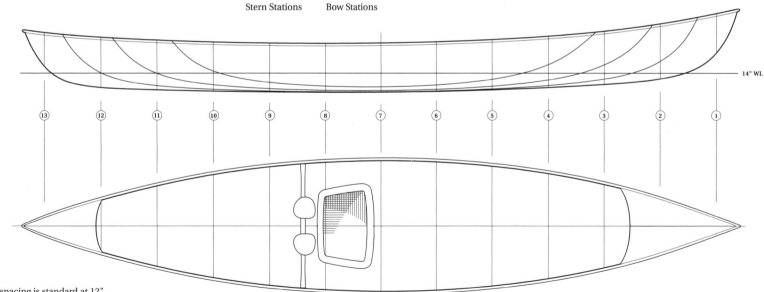

Station spacing is standard at 12"

PIPE DREAMS TO PAPER

Bob's Special: a "Chestnut" classic

From the 1950 Chestnut Canoe Company catalog: "The Chestnut 50-lb. Special has been designed to meet a certain demand for an extremely lightweight canoe of good carrying capacity and has proved very popular. Owing to its width and flat bottom, it is very steady, and the ends are low, making it easy to portage through the brush."

Forty years later, this remains one of Chestnut's better-known models, favored especially by anglers and solo trippers, since the moderate rocker and soft bilges make it a great canoe for traditional-style solo paddling. To adapt to strip planking, some modifications were made: the severe hollows near the waterline toward the ends of the canoe were reduced, and the sheer-line was given a less pronounced rise near the ends. We feel the changes produce a more pleasant boat all-round.

TABLE OF HEIGHTS Dimensions are in feet-inches-eighths

Station	0	1	2	3	4	5	6	7
Sheer	0-08-0	0-07-7	0-07-5	0-07-1+	0-06-5	0-05-5+	0-04-3+	0-02-3
Butt 2"	1-08-5	1-08-5	1-08-4+	1-08-4	1-08-2+	1-07-7	1-06-6	
Butt 4"	1-08-4	1-08-4	1-08-3+	1-08-2	1-07-7	1-06-7+	1-03-6	
Butt 6"	1-08-2+	1-08-2+	1-08-1+	1-07-7	1-07-1	1-05-1+		
Butt 8"	1-08-0+	1-08-0	1-07-6	1-07-1+	1-05-7			
Butt 10"	1-07-5	1-07-4	1-07-1	1-06-1+	1-03-4+			
Butt 12"	1-07-0+	1-06-7	1-06-2	1-04-5				
Butt 14"	1-06-2	1-05-7+	1-04-6+					
Butt 16"	1-05-0	1-04-3						
Profile	1-08-5+	1-08-5+	1-08-5+	1-08-5	1-08-4	1-08-2	1-07-7	1-06-6+

TABLE OF HALF-BREADTHS

Station	0	1	2	3	4	5	6	7
Sheer	1-04-7	1-04-3	1-03-0+	1-01-0	0-10-3+	0-07-3	0-04-2	0-00-7+
WL 4"								0-01-0+
WL 6"						0-07-3+	0-04-3	0-01-2
WL 8"		1-04-3	1-03-1	1-01-1+	0-10-5	0-07-5	0-04-4	0-01-3
WL 10"	1-05-3	1-04-7	1-03-4	1-01-3+	0-10-6+	0-07-6	0-04-5	0-01-3+
WL 12"	1-05-5+	1-05-1+	1-03-6	1-01-4+	0-10-6+	0-07-6	0-04-5	0-01-4
WL 14"	1-05-5+	1-05-1	1-03-5	1-01-3	0-10-4+	0-07-4	0-04-3+	0-01-3
WL 16"	1-04-7	1-04-2+	1-02-6	1-00-4	0-09-6	0-06-6+	0-03-7	0-01-0+
WL 18"	1-02-4	1-01-7+	1-00-3+	0-10-2+	0-07-6+	0-05-1+	0-02-5+	0-00-3
WL 20"	0-08-4	0-08-1	0-07-1	0-05-4+	0-03-5	0-01-4		

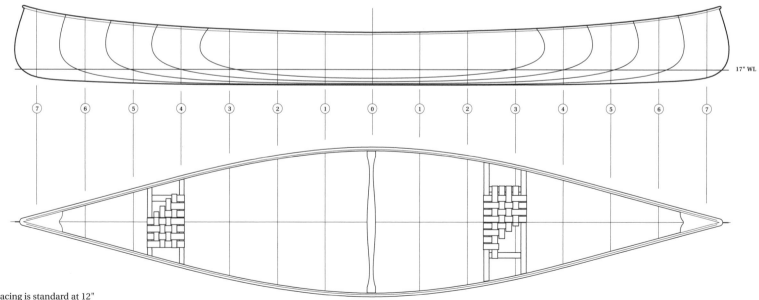

Distance from Station 6 to forward edge of inside stem:

WL	2"	1-03-0
WL	4"	1-03-5+
WL	6"	1-04-2+
WL	8"	1-04-7
WL	10"	1-05-2+
WL	12"	1-05-3+
WL	14"	1-05-2+
WL	16"	1-04-4
WL	18"	1-02-2
WL	20"	1-08-7+

BOB'S SPECIAL SPECIFICATIONS

Length: 15' 0"
Beam: 36"
Beam WL: 32"
Depth: 12' ½"
Draft: 4"
Weight: 40 to 50 lbs.

Design © Ted Moores/Steve Killing

BASELINE

4" WL

STATION 7

STATION 0

17" WL

17" WL

⑦ ⑥ ⑤ ④ ③ ② ① ⓪ ① ② ③ ④ ⑤ ⑥ ⑦

Station spacing is standard at 12"

Hiawatha: a light-displacement, easy-paddling canoe

This Bear Mountain design has a traditional sheer-line and bow profile reminiscent of the early "Canadian" style canoe. Below the waterline, the hull is a more modern shape for paddling efficiency. The hull is a shallow arch with a moderately flat keel-line that flows into a vee at the bow for directional stability, speed and maneuverability.

The Hiawatha is a general-purpose recreational canoe of light displacement, designed in the tradition of contemporary American cruisers, achieving its optimum waterline shape when paddled level, rather than heeled over. A good solo canoe, it is also very fast and responsive with a double paddle. In 1999, we redesigned the hull to add stability and to increase performance. The essential flavor of the boat, however, has remained.

TABLE OF HEIGHTS Dimensions are in feet-inches-eighths

Station	0	1	2	3	4	5	6
Sheer	0-11-0+	0-11-0+	0-11-0+	0-11-0	0-10-6	0-10-0	0-080
Butt 2"	1-10-7	1-10-6+	1-10-6	1-10-5	1-10-3	1-09-7	1-08-4+
Butt 4"	1-10-6	1-10-5+	1-10-4+	1-10-2+	1-09-7	1-08-6	
Butt 6"	1-10-5	1-10-4	1-10-2+	1-10-0	1-09-1	1-06-1+	
Butt 8"	1-10-3	1-10-2	1-10-0	1-09-2+	1-07-5		
Butt 10"	1-10-0	1-09-6+	1-09-3	1-08-1+			
Butt 12"	1-09-3	1-09-1	1-08-2+	1-05-1+			
Butt 14"	1-08-2	1-07-6	1-05-4				
Butt 16"	1-05-3+	1-00-5					
Profile	1-11-0	1-11-0	1-10-7	1-10-6+	1-10-6	1-10-4+	1-10-2+

TABLE OF HALF-BREADTHS

Station	0	1	2	3	4	5	6
Sheer	1-04-4	1-03-7+	1-02-4	1-00-3	0-09-5+	0-06-5+	0-03-4
WL 10"							0-03-6
WL 12"	1-04-4	1-04-0	1-02-4	1-00-3	0-09-6	0-06-6+	0-03-7
WL 14"	1-04-4+	1-04-0	1-02-4	1-00-3	0-09-6	0-06-6+	0-03-7
WL 16"	1-04-3	1-03-6+	1-02-3	1-00-2	0-09-4+	0-06-5	0-03-5+
WL 18"	1-03-6	1-03-1+	1-01-6+	0-11-5+	0-09-0	0-06-0+	0-03-2
WL 20"	1-02-2	1-01-6	1-00-3	0-10-2	0-07-5	0-04-7	0-02-3
WL 22"	0-10-0	0-09-3+	0-07-7+	0-05-7	0-03-5	0-01-6	0-00-4+

Distance from Station 6 to forward edge of inside stem:

WL	2"	1-00-7+
WL	4"	1-02-4+
WL	6"	1-03-7+
WL	8"	1-05-0+
WL	10"	1-05-6
WL	12"	1-06-0+
WL	14"	1-06-0+
WL	16"	1-05-4+
WL	18"	1-04-4
WL	20"	1-02-2+
WL	22"	0-06-7+

HIAWATHA SPECIFICATIONS

Length: 15' 1½"
Beam: 33½"
Beam WL: 31"
Depth: 12' ¼"
Draft: 4¼"
Weight: 40 to 50 lbs.

Design © Ted Moores/Steve Killing

BASELINE
4" WL
STATION 7
STATION 0
19" WL

19" WL

⑦ ⑥ ⑤ ④ ③ ② ① ⓪ ① ② ③ ④ ⑤ ⑥ ⑦

Station spacing is standard at 12"

Ranger: a pocket-size Prospector

The Prospector model originally built by the Chestnut Canoe Company was made in lengths from 12 to 18 feet. This model, the 15-foot Ranger, has a sweet shape, and Ron Frenette of Canadian Canoes decided we should have it in our range of plans. It has the same end shape and highly rockered hull of our 16-foot Prospector. It is stable and strong, making it a good load carrier. If you are looking for a boat with some history and good all-round paddling characteristics, this might be the one.

Table of Heights Dimensions are in feet-inches-eighths

Station	0	1	2	3	4	5	6	7
Sheer	0-11-5+	0-11-5	0-11-4	0-11-1+	0-10-2+	0-08-5+	0-06-2	0-02-3
Butt 2"	2-00-5+	2-00-5+	2-00-5	2-00-4	2-00-2	1-11-5	1-10-1+	0-00-0
Butt 4"	2-00-5	2-00-4+	2-00-4	2-00-2+	1-11-7	1-10-6+	1-07-2+	
Butt 6"	2-00-4	2-00-3+	2-00-2+	2-00-0+	1-11-2+	1-09-2+		
Butt 8"	2-00-2+	2-00-2	2-00-0+	1-11-5	1-10-3	1-06-1+		
Butt 10"	2-00-0+	2-00-0	1-11-6	1-11-0	1-08-5+			
Butt 12"	1-11-5	1-11-4	1-11-1	1-09-6+				
Butt 14"	1-11-0	1-10-6+	1-10-0+	1-02-6+				
Butt 16"	1-09-5+	1-09-1+						
Profile	2-00-6	2-00-5+	2-00-5+	2-00-4+	2-00-3+	2-00-0	1-11-3	1-09-2+

Table of Half-Breadths

Station	0	1	2	3	4	5	6	7
Sheer	1-04-3	1-04-0	1-03-0	1-01-2+	0-11-0	0-08-0+	0-04-5+	0-00-6+
WL 2"								
WL 4"							0-01-0	
WL 6"							0-01-2	
WL 8"							0-04-7	0-01-3+
WL 10"						0-08-2	0-05-0+	0-01-4
WL 12"	1-04-3+	1-04-0+	1-03-1	1-01-4	0-11-2	0-08-3+	0-05-1	0-01-4
WL 14"	1-04-6+	1-04-3+	1-03-4	1-01-7	0-11-4	0-08-4	0-05-0+	0-01-4
WL 16"	1-05-1	1-04-6	1-03-6	1-02-0+	0-11-5	0-08-3+	0-04-7	0-01-3
WL 18"	1-05-2+	1-04-7	1-03-6+	1-02-0+	0-11-3	0-08-0+	0-04-4	0-01-1
WL 20"	1-05-0+	1-04-5	1-03-3+	1-01-3+	0-10-4+	0-07-0+	0-03-5	0-00-5
WL 22"	1-03-5	1-03-2	1-02-0+	0-11-6	0-08-5	0-05-2	0-02-1+	
WL 24"	0-10-3	0-10-0	0-08-5+	0-06-3+	0-03-4+	0-00-2+		

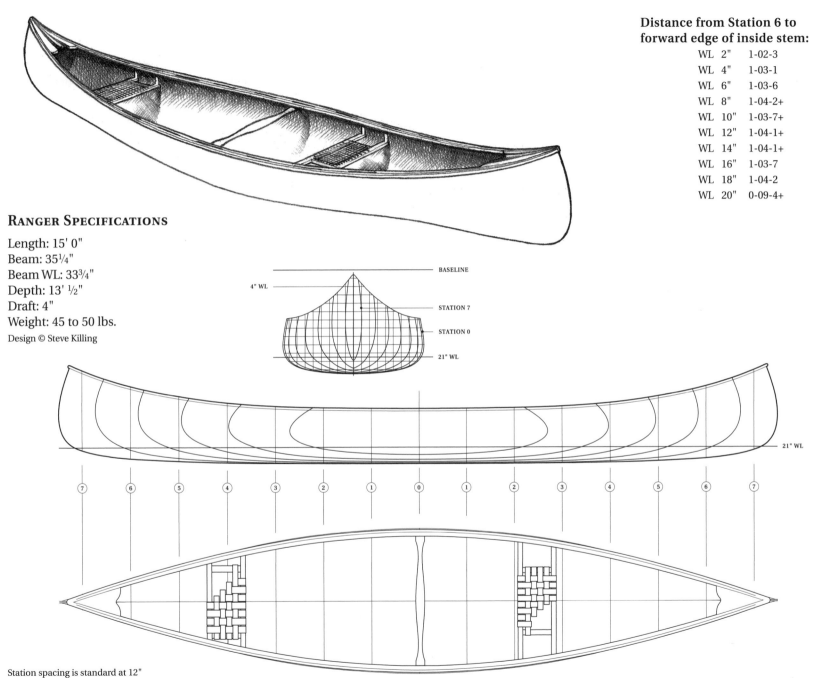

WL	2"	1-02-3
WL	4"	1-03-1
WL	6"	1-03-6
WL	8"	1-04-2+
WL	10"	1-03-7+
WL	12"	1-04-1+
WL	14"	1-04-1+
WL	16"	1-03-7
WL	18"	1-04-2
WL	20"	0-09-4+

RANGER SPECIFICATIONS

Length: 15' 0"
Beam: 35¼"
Beam WL: 33¾"
Depth: 13' ½"
Draft: 4"
Weight: 45 to 50 lbs.

Design © Steve Killing

BASELINE

4" WL

STATION 7

STATION 0

21" WL

21" WL

⑦ ⑥ ⑤ ④ ③ ② ① ⓪ ① ② ③ ④ ⑤ ⑥ ⑦

Station spacing is standard at 12"

Huron Cruiser: traditional yet sleek

The lines for this canoe were taken from an original "Huron" built in cedar/canvas by the Peterborough Canoe Company.

According to the Peterborough Canoe Company catalog, "They have good carrying capacity while retaining a light draft and are an easy paddling craft that can be handled well in rough or swift waters. The gunwhale line is straighter in these models and is lowered at bow and stem, thus offering less wind resistance." The rounded bottom may reduce carrying capacity, but the paddler can expect a quick and responsive craft.

On the original, two optional keels were offered: the shoe keel (1/2" thick by 1 3/4" wide) for added protection; and a lake keel (7/8" thick by 3/4" wide, tapered to 3/8") for a small increase in directional stability.

TABLE OF HEIGHTS Dimensions are in feet-inches-eighths

Station	0	1	2	3	4	5	6	7
Sheer	0-08-2+	0-08-2	0-08-0+	0-07-5+	0-07-0	0-05-7	0-04-3+	0-02-1+
Butt 2"	1-09-5+	1-09-5	1-09-4+	1-09-3+	1-09-2	1-08-6+	1-07-6+	0-00-0
Butt 4"	1-09-4+	1-09-4	1-09-3	1-09-1+	1-08-6+	1-07-7+	1-04-4	
Butt 6"	1-09-3	1-09-2+	1-09-1	1-08-6+	1-08-1	1-06-1		
Butt 8"	1-09-0+	1-09-0	1-08-6	1-08-2	1-06-7			
Butt 10"	1-08-5	1-08-4+	1-08-1+	1-07-2	0-08-4			
Butt 12"	1-08-0	1-07-6+	1-07-1+	1-05-0+				
Butt 14"	1-06-6+	1-06-4	0-08-2+					
Butt 16"	1-03-1+							
Profile	1-09-6	1-09-5+	1-09-5+	1-09-4+	1-09-3+	1-09-1+	1-09-0	1-08-0

TABLE OF HALF-BREADTHS

Station	0	1	2	3	4	5	6	7
Sheer	1-03-2+	1-03-0	1-01-7+	1-00-1	0-09-6+	0-07-0+	0-04-1+	0-01-4
WL 4"								0-01-5
WL 6"						0-07-0+	0-04-2+	0-01-6
WL 8"				1-00-1+	0-09-7+	0-07-2	0-04-3+	0-01-7
WL 10"	1-03-5	1-03-2+	1-02-2+	1-00-4	0-10-1	0-07-3	0-04-4+	0-01-7+
WL 12"	1-03-7	1-03-4+	1-02-4	1-00-5	0-10-1+	0-07-3+	0-04-4+	0-01-7+
WL 14"	1-04-0	1-03-5	1-02-4+	1-00-5	0-10-1+	0-07-3	0-04-3+	0-01-6+
WL 16"	1-03-6+	1-03-3+	1-02-3	1-00-3	0-09-7	0-07-0	0-04-1	0-01-4+
WL 18"	1-02-6+	1-02-3+	1-01-3	0-11-3+	0-08-7	0-06-0+	0-03-3	0-01-0
WL 20"	1-00-0	0-11-5	0-10-4	0-08-5	0-06-2	0-03-7	0-01-6	0-00-0

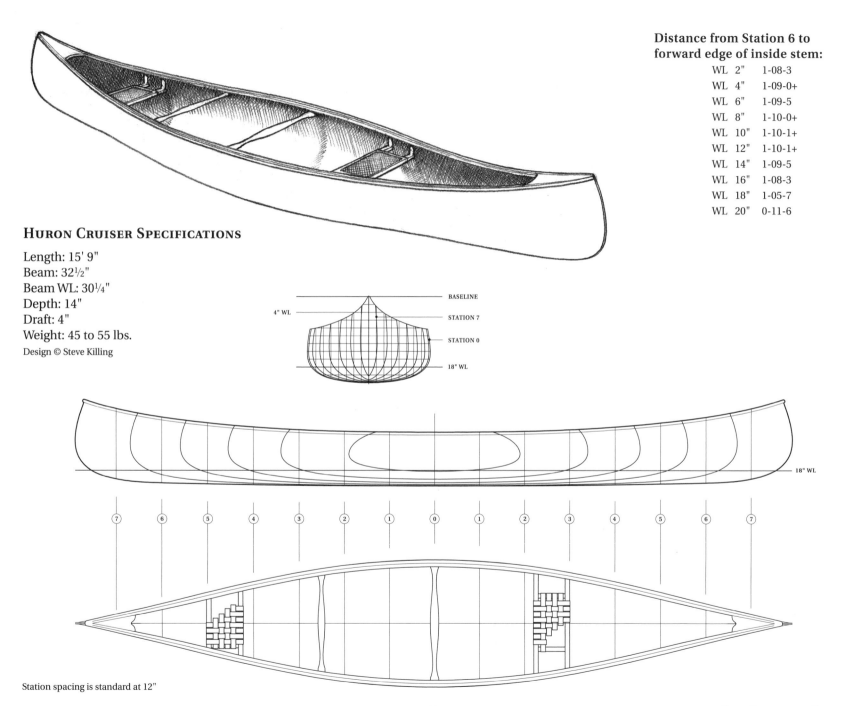

Distance from Station 6 to forward edge of inside stem:

WL	2"	1-08-3
WL	4"	1-09-0+
WL	6"	1-09-5
WL	8"	1-10-0+
WL	10"	1-10-1+
WL	12"	1-10-1+
WL	14"	1-09-5
WL	16"	1-08-3
WL	18"	1-05-7
WL	20"	0-11-6

HURON CRUISER SPECIFICATIONS

Length: 15' 9"
Beam: 32½"
Beam WL: 30¼"
Depth: 14"
Draft: 4"
Weight: 45 to 55 lbs.

Design © Steve Killing

BASELINE

4" WL

STATION 7

STATION 0

18" WL

18" WL

7 6 5 4 3 2 1 0 1 2 3 4 5 6 7

Station spacing is standard at 12"

PROSPECTOR: AN IDEAL ALL-ROUND CANOE

The Chestnut Canoe Company built this "workhorse of the North" to meet the specific needs of the prospector—good maneuverability through whitewater and wilderness, with the capacity to carry substantial loads. It features a flattened, shallow-arch hull, with its fullness carried into the bow and stern, good depth amidships to maintain freeboard and deepened ends to keep paddlers and gear dry. The rockered keel-line makes it particularly maneuverable in whitewater. As canoeist-filmmaker Bill Mason wrote, "It is amazing that such a large-volume tripping canoe can also be so beautiful to paddle solo in the leaned position—canoe ballet, as I call it. It is the ideal all-round canoe."

TABLE OF HEIGHTS   Dimensions are in feet-inches-eighths

Station	0	1	2	3	4	5	6	7
Sheer	0-10-4+	0-10-3+	0-10-1+	0-09-5	0-08-6+	0-07-5	0-06-0	0-03-3
Butt 2"	2-01-0	2-01-0	2-00-6	2-00-3+	2-00-0	1-11-2	1-09-6+	1-05-2
Butt 4"	2-00-7+	2-00-7	2-00-5	2-00-2	1-11-4+	1-10-3	1-07-4	
Butt 6"	2-00-6	2-00-5+	2-00-3+	1-11-7	1-11-0	1-09-0+		
Butt 8"	2-00-4	2-00-3	2-00-0+	1-11-3+	1-10-0+	1-06-1		
Butt 10"	2-00-1	2-00-0	1-11-4+	1-10-5+	1-08-3			
Butt 12"	1-11-4+	1-11-3+	1-10-6+	1-09-3				
Butt 14"	1-10-6	1-10-4	1-09-4	1-05-3				
Butt 16"	1-09-0+	1-08-3+						
Profile	2-01-0+	2-01-0	2-00-6+	2-00-5	2-00-2	1-11-6	1-11-0+	1-09-5+

TABLE OF HALF-BREADTHS

Station	0	1	2	3	4	5	6	7
Sheer	1-04-7+	1-04-5	1-03-5+	1-02-0+	0-11-6	0-08-7	0-05-6	0-02-4+
WL 4"								0-02-5
WL 6"							0-05-6	0-02-6
WL 8"						0-08-7	0-05-6+	0-02-6+
WL 10"				1-02-0+	0-11-6	0-09-0	0-05-7	0-02-7
WL 12"	1-05-0+	1-04-6	1-03-6+	1-02-1+	0-11-7	0-09-0	0-05-7	0-02-6+
WL 14"	1-05-1+	1-04-7	1-03-7	1-02-2	0-11-6+	0-08-7+	0-05-5+	0-02-5
WL 16"	1-05-2	1-04-7+	1-03-7	1-02-1+	0-11-5+	0-08-5	0-05-2+	0-02-2
WL 18"	1-05-1	1-04-6	1-03-5+	1-01-6+	0-11-2	0-08-0+	0-04-5+	0-01-6
WL 20"	1-04-4+	1-04-1+	1-03-0+	1-01-0+	0-10-2+	0-07-0	0-03-5	0-01-0
WL 22"	1-03-1	1-02-5+	1-01-3+	0-11-1+	0-08-1	0-04-6	0-01-6	
WL 24"	0-10-5	0-10-0+	0-08-3+	0-05-5	0-02-1			

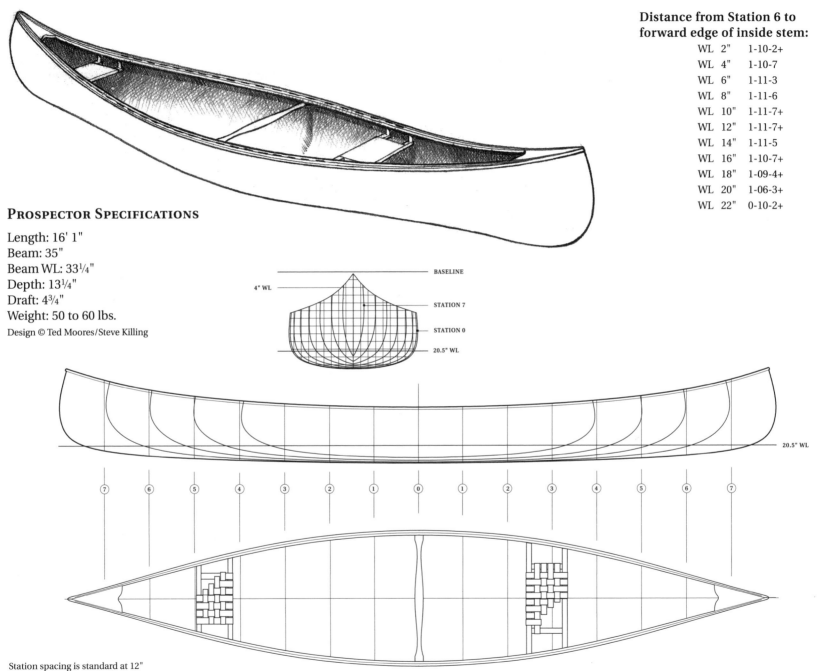

Distance from Station 6 to forward edge of inside stem:

WL	2"	1-10-2+
WL	4"	1-10-7
WL	6"	1-11-3
WL	8"	1-11-6
WL	10"	1-11-7+
WL	12"	1-11-7+
WL	14"	1-11-5
WL	16"	1-10-7+
WL	18"	1-09-4+
WL	20"	1-06-3+
WL	22"	0-10-2+

PROSPECTOR SPECIFICATIONS

Length: 16' 1"
Beam: 35"
Beam WL: 33¼"
Depth: 13¼"
Draft: 4¾"
Weight: 50 to 60 lbs.

Design © Ted Moores/Steve Killing

BASELINE

4" WL

STATION 7

STATION 0

20.5" WL

20.5" WL

⑦ ⑥ ⑤ ④ ③ ② ① ⓪ ① ② ③ ④ ⑤ ⑥ ⑦

Station spacing is standard at 12"

FREEDOM: A MODERN, EFFICIENT TRIPPING CANOE

The Freedom features an asymmetrical hull with a slim bow, a maximum beam aft of the middle and filled-out stern sections to reduce resistance. The gently rockered profile lets the boat turn with ease. Because of the slight tumblehome, this canoe is a wonderful solo boat but is also a great two-person tripper.

Designed by Steve Killing, who is better known for his yachts and America's Cup sailing designs, the Freedom 17 incorporates many of the hull-shape subtleties learned from his extensive paddling, sailing and rowing experience. The result is a tripping canoe that is both easy to plank and to paddle.

TABLE OF HEIGHTS Dimensions are in feet-inches-eighths

Station	16	15	14	13	12	11	10	9	8	7	6	5	4	3	2	1	0
Sheer	0-03-5	0-04-6	0-05-5	0-06-2+	0-06-6	0-07-0+	0-07-1+	0-07-1	0-07-0	0-06-6	0-06-3	0-05-7	0-05-1+	0-04-3+	0-03-4+	0-02-5	0-01-4+
Butt 2"		1-06-3+	1-07-2	1-07-4+	1-07-6	1-07-6+	1-07-7	1-07-7	1-07-7	1-07-6+	1-07-5+	1-07-4+	1-07-3	1-07-0	1-06-3+	1-05-0	
Butt 4"		1-04-0+	1-06-4	1-07-1+	1-07-4	1-07-5	1-07-5+	1-07-5+	1-07-5+	1-07-5	1-07-4	1-07-2	1-06-7+	1-06-3	1-05-1+		
Butt 6"			1-05-1+	1-06-4	1-07-1	1-07-3	1-07-3+	1-07-4	1-07-3+	1-07-2+	1-07-1	1-06-6+	1-06-2+	1-05-2+	1-00-5+		
Butt 8"				1-05-4+	1-06-4+	1-07-0	1-07-1	1-07-1+	1-07-1	1-07-0	1-06-5+	1-06-2	1-05-3	1-02-6+			
Butt 10"				1-02-6	1-05-5+	1-06-3+	1-06-5+	1-06-6+	1-06-5+	1-06-4	1-06-1	1-05-3	1-03-3				
Butt 12"					1-03-5+	1-05-4+	1-06-0+	1-06-2	1-06-1	1-05-6+	1-05-1+	1-03-3+					
Butt 14"						1-03-3+	1-05-0+	1-05-3	1-05-2	1-04-5	1-02-5						
Butt 16"								1-03-1	0-07-6+								
Profile	1-06-2+	1-07-2+	1-07-5	1-07-6+	1-07-7+	1-08-0	1-08-0+	1-08-0+	1-08-0	1-08-0	1-07-7+	1-07-6+	1-07-5	1-07-3+	1-07-1	1-06-5+	1-05-2+

TABLE OF HALF-BREADTHS

Station	16	15	14	13	12	11	10	9	8	7	6	5	4	3	2	1	0
Sheer	0-01-4	0-04-6	0-07-5+	0-10-2+	1-00-4	1-02-2	1-03-3+	1-04-0	1-03-7	1-03-2	1-02-1	1-00-5	0-10-6+	0-08-6	0-06-3+	0-03-7+	0-01-2
WL 2"																	0-01-1+
WL 4"	0-01-4														0-06-3+	0-03-7	0-01-1+
WL 6"	0-01-4	0-04-6	0-07-5+									1-00-5	0-10-6+	0-08-6	0-06-3	0-03-6+	0-01-1
WL 8"	0-01-4	0-04-6	0-07-5+	0-10-2+	1-00-4+	1-02-3	1-03-4+	1-04-0+	1-04-0	1-03-2+	1-02-2	1-00-6	0-10-7	0-08-5+	0-06-2+	0-03-6	0-01-0+
WL 10"	0-01-3+	0-04-5+	0-07-5+	0-10-3	1-00-5+	1-02-4	1-03-6	1-04-2+	1-04-1+	1-03-4	1-02-2+	1-00-6	0-10-7	0-08-5	0-06-1+	0-03-5	0-01-0
WL 12"	0-01-3	0-04-4+	0-07-5	0-10-2+	1-00-5+	1-02-4+	1-03-6+	1-04-3	1-04-2	1-03-4+	1-02-2+	1-00-6	0-10-6	0-08-4	0-06-0+	0-03-4	0-00-7+
WL 14"	0-01-2	0-04-3+	0-07-3+	0-10-1	1-00-4	1-02-3	1-03-5+	1-04-2	1-04-1	1-03-3	1-02-1	1-00-4	0-10-4	0-08-1+	0-05-6	0-03-2	0-00-6
WL 16"	0-01-0	0-04-0	0-06-7	0-09-4	0-11-6+	1-01-5+	1-03-0	1-03-4	1-03-3	1-02-4+	1-01-2+	0-11-5	0-09-5	0-07-3	0-05-0	0-02-5+	0-00-3+
WL 18"	0-00-1+	0-02-4+	0-05-0	0-07-2+	0-09-3+	0-11-1+	1-00-2	1-00-5+	1-00-3+	0-11-5	0-10-3	0-08-6	0-06-6+	0-04-6+	0-02-6+	0-10-0+	
WL 20"						0-00-3	0-00-7+	0-01-0	0-00-6	0-00-1							

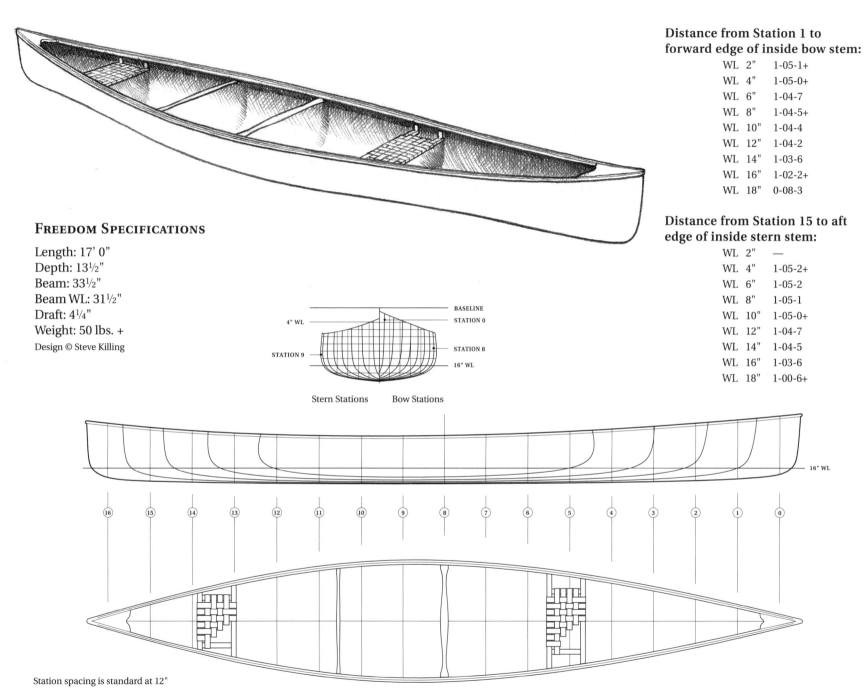

Distance from Station 1 to forward edge of inside bow stem:

WL	2"	1-05-1+
WL	4"	1-05-0+
WL	6"	1-04-7
WL	8"	1-04-5+
WL	10"	1-04-4
WL	12"	1-04-2
WL	14"	1-03-6
WL	16"	1-02-2+
WL	18"	0-08-3

Distance from Station 15 to aft edge of inside stern stem:

WL	2"	—
WL	4"	1-05-2+
WL	6"	1-05-2
WL	8"	1-05-1
WL	10"	1-05-0+
WL	12"	1-04-7
WL	14"	1-04-5
WL	16"	1-03-6
WL	18"	1-00-6+

FREEDOM SPECIFICATIONS

Length: 17' 0"
Depth: 13½"
Beam: 33½"
Beam WL: 31½"
Draft: 4¼"
Weight: 50 lbs. +

Design © Steve Killing

BASELINE
STATION 0
4" WL
STATION 8
STATION 9
STATION 15
16" WL

Stern Stations   Bow Stations

16" WL

16 15 14 13 12 11 10 9 8 7 6 5 4 3 2 1 0

Station spacing is standard at 12"

Redbird: a fast, light day-tripper

This Bear Mountain design is an efficient wilderness canoe that has proven exceptionally seaworthy, even in the North Sea and in the heavy seas around the Magdalen Islands in the Gulf of St. Lawrence. Its keelless shallow-arch hull with moderate rocker combines with a long waterline and fine entry to make it a fast, responsive boat. The bow and stern pro- files are reminiscent of the Long Nose Ojibwa Rice Harvesting canoe. The sides have a moderate tumblehome that adds lateral strength and allows outwales wide enough to turn aside waves. The boat was refaired in 1998 by Steve Killing, and in doing so, he added a little more stability, creating a canoe equally suited to experienced paddlers and talented novices.

TABLE OF HEIGHTS   Dimensions are in feet-inches-eighths

Station	0	1	2	3	4	5	6	7	8
Sheer	0-10-2	0-10-2	0-10-1	0-09-7	0-09-4	0-08-7+	0-08-0	0-05-7	0-01-4
Butt 2"	1-09-7	1-09-6+	1-09-6	1-09-4+	1-09-2+	1-08-7	1-08-1+	1-06-7	
Butt 4"	1-09-5+	1-09-5+	1-09-4	1-09-2	1-08-7	1-08-1+	1-06-7	0-09-1	
Butt 6"	1-09-4	1-09-3+	1-09-1+	1-08-6+	1-08-1+	1-07-0+	0-08-1	.	
Butt 8"	1-09-1+	1-09-0+	1-08-6	1-08-1+	1-07-2	1-05-0+			
Butt 10"	1-08-6	1-08-4+	1-08-1	1-07-2	1-05-3+				
Butt 12"	1-08-1	1-07-7	1-07-1+	1-05-4+					
Butt 14"	1-07-1+	1-06-6+	1-05-2+						
Butt 16"	0-10-7	1-01-4							
Profile	1-10-0	1-10-0	1-09-7	1-09-6+	1-09-5	1-09-3+	1-09-1	1-08-6	1-08-0

TABLE OF HALF-BREADTHS

Station	0	1	2	3	4	5	6	7	8
Sheer	1-03-6+	1-03-4	1-02-4+	1-01-0+	0-11-0	0-08-5	0-05-7+	0-03-1	0-00-2+
WL 2"									0-00-3
WL 4"									0-00-6+
WL 6"								0-03-1	0-01-2
WL 8"							0-05-7+	0-03-5+	0-01-4+
WL 10"				1-01-0+	0-11-0+	0-08-6	0-06-3	0-04-1	0-01-6+
WL 12"	1-04-1+	1-03-6+	1-02-6	1-01-2	0-11-2	0-09-0	0-06-5+	0-04-3	0-01-7
WL 14"	1-04-3+	1-04-0	1-02-7	1-01-2	0-11-2	0-09-0	0-06-5	0-04-2	0-01-6
WL 16"	1-04-2+	1-03-6+	1-02-4+	1-00-7	0-10-6+	0-08-4	0-06-1	0-03-5+	0-01-2+
WL 18"	1-03-3	1-02-6+	1-01-3+	0-11-5	0-09-4+	0-07-2	0-04-7	0-02-5+	0-00-6
WL 20"	1-00-3+	0-11-6+	0-10-3	0-08-4+	0-06-4+	0-04-3	0-02-3	0-01-0	

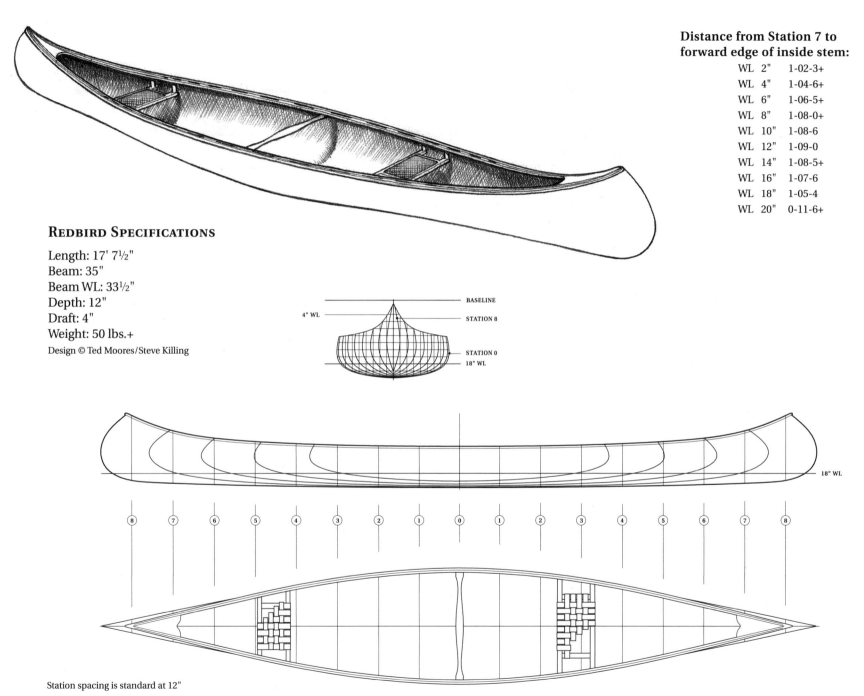

Distance from Station 7 to forward edge of inside stem:

WL	2"	1-02-3+
WL	4"	1-04-6+
WL	6"	1-06-5+
WL	8"	1-08-0+
WL	10"	1-08-6
WL	12"	1-09-0
WL	14"	1-08-5+
WL	16"	1-07-6
WL	18"	1-05-4
WL	20"	0-11-6+

Redbird Specifications

Length: 17' 7½"
Beam: 35"
Beam WL: 33½"
Depth: 12"
Draft: 4"
Weight: 50 lbs.+

Design © Ted Moores/Steve Killing

BASELINE
4" WL
STATION 8
STATION 0
18" WL

18" WL

⑧ ⑦ ⑥ ⑤ ④ ③ ② ① ⓪ ① ② ③ ④ ⑤ ⑥ ⑦ ⑧

Station spacing is standard at 12"

PREPARATIONS

Setting Up the Workshop

THE INTEGRITY OF THE BOATBUILDER IS HIS MOST VALUABLE ASSET.

—Bud McIntosh

Judging from the meticulous craftsmanship of a classic Otonabee cedarstrip—or a modern Bear Mountain canoe—one would think that each had emerged from an orderly shop equipped with the finest in precision tools. A glimpse into some of the workshops we've built in, however, would be as reassuring as the fading photographs of Thomas Gordon's boatworks.

Canoebuilders, it seems, have always plied their trade in cramped and cluttered quarters. Gordon's canoes took shape in an abandoned church on a Lakefield back street; a dilapidated farm-implement outlet on the outskirts of Bancroft was the early home of Bear Mountain canoes.

Ultimately, a canoe can be built anywhere, with very little equipment—only the quality of materials can never be compromised.

WORKPLACE

A boat shop is wherever you make it. An empty hayloft may seem an appropriate, even romantic, workshop, set amidst curious spiders and darting swallows. But slanting shadows through the barnboard, dusty residues and shifting temperatures make it less than ideal.

In selecting your own boat shop, consider the amount of space and the degree of control over climate and ventilation it offers. While perfect conditions are desirable, you will undoubtedly have to make compromises. After all, it is better to put up with a second-class shop than to abandon your dream canoe.

WILL IT FIT?

The workshop need not be huge, but to be comfortable, there should be at least 3 feet, free and clear, around the whole canoe. During those times you need a helper, tripping over each other will hamper both your mood and efficiency.

When sizing up a potential boat shop, remember that what came in as thin, flexible pieces of wood must go out as a full-size canoe. This may seem like an old joke, but it happens. One Scarborough builder had to remove a window and two rows of bricks to get his canoe to water.

Aside from the strongback and emerging canoe, you need room for a bench or work surface to hold tools, materials and mugs of coffee, a place to store strips where they won't get mangled and, if you are machining your own parts, enough room to rip lumber. Electrical outlets will be appreciated, and a level floor is a real bonus.

One essential piece of furniture cannot be overlooked—a moaning chair. This will be your haven of despair and delight, where you can rest and eye your fledgling craft, check your plans, pick out flaws before they become fatal and dream of crackling campfires and foaming rapids.

CLIMATE CONSIDERATIONS

Temperature and humidity are crucial to the resin-curing process: the closer these conditions are to the ideal, the easier the resin will be to work with. For every increase of 18 Fahrenheit degrees, cure time can be cut in half. The longer the drying period, the greater the risk of contamination by dust and humidity. Although the resin will eventually cure, working times will be less predictable and schedules may be disrupted.

Extremely hot temperatures can be just as damaging. When a builder in California's Napa Valley laid up his canoe, the temperature soared to 90 degrees F, setting the resin almost as fast as he brushed it on. Ideal conditions are 60 to 70 degrees, with a relative humidity of 45 to 65 percent. Even slightly cooler temperatures can make the resin hard to work and can produce a milky finish.

If you work in winter, be sure the space can be adequately heated. The temperature of the wood surface is more critical than the air temperature, so if you are heating the area just for lay-up, allow enough time for the hull to warm up.

Average room lighting is not enough for boatbuilding. Hang several 200-watt bulbs directly over the work space. Intense direct light will eliminate shadows, helping you spot humps in the hull and assuring thorough epoxy coating of the cloth. One builder from North Augusta, Ontario, learned of the inadequacy of his gloomy workshop in a painful first-day launch. He thought his finished canoe looked great—until the unforgiving light of day made the resin runs and bare patches glaringly obvious for the first time.

CAN YOU BREATHE?

Ventilation is a major consideration when working with petrochemicals, especially if the fumes can seep from the workshop into living areas. Epoxy resin is not as foul as polyester resin, but some varnishes are much worse. The fumes can be cloying, choking off oxygen and causing headaches, nausea, dizziness and, occasionally, respiratory problems. Wood dust, especially from red cedar, can be just as hazardous.

To keep the air clear, your boat shop should have operable windows for good cross-ventilation or an exhaust fan to suck out dust and fumes. Even in a well-ventilated space, there will be times during the construction of your canoe when you require lung protection. Be sure to read the safety material included with the instructions, and heed the warnings.

OPTIONS

Basements and garages are most often pressed into service as boat shops. Though basements offer better climatic control, working in such close proximity to living quarters can be harmful to more than your health—many woodstrip/epoxy canoes have taken shape in basements to the tune of continuous objections from cohabitants.

"I built in the basement, which was large, dry and well lit," said one young Ottawa builder. "It was suitable for me, though I'm not sure my parents would agree."

For about 12 years, we worked in a shop built on the back of the house. We avoided dust and fume problems by using two exhaust fans. A fan in a basement window, correctly positioned, will draw dust and fumes away from the interior toward the outside. As for noise, plan those stages so that the household isn't unduly disturbed.

A garage may be a little cramped, but it solves fume and dust problems. Unless it is heated, your efforts will be limited to warm weather, which brings its own curse. Ruby-bellied mosquitoes permanently adorned the canoe of one enthusiast who built at the peak of the bug season. A garage boat shop may also bring out onlookers, with their well-intentioned advice and cryptic assessments of your progress.

If you build outside, the canoe should be shaded. Direct sun can cause bubbles in uncured resin and cloud a finish coat. Even indoors, do not position the strongback where the sun's ultraviolet rays can fall directly on the hull for long periods of time. If it must be exposed to sunlight, cover the hull between sessions until it is protected with UV-shield varnish.

If the basement, garage, backyard and shed are not quite right for the job, follow the example of a Georgia canoeist, who, having assembled his boatbuilding materials, added a sunroom/boat shop to his house to have a proper place in which to create his canoe.

EQUIPMENT

A woodstrip canoe can be built with a bare minimum of tools. One teenager did the job with hand tools borrowed from a sympathetic and generous neighbor.

While the variety of equipment you have to work with has no direct bearing on the quality of the boat you build, you will do it in less time and with less frustration if you are properly outfitted.

Following is a list of required tools. To get the most out of them, keep them clean, sharp and accessible. A detailed list of required tools appears with each stage of the construction process.

Aside from conventional tools, you will occasionally need some equipment that is easily made from scrap wood. Directions are sprinkled throughout the text for handy devices, such as spring fingers, push sticks and slide rules. There are also instructions for several different "jigs," indispensable forms that hold a piece of work in place or guide a tool during repetitious operations. Though at first these may not seem worth the effort involved to make them, they will ease construction remarkably and, more important, will introduce you to the ingenious world of homemade tools.

THE RIGHT TOOLS

TOOL	USE	COMMENTS	SOURCE
Cutting Tools			
Portable circular saw (optional)	Cutting strongback parts.		
Saber saw	Cutting out station molds and decks.	Alternative: band saw.	Hardware
Crosscut handsaw	Cutting straight lines.		Hardware
Coping saw	Trimming planks.	Alternatives: Japanese razor saw, dovetail saw or backsaw.	Hardware
Table saw	Ripping planking, gunwales, keel.	Use hollow-ground combination planer blade.	Hardware
Dovetail saw	Cutting hardwood trim and planking to length.	Alternatives: fine-tooth hacksaw, backsaw, razor saw.	Hardware
Utility knife	Trimming fiberglass cloth.	Keep sharp blades available.	Hardware
Scissors	Cutting fiberglass cloth.	Don't use your best pair.	Hardware
Shaping and Fairing Tools			
Block plane	Fairing the hull and stems; shaping the ends of the planks where they meet at the bottom of the hull; fitting decks; shaping gunwales.	Alternative: spokeshave. Buy a good one. Low angle preferred.	Woodwork supply; hardware
Surform	Shaping curved surfaces; shaping cured epoxy.	Flat and curved bottom blades.	Hardware
Spokeshave	Smoothing compound curves as in shaping thwarts; fairing hull in tight spots where plane won't fit.	Very handy general workshop tool. Buy a good one. Flat sole.	Woodwork supply
Paint scraper	Rough-shaping hull; cleaning up epoxy.	Buy extra blade.	Hardware or paint store
Cabinet scraper	Shaping hardwood.	Nice-to-have shaping and smoothing tool.	Woodwork supply
Rasp (optional)	Shaping and rounding edges on epoxy and trim.	Both round and flat are useful.	Hardware
Router (optional)	Shaping trim; putting bead-and-cove edge on planking.	Must be used in a router-table setup for planking. Hand-held on trim.	See Sources (page 202)
$\frac{1}{4}$" and $1\frac{1}{4}$" chisel	Shaping and fitting.	Very useful.	Woodwork supply; hardware
Sharpening stone	Maintaining keen edge on cutting tools.	Sharp tools are safer than dull ones.	Woodwork supply

TOOL	USE	COMMENTS	SOURCE
Mill file	Sharpening scraper blade; smoothing metal edges on bolts, stem bands.	Use a file card to keep it clean.	Woodwork supply; hardware

Sanding Tools

TOOL	USE	COMMENTS	SOURCE
Sanding block	Makes the most of your sandpaper.	Buy shaped rubber block, or make from scrap wood or foam.	Hardware
Long board	Alternative to power sander; easier to avoid low spots	Also called file board (Speed File). Use with sandpaper for rough and fine sanding of hull.	Woodwork supply
5" round or 6" random orbital sander	Ideal for almost all sanding operations.	Fairly inexpensive, easily controlled power tool that will save a lot of time.	Hardware
Tack cloth	Wiping off sanded surfaces before applying finish.	Indispensable.	Hardware

Fastening Tools

TOOL	USE	COMMENTS	SOURCE
Staple gun	Fastening planks to stations.	For use with $9/16$" staples.	Hardware
Staple puller	Lifting staples.	Tack puller, or bend and pad end of flat screwdriver.	Hardware
Needle-nose pliers	Removing staples once heads are exposed.		Hardware
Screwdrivers	To fit screws you are using.		Hardware
Drill and wood bits	Predrilling and countersinking screw holes; driving screws.	Hand or power drill; countersink bit to fit screw sizes.	Hardware
Counterbore and plug cutter (optional)	Counterboring screw holes for plugs in gunwales and seats.		Hardware
C-clamps	Clamping stems, gunwales, decks and thwarts.	Minimum half-dozen $2\frac{1}{2}$"; more will speed up some jobs; make your own.	Hardware
Center punch	Starting holes in brass stem band.		Hardware

Fiberglassing Tools

TOOL	USE	COMMENTS	SOURCE
Mixing containers	Mixing resin and hardener.	Use paper coffee cups or small tin cans. You will need about 1 dozen.	
Tin pie plate (optional)	Pouring out mixed resin before application.	Resin will not set as fast in a thin layer.	
Stir sticks	Mixing resin and hardener.	Scraps of planking or tongue depressors.	
Syringe	Applying glue to bead-and-cove planking.	Curved nozzle is best.	Woodwork supply; resin supplier

TOOL	USE	COMMENTS	SOURCE
Glue brushes	Gluing gunwales and trim.	Small, disposable. Acid brushes.	Hardware; resin supplier
Epoxy roller (optional)	Applying last coats of epoxy; varnishing.	$\frac{1}{8}$" foam; no substitutes.	Resin supplier
Squeegee	Leveling first coat of resin and applying second coat.		Resin/body-shop supplier
Paintbrush	Applying first and last coat of epoxy and varnishing.	One $2\frac{1}{2}$" to 3" short-bristled, cheap. One 2" to 3", good quality.	Hardware; paint store
Mini-pumps	Dispensing resin and hardener; one shot of each gives desired resin/hardener ratio.		Resin supplier
Putty knife	Cleaning up excess glue; applying filler.	A flexible blade is desirable.	Hardware
Clean rags	Cleaning up.	Keep large supply on hand; white, cotton.	

Measuring Tools

Metal tape measure			Hardware
Tri-square	Setting up mold.	Small (12") metal.	Hardware
Level	Setting up mold.	2-foot size.	Hardware
Taut line	Determining long, straight lines.	Heavy fishing line.	Hardware

Safety

Dust mask or respirator	Machining and sanding.	Disposable model or one with replacement filters.	Hardware; paint store; body-shop supply
Waterless hand cleaner	Clean skin without using solvents.		Epoxy/body-shop supplier
Gloves	Preventing epoxy skin irritation.	Disposable plastic; surgeon's gloves are ideal. Work gloves.	Hardware; paint store; drugstore
Fan	Controlling dust and fumes.	Window fan is acceptable.	
Basic first-aid kit			
Fire extinguisher		Appropriate for solvent and wood fires.	
Barrier cream	Prevents skin irritation.	Use above gloves; bad reaction if used under.	Epoxy supplier
Eye protection			
Step stool or milk crate	Improve perspective and safety.	Be sure it is absolutely stable.	

MATERIALS

Wood is a traditional boatbuilding material, and there are purists who maintain it is still the best. Unfortunately, wood and water are not compatible in the long run.

The boatbuilder, unlike the cabinetmaker, must consider how water transforms wood's physical characteristics. Successive cycles of moisture and dry storage weaken wood, accelerating its deterioration. Exposed to water, wood becomes dimensionally unstable, swelling and shrinking. Water, together with air, warmth and food, promotes rot fungus, the bane of wooden-boat owners.

The monocoque structure described in this book has revolutionized wooden-boat building, because it sandwiches wood inside a sheath of epoxy resin and fiberglass cloth, stabilizing its moisture content and eliminating dry rot. Thus protected, wood becomes a dimensionally stable and reliable building material. This method is not a compromise, as some suggest, but an improvement, enhancing the natural buoyancy, strength and stiffness of wood with the durability of modern materials.

WOOD

Wood not only gives your canoe its warm, sensuous beauty but also is the vital structural core of the monocoque system. Shaping itself smoothly to form, it offers

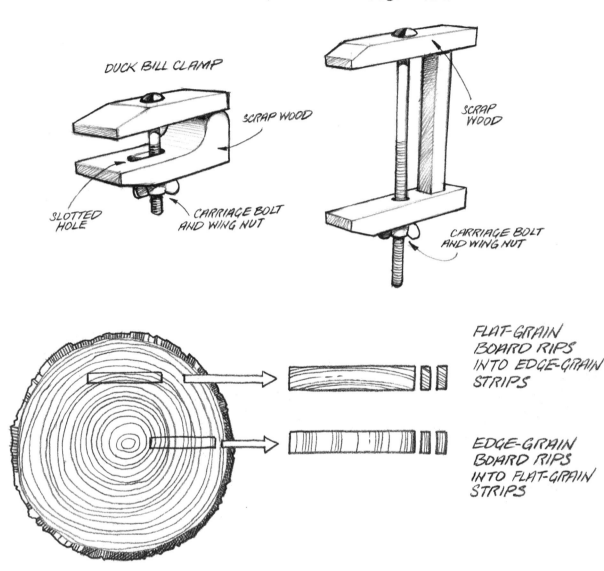

Top: Homemade clamps can easily be made from scraps of wood— a wise economy measure for a project that uses dozens of clamps. *Above:* The grain of your wood strips affects their color, texture and workability: edge-grain strips are more uniform and easier to work; flat-grain strips are harder to sand but are visually more interesting.

good strength for its weight and volume. Above all, it is tough, naturally buoyant and elastic. It is nature's own fiber-reinforced plastic, with cellulose fiber cells bonded together by lignin.

Different species of wood vary tremendously in their weight, strength and workability. No single species is best for woodstrip/epoxy canoes. Your choice will depend on what you expect of your canoe, what is available locally and your budget. The epoxy sheath itself imposes little restriction, since, unlike polyester, it bonds with most woods, however resinous or close-grained.

Throughout this book, wood sizes are given in actual, or dressed, dimensions, except in the materials list (see The Right Materials, page 75), where nominal dimensions are listed, because that is how lumber is sold. The two compare as follows:

Nominal	Dressed
1"	$3/4$"
2"	$1\frac{1}{2}$"
4"	$3\frac{1}{2}$"
6"	$5\frac{1}{2}$"
8"	$7\frac{1}{4}$"
10"	$9\frac{1}{4}$"

Planking
In selecting wood for your strips, the primary considerations are weight, workability, size and aesthetic appeal. Because the epoxy seals the planks from moisture and air, rot resistance is not important.

Lightness is usually prized in canoe wood, but if the boat will be used roughly or if it is not going to be portaged a lot, you may choose to sacrifice low weight for strength.

When lumber is sawn from a tree, it has either edge or flat grain (see page 66). In terms of strength, this is not a major consideration because these planks are so small, but it does affect workability, color and texture. Edge-grain strips are easier to sand and more uniform visually. Flat-grain strips are a little denser, harder to sand, but more interesting in color and texture.

The fewer knots and swirls in the wood, the straighter the grain, making the wood less prone to splitting and easier to rip on the saw. To get the maximum number of full-length strips with the fewest headaches, buy the best-quality lumber you can find, with as few knots as possible.

The wood you buy should have no more than 12 percent moisture content, since dry wood is stronger, stiffer and lighter than wet. It does not matter whether it is air- or kiln-dried, although the latter is more brittle. Dry wood will rip cleanly; wet wood will fuzz as it goes through the saw. If the wood seems damp when you rip it, machine the strips and stack them for a week or so before planking the canoe.

Buy boards a foot longer than the canoe and as wide as is practicable. Wider boards cost more but result in less waste when ripped

into strips. A good compromise is 1-by-6-inch lumber, dressed to $3/4$ inch. A 16-foot canoe will require about 50 board feet.

Instead of buying dimensional lumber, you can buy the planking precut (see Sources, page 201). It will cost more but will eliminate a lot of frustration. If you buy precut planking, look for a supplier that offers bead-and-cove edging.

If you can find only short planking, it's not a problem. In fact, it may be an opportunity for creativity. If you want to produce a feature pattern on the sides of the hull with different-colored wood, short planks are ideal. They can easily be joined on the mold by cutting the ends of the planks square, applying glue to the cut ends and butt-joining them in position.

Trim
Because the trim forms the structural skeleton of the canoe, hardwood should be used. Dense species like oak and ash can be pared down for sleek lines without sacrificing strength. The specific gravity of hardwoods varies considerably, so weight can be cut simply by choosing a lighter species. Since trim accounts for up to half the weight of a canoe, you will be grateful for any savings when you hoist the boat over long portages.

Finding hardwood in lengths long enough for gunwales might be difficult, though short pieces

can be glued with a scarf joint (see page 82). As in planking, look for clear, straight grain; when you try to twist a gunwale into its compound bend, it will break at the knots.

Beyond its practical function, trim can be the vehicle for those frivolous aesthetic touches that set your canoe apart from all others, be it a coaming of exotic purple heartwood against a golden deck of bird's-eye maple or a creamy Sitka spruce inwale accented with black-cherry scuppers. Where weight, expense and clear, long lengths are not an issue, select woods for their eye appeal and for their fine finish alone.

The woods listed in the chart are only the most common species used in canoes. The choice is unlimited. Peterborough builders used butternut to trim and plank canoes and often added a racing stripe of black walnut. Rushton shaped his thwarts in maple. White cedar is a prime canoe wood but almost impossible to get, perhaps because in the 1880s, it was considered the best of all woods for lightweight watercraft and was exported to discriminating boatbuilders all over the world.

Finding good wood has always been a challenge for boatbuilders. Rushton himself had to turn to West Coast lumber as an alternative to dwindling eastern supplies. Clear, long timbers are even more elusive today.

Local lumberyards may have

the wood, but prices will be high and selection limited. Specialty wood stores offer the best quality and selection at premium prices. If you can find a wholesale lumber dealer who will sell retail, the price and selection will be tops but the quality will be hard to judge, because the boards will not be dressed. Lumber mills offer the best price and maintain the tradition of using local woods, but quality will depend on timber stands in the area. The lumber will not be dressed, and the moisture content may be unpredictable.

Wherever you buy it, take the time to select your wood carefully. Look for long, straight, clear planks that are dressed to an even thickness and free of gouges, splits or planer skips. As you sort through the stack, keep the color of your canoe in mind. Be picky—this wood is going to keep you and yours afloat long after that impatient clerk has retired.

RESIN

In the monocoque structure, resin is the vital link between cloth and wood. It is more than just a glue and a glassy shell—it penetrates the core, bonding wood, cloth and plastic into a cohesive whole.

Two major types are used in boatbuilding—polyester and epoxy. Each is a petrochemical-based liquid that becomes solid when a catalyst or curing agent is added. When we first started to

build strip canoes, we brushed polyester over the planking but soon found it inadequate as a sheathing system.

Epoxy is more expensive than polyester, but its advantages more than justify the cost. Unlike the linear-chain polyesters, epoxy is composed of multidirectional interlocking-molecule chains. Composed of 100 percent solids, it shrinks only imperceptibly as it cures.

Because it is compatible with wood's own natural resins, epoxy bonds chemically as well as mechanically with all species, which means that builders can use less epoxy and cloth, dramatically reducing weight and costs without having to flinch every time their canoes scrape a rock.

Properly formulated and applied, epoxy has proved superior to polyester in flexibility, resilience and impact resistance. In a test reported in *WoodenBoat* magazine in July/August 1977, a coat of epoxy, though half as thick, had twice the impact resistance of polyester on wood.

Epoxy can be toxic when absorbed through the skin; people who are highly sensitive may break out in a rash. As a precaution, it should never be handled without first protecting your skin from exposure. That means wearing long sleeves and gloves (see the safety advice on page 144).

Not all epoxies will give your wood a clear, tough sheath. There

are as many formulations of the resins as there are applications, but the best is the one with the fewest restrictions and the most predictability.

When mixed, epoxy should be thin enough to saturate the cloth and surface wood fibers but thick enough to handle on a vertical plane without sagging or running. You should be able to recoat within a few hours and sand within a day. (Some we have tested were still rubbery after two weeks.) Finally, the epoxy should cure with good clarity, adding no objectionable tint to the wood. One brand was fine over dark planking but turned Sitka spruce an ugly greenish yellow.

A handful of epoxies are designed specifically for marine use. Bear Mountain Boat Shop has tested most, and of these, WEST SYSTEM™ epoxy by Gougeon Brothers Inc. seems best suited for the monocoque method (see Sources, page 201). We've been using it for more than 20 years. Over the years, the Gougeons have continually improved their product, making it safer to use and more user-friendly. Their technical backup is excellent, and their concern for safety heartening.

Always use WEST SYSTEM™ 207 slow hardener for sheathing a woodstrip canoe. The fast formula tends to set before it can saturate the fiberglass and wood fibers, and it cures so quickly that maintaining a wet edge is impossible.

For a 16-foot canoe, you will need approximately 18 pounds (2 U.S. gallons) of resin and the appropriate amount of hardener. (Buy the calibrated pumps that handily dispense the resin and hardener in accurate proportions.) This should provide three coats both inside and out, with enough left over to glue the trim.

Stored in a cool place, resin and hardener have a shelf life of about a year. When you are ready to lay up your canoe, mix and apply the epoxy according to manufacturer's instructions, with strict attention to your workshop conditions.

Before using the resin, read and understand the safety information on page 144. If you are considering a resin system other than WEST, talk to someone who has used it. Ask about workability, cure time, smell, sandability, color and aging properties. Find out about the company's technical support and safety information. Whatever you decide, don't take a chance on your boat or your health just to save a few dollars.

CLOTH REINFORCEMENT

Although wood and epoxy alone would give your canoe good end-to-end strength, the cloth reinforcement ties the strips together across the grain, effectively taking the place of ribs. The cloth also ensures that a minimum consistent thickness of epoxy is applied on the hull.

Fiberglass cloth is a convenient,

THE RIGHT WOODS

NAME	ADVANTAGES	DISADVANTAGES	USE
Western red cedar (*Thuya plicata*)	Light; workable with hand tools; good color range; available in long lengths; close, straight, even grain.	Red cedar is a little more brittle than white.	Ideal for planking.
Sitka spruce (*Picea sitchensis*)	Very good strength-to-weight ratio; sapwood pale yellow, heartwood brown; available in long, clear lengths; does not sand as fast as cedar, but tougher, nearly nonresinous; elastic; straight, even grain.	Adds 5 to 6 pounds more weight to 16-foot canoe than cedar.	Ideal for planking, yokes and spars; use on hull bottom and high-stress areas for extra strength; good for trim if weight a primary consideration.
Redwood (*Pinus sylvestris*)	Workability comparable to cedar; fairly dark color; available in long, clear lengths; straight grain.	Heavier than cedar; fairly brittle; moderately resinous; soft.	Suitable for planking.
Ash (*Fraxinus*)	Good bendability; strong for its weight; wears well; fair workability; very tough and elastic.	For high finish, use filler; not durable when exposed to weather; coarse texture.	Ideal for trim (keel, gunwales, seat frames, decks, stems).
Oak (*Quercus*)	White more bendable than red; red coarse, white fine-textured; attractive grain; tough, durable.	Poor workability with hand tools; hard to get good finish; open grain, use filler; heavy; hard to glue.	Suitable for trim.
Cherry (*Prunus*)	Beautiful; good workability; reasonably light for strength; ages well; takes finish well.	Does not bend as well as ash; not readily available, especially in long lengths.	Suitable for trim.
Mahogany (more than 60 different tropical species are sold under this name)	Good workability with hand tools; lighter than cherry; available in long lengths; highly figured, brown to red.	Open grain, use filler for good finish; hard to find good quality; some types susceptible to splits.	Suitable for trim; Honduras and African mahogany are most desirable.

effective, relatively inexpensive reinforcement for woodstrip canoes. It is made from fine, continuous filaments of molten glass, spun into thread and woven together as cloth. When wetted out, it becomes completely transparent, revealing the beauty of the wood.

Sold by the running yard, fiberglass cloth comes in various widths and weights. We recommend a single sheet of 6-ounce 50- or 60-inch cloth the length of the canoe for the inside of the hull and a single sheet a foot longer than the canoe for the outside.

We found that ¼-inch cedar between layers of 6-ounce glass cloth did not fail until subjected to a load of 221 pounds. An additional layer of 6-ounce cloth (such as might be applied to a canoe's bottom) increased the failure point by more than 100 percent (to 450 pounds), though it added only 25 percent more weight.

If you are more interested in weight than in strength, buy a lighter (4-ounce) cloth. On the other hand, if your boat will be put to hard use, you may want to increase the cloth weight in some areas, gaining extra strength at the expense of clarity. Whatever the weight, be sure that the cloth you buy is carefully rolled—not folded—because creases will not come out. A wrinkle in the cloth may be permanently visible on the hull of your boat.

All fiberglass cloths look the same, but they're not. After the glass fibers are woven into cloth, the fabric is fired to remove all residual wax and oil and then is finished with a coupling agent. This coupling agent is the interface between the glass and the resin, ensuring that the bond does not deteriorate. Many different finishes are available, but few are compatible with epoxy for wooden-boat building. To be sure, buy your cloth from the epoxy dealer and ask if the finish is compatible with the epoxy you will use.

Cloth adds toughness to a canoe, but it also adds weight, so builders are always experimenting with new "miracle" fabrics that claim to be light and durable. Unfortunately, most have proved unsuitable for wood-strip/epoxy canoes.

A modacrylic fabric like Dynel withstands scuffing and abrasion very well. Half the weight of fiberglass, it drapes softly and is easily saturated with resin. It is highly absorbent, however, puffing up to twice the thickness of fiberglass with a rough, hard-to-sand surface. Despite superior abrasion resistance, its impact resistance is the same as that of fiberglass.

A polypropylene fabric, such as Vectra or Versatex, weighs a third as much as fiberglass but has 15 times the tear strength and twice the impact and abrasion resistance. It takes contours well but, being lightweight, tends to "float" on the resin and fuzzes badly when sanded. The weave will become visible after a few seasons of exposure.

An aramid fabric like Kevlar-49 has such a high tensile strength that you need carbide-tipped cutting tools. Its impact resistance lies somewhere between fiberglass and polypropylene. It does not work particularly well with wood, remains a yellow-brown color when wetted out and, at 10 times the price of fiberglass, has no place in woodstrip-canoe construction.

Generally, the alternatives are more expensive and less transparent than fiberglass is. Most important, they are much more elastic than wood, flexing greatly under stress: they will tend to stretch while the wood is breaking. For woodstrip construction, the cloth should have a stretch factor close to that of the wood core so that the two will work together under impact, each compounding the strength of the other.

At this writing, we consider fiberglass the best mate for wood and epoxy in the average cruising canoe. If you want extra protection in the high-abuse zone below the waterline, lay a narrow panel of polypropylene over the keel-line. Fiberglass laid over top eliminates floating or sanding problems.

GLUE

Among the vast array of adhesives available today, only a few are appropriate for building wood-strip canoes. The glue that holds the planks together must bond with little clamping pressure and have some gap-filling properties. It

should be easy to mix and spread, have a comfortably long pot life but dry reasonably fast under average conditions to a color that blends with your planking. It must be easily sanded, compatible with epoxy resin and relatively non-toxic, because you will be exposed to its fumes and dust.

Since the epoxy coating on both sides of the hull effectively stabilizes the moisture content of the planking, waterproof glue is not necessary here. On the other hand, because it will not be encased in epoxy, glue for the trim must be completely waterproof. The types described below are commonly available from hardware stores or marine suppliers.

All-Purpose Wood Glue

Yellow carpenter's glues like Elmer's have become the glue of choice for edge-gluing strip planking. They are widely available, inexpensive and nontoxic, possess good gap-filling properties and clean up with water. Unlike the white glue of the past, they sand well with sharp paper at slow speeds. Yellow glue dries fast to an opaque white or clear color, making it suitable for light-colored planking. For dark-colored planking or to accent the plank seam, use Lee Valley Cabinetmaker's Glue 202 GF, which dries to a mid-tone brown.

The original Titebond is also an acceptable choice, but avoid Titebond II. Although it is promoted

as a great boatbuilding glue, it is not appropriate for edge-gluing the planking, because it has very little body and takes a long time to set up.
Solvent: water
Required: 1½ quarts
Recommended: planking

Urea Formaldehyde Resin Glue

Also known as plastic resin glue, this is sold as a light brown powder that is mixed with water to the consistency of cream. It has a long pot life (three to four hours) and will bond with hand pressure. Though not as good as epoxy, its gap-filling properties are adequate, and it sands beautifully. Curing temperatures are not critical, but it is moderately toxic and should be used with gloves.

Because it is water-resistant, not waterproof, it is most appropriate for planking, where it is sealed in epoxy. It dries to a straw color and can be wiped off with water within 20 minutes. Although sometimes hard to find, it is a traditional boatbuilding glue, because it is easy to work with and inexpensive. Note: Two-part urea adhesives have entirely different characteristics.
Solvent: water
Required: 1½ pounds
Recommended: planking

Epoxy Resin Glue

Developed during World War II, epoxy was used by the aircraft industry a decade before boatbuilders

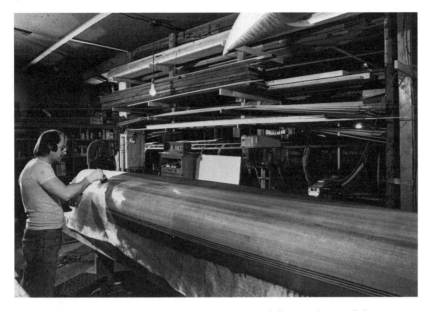

A neat workshop, with the wood strips stored flat and out of the way yet handy to the mold, expedites construction.

discovered it. Its superior bond makes it the most promising, though most expensive, boat-building adhesive. Colorless and waterproof, epoxy creates a strong, flexible bond that does not require a precise fit or clamping pressure. Its gap-filling capacity is unexcelled, because the resin film between surfaces makes the joint stronger. Though correct temperature and humidity are important for proper curing, epoxy glue sands extremely well when hard.

To use as glue, blend resin and hardener in the correct ratio, stir well, then add two or three pinches of #403 Microfibers filler. These fine cotton fibers thicken the epoxy slightly, giving it extra strength and body without affecting its ability to penetrate the wood. Epoxy glue has a pot life of about a half an hour, which makes it inappropriate for the job of gluing planking. Glued joints harden enough in six to eight hours for clamps to be removed. Before it sets, excess epoxy should be wiped off with a cloth dipped in solvent. Although #403 Microfibers filler is nontoxic, always wear gloves when using it, because the epoxy itself can cause skin irritation.

This glue is ideal for trim but tends to be too messy for planking because of its short pot life and finicky handling. It can also be used as a wood filler by adding sanding dust to improve body and to color-match the wood.

Note that epoxy glue is not the same thing as epoxy resin and hardener. For resin and hardener to serve as a glue, it must first be thickened with sanding dust or with a proprietary product such as #403 Microfibers.

Solvent: acetone or lacquer thinner

Required: small amount; small bag #403 Microfibers

Recommended: trim, stems

Resorcinol Resin

Introduced in the early 1940s, this waterproof glue is sold as a water-soluble powder or a two-part system of liquid resin and powdered catalyst. Since it requires a precise fit, high pressure and warm temperatures for a good bond, it is not suitable for strip gluing. It can be used for waterproof joints in the trim, however, and is ideal for gluing oak. Besides being fairly expensive, it cures to a brownish purple color, which, if not part of the design, can be objectionable.

Not recommended.

VARNISH

Varnish is more than cosmetic. It protects epoxy from the sun's damaging ultraviolet rays and keeps water from penetrating the trim.

Buy a high-quality spar varnish with a UV shield. Made from tung oil, with hardeners and pigments added, spar varnish is easy to work with and has a pleasant smell. It is expensive, however, and this is a clear case of getting what you pay for. Buy top quality, and expect to pay a premium price.

Do not substitute standard polyurethane varnish. Although it is cheaper, polyurethane varnish is brittle, has a tendency to peel and yellow and probably will not have UV filters.

Some of the two-part polyurethanes are worth considering. They are tougher but are very expensive and can be toxic if sprayed.

Solvent: mineral spirits

Required: 2 quarts

SOLVENTS

You will need two different solvents—one for epoxy and one for varnish.

With epoxy, the solvent is used to clean uncured resin from your tools and mop up spills. You will also need to wipe down the surface of the hull with solvent before applying the resin coats.

Lacquer thinner, acetone and methylene chloride are all good epoxy solvents. Acetone is an excellent cleaner, but it is expensive and evaporates quickly. Methylene chloride is not as flammable as the others, but it is expensive and not readily available. Lacquer thinner, though not as effective as the other two, will do the job nicely and is both cheaper and easy to find. Buy it from an automobile body-shop supplier. It comes in several grades, but since you are using it for cleaning up, buy the cheapest. A quart should be sufficient.

For varnishing, buy a quart of mineral spirits. Varsol, made by Esso, is good, but buy the cheapest.

Polyclens is an excellent brush cleaner that is worth keeping in the workshop all the time. Pour an inch of the pleasant-smelling pink liquid in a can, and soak your brush after removing the bulk of the resin or varnish with solvent. Wash under the tap and hang to dry, and your brush will come out like new.

Do not use these solvents for cleaning your hands. They are irritants and strip your skin of its natural protective oils. Instead, keep a can of waterless hand cleaner in the shop, or use soap and water.

ABRASIVES

Think of sandpaper as a surface of sharp cutting tools. On coarse-grit paper, the cutters are large and far apart; they cut deep, widely spaced grooves. On fine-grit paper, the cutters are small and closer together, making many close, shallow cuts.

Coarse-grit paper is more suitable for power sanding, because it takes many passes before the cuts overlap. Finer grits are more suited to hand sanding, since they cut more evenly on each pass.

The space between the grit particles has a lot to do with how well sandpaper works in different applications. The larger the space, the more dust it will hold before it plugs up and the paper becomes ineffective.

The trick is to find a balance between the grit becoming dull and the spaces between the grit clogging with dust. Sanding 120-grit Garnet paper, if used to sand epoxy, would quickly plug, while the same grit on silicone-carbide open-coated paper would stay clean and would cut until the grit wore out.

There is a big difference, too, in the quality of sandpapers and the glue that attaches the grit. With cheap backings and glues, the grit falls off when the sandpaper is bent. This becomes important when choosing paper for hand-sanding curves. Cloth-backed resin-bonded sanding belts are excellent for this job.

The ideal is a sandpaper on which the grit stays sharp and in place; the paper doesn't plug up and fall apart. For your canoebuilding project, we recommend aluminum-oxide resin bonded to a good backing for sanding both wood and epoxy. Silicone-carbide open-coated paper is the best choice for sanding epoxy and varnish.

You will need a medium 80-grit paper for rough-shaping the wooden hull and for rough-sanding the epoxy. To shape the hardwood trim and to finish-sand the planking and epoxy, use 120-grit paper. I don't recommend going finer than 120-grit on the epoxy

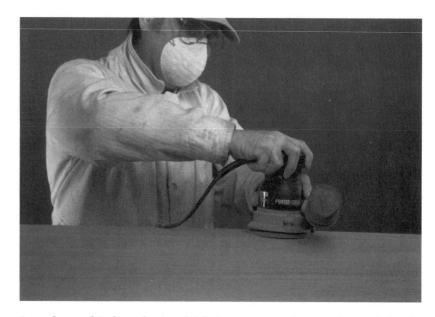

A random orbital sander is a fairly inexpensive time-saving tool that is ideal for almost all sanding operations in the canoebuilding process.

finish; 120-grit leaves enough bite to give the varnish a good mechanical bond with the epoxy surface. But you'll need a very fine 220-grit for finish-sanding the hardwood trim and sanding between the varnish coats.

We've noticed that with a good resin-bonded disc, the finer grits are as aggressive as a coarser, cheaper production paper disc. They give a very controlled rate of material removal and arrive closer to the desired surface faster. If you are worried about removing too much too fast, consider using good paper on a random orbital sander to sand both the planking and the epoxy on the hull, using only 120-grit rather than starting with 80-grit. Doing all the sanding with 120-grit will use more discs and will be a little slower-going, but it is aggressive enough to get the job done. And if this is your first boat, you will appreciate the added control.

It is hard to say how much sandpaper you are going to need, but the best place to buy it is at a body-shop supplier, where you can get it in bulk instead of in high-priced packets of five sheets or discs.

STEM BAND

The brass stem band is a protective device that gives your canoe a natty, nautical look. If you have a keel, you will need enough brass to cover the full length of the boat, stem to stem, plus an inch or two extra at each deck. It comes in 10-foot lengths, $3/8$ by $3/16$ inch.

You can substitute aluminum, but it is not as tough, nor does it look as traditional. You may have some trouble finding brass banding, but the effect is worth the effort (see Sources, page 200).

FASTENERS

Ever since the first primitive boat moved past the one-log stage, people have had to use their ingenuity to tie the boat parts together. The Norse used rawhide strips, the Romans hammered bronze and copper pins, and North American Indians laced black-spruce roots. Gluing the planks together and sealing them in resin eliminate much of the need for fasteners, but you still have to tie the gunwales, thwarts, seats and decks to the hull.

Except in the strongback, screws must be noncorrosive, which eliminates the common steel variety. Brass screws are the traditional choice; the color melds beautifully with the canoe's wood hues, but they are soft and require extra care to prevent the heads from twisting off. (This can be avoided by first twisting in a steel screw to cut threads in the wood.) Bronze is a tougher traditional screw but hard to find. Stainless-steel screws are the easiest to use and can usually be found at a marine supply.

You will also need staples with a medium crown ($1/2$ inch) for fastening planking to the stations. Instead of staples, 1-inch finishing nails can be used.

COST

Price often starts out as the primary motivation for building a woodstrip/epoxy canoe, and rightly so. You will definitely save money by building, rather than buying, this type of canoe, which, in 1999, sold for prices ranging from $2,500 to $12,000.

Even buying the most expensive lumber, you should be able to build any of the designs in this book for $750 to $1,200 (at 1999 material prices). You should be able to buy a complete kit of machined parts for around $1,300. (These prices are given in Canadian dollars.)

This is obviously not a cheap way to build, but doing it yourself will realize significant savings, even without considering the priceless personal touches you will build into your own boat. As most builders will tell you, their dollar investment was more than repaid long before their canoe took its maiden voyage. The pleasure and satisfaction of spending quality time producing something with your own hands and ingenuity cannot be calculated in currency.

On page 75, you'll find a shopping list of all the materials needed to complete this project, together with their dimensions

Avoid hazards by wearing dust mask, gloves, and ear and eye protection.

and quantities. Check Sources, page 200, and shop around for the best quality at the best price.

SAFETY

The expression "safety is no accident" may be a cliché, but it is nevertheless true. The pleasure of building your own canoe will soon dissipate if a preventable accident occurs.

All the usual safety precautions of a home workshop apply to canoebuilding. Keep flammable liquids tightly capped in a safe place, and do not smoke. Keep your work area well lit, clean and organized. Work at a comfortable height whenever possible. Keep a fire extinguisher and first-aid kit within easy reach at all times.

Working with epoxy imposes its own extra measure of caution. Do not let children or pets in your work area during lay-up. The process is messy enough without having to worry about small bodies. Ventilate the area well. Deposit resin and solvent washes in a metal can, and store it outside, away from combustibles.

Resin dust can also be highly flammable. One builder lit a cigarette after sanding down his fiberglassed hull and snapped the lighter shut on his knee. The dust on his clothes caught fire, enveloping him in a flash of flame. Luckily, he escaped with only singed body hair and a racing heart.

Epoxy resins and hardeners have a reputation as skin sensi-

tizers, though WEST SYSTEM™ epoxy seems to have relatively low toxicity. The hardener is a more serious irritant than the resin, but skin contact should be rigorously avoided with both. Never handle either without wearing rubber gloves and applying barrier cream to skin exposed between gloves and sleeves. Also take care to protect your eyes from splashes of hardener by wearing safety glasses. If you do get some in your eye, flush it out with water for at least 15 minutes and see a doctor. If you develop a rash while working with epoxy, stop using it and consult your physician.

During epoxy lay-up, wear old clothes. What you spill will be a lifelong memento. Wear a dust mask or respirator to filter out the fumes and particles produced by machining wood and applying and sanding epoxy and varnish. Goggles, if kept clean, will protect your eyes during the ripping process.

Detailed safety instructions for working with wood and with epoxy are included just before these steps in the canoebuilding process. Take the precautions advised, and make this boatbuilding project a successful and safe one.

Keep the workshop clean and organized at every stage of the project.

LUMBER

Strongback:

2 sheets 4' x 8' x ³/₄" plywood or particleboard

Molds:

2 sheets 4' x 8' x ³/₈" to ¹/₂" plywood or particleboard

One 1¹/₂" x 1¹/₂" x 10" softwood mold block per station

Four 1" x 1" softwood corner blocks just less than stem height

Stems:

¹/₄" x ⁷/₈" lengths of hardwood, 40" to 50" (about 4" longer than the stem); 3 per stem (12 pieces for inside and outside stems)

Planking:

50 to 60 board feet of 1" softwood, 12" longer than canoe

Inwales & Outwales:

Four ³/₄" x ⁷/₈" x desired width hardwood, about 4" longer than the distance along the sheer from stem to stem

Decks:

Two ³/₄" to 1" x desired width hardwood x length of deck

Thwarts:

One or two ³/₄" x 2¹/₂" to 3" hardwood x width of canoe

Seat Frames:

Two ⁷/₈" x 1¹/₂" x 7' hardwood

Two ³/₈" x 12" hardwood dowels (or 8 dowel pins per seat)

FASTENERS

Strongback:

2 pounds 1⁵/₈" drywall screws

Setting Up Mold:

Some of above

Planking:

1 box ⁹/₁₆" staples for bead and cove

Inwales:

1 box (100) ¹/₂" #4 flathead non-corrosive wood screws

Outwales:

1 box (100) 1¹/₂" #8 flathead non-corrosive wood screws if the heads are set flush

1 box (100) 1¹/₄" #8 flathead non-corrosive wood screws if the heads are plugged

Decks:

Twelve 1¹/₂" or 1³/₄" #8 flathead noncorrosive wood screws

Seats:

Four ³/₁₆" x 4" to 6" carriage bolts or 10/24 machine screws with nuts and washers per seat

Thwarts:

Four ³/₁₆" x 2" carriage bolts or 10/24 machine screws with nuts and washers per thwart

Stem Bands:

Two ³/₈" x ³/₁₆" brass stem band x desired length

¹/₂" or ³/₄" #4 flathead brass screws

SHEATHING

Fiberglass Cloth (6 oz.):

1 piece 60" wide (or as required) x canoe length for inside hull

1 piece 60" wide x canoe length plus 12" for outside hull

Epoxy Resin:

2 gallons epoxy resin and hardener

Spar Varnish:

2 quarts

GLUING

Planking:

1 quart yellow carpenter's glue

Epoxy resin and 1 small bag #403 Microfibers

Trim and Filler:

Epoxy resin mixed with #403 Microfibers and #410 Microlight

SOLVENTS

1 quart lacquer thinner for epoxy

1 quart mineral spirits for varnish

1 pint Polyclens for brushes

MISCELLANEOUS

2 to 3 sheets of largest-size carbon paper for molds

1 roll 1" masking tape

1 bar paraffin or packing tape for mold release

1 package disposable paint filters for varnish

24 sheets #80 sandpaper

24 sheets #120 sandpaper

6 sheets #220 sandpaper

6 sheets #240 wet sandpaper

Pencil and/or ballpoint pen

Garbage can and bags

Broom and dustpan

CHAPTER 6

MATERIAL MATTERS

Machining the Wood

ARE WE QUITE SURE THAT THERE IS NO FEELING IN THE "HEART OF OAK," NO SENTIMENT UNDER BENT BIRCH RIBS; THAT A CANOE, IN FACT, HAS NO CHARACTER?

—John MacGregor

Having chosen the design of your canoe and bought all the necessary materials, there is a real temptation to plunge ahead into the construction of the hull. It is possible, of course, to swing into action, but in doing so, you will find that progress on the canoe is repeatedly delayed as you stop to machine the parts for the next stage of construction.

Because the making of parts can account for up to a quarter of your total boatbuilding hours, some builders prefer to do all the machining at once so that when the hull is complete, there is no delay fitting in the seats, thwarts, deck and other parts that transform the hull into a canoe.

One Ottawa man leisurely machined the parts and prepared the mold one winter, built the hull the next and happily launched his new canoe on a sunny May morning more than two years after beginning his project.

We prefer to prepare the planking and build the hull, then make the pieces as they come up in the canoebuilding process. Making the next part often becomes a fill-in job during pauses in construction. For novices whose woodworking skills will steadily improve as they work through the steps, it may be wise to save the machining of visible parts until they are comfortable with the tools and techniques.

It all depends on the pace and priorities of the builder. Whatever order you choose, it should fit your own schedule and temperament.

For the sake of convenience, however, the machining of all the parts has been gathered within this single chapter. The specifications for each part, of course, will be dictated by the size and shape of your canoe, but there are few other restrictions. Armed with what you learn from this chapter, you should be able to let your imagination wander through all sorts of possibilities.

In each section, the machining instructions begin with a basic approach, then proceed through increasingly interesting variations to the most exquisitely complex. The difference between approaches is usually not dependent on woodworking skill so much as on patience and dedication to your personal concept of the ideal canoe.

THE PLANKING

RIPPING THE PLANKING

This is the first real step in building your canoe—slicing those long, hefty boards into thin, supple strips that will bend to an elegant shape and eventually sustain you through heavy waves or swirling rapids.

Ripping the planks is not difficult, provided you take time to set up the equipment and the work area first. Your overriding aim in this process is to produce long planks of uniform ¼-inch thickness along their full length.

This can be done using either a table saw or a band saw. The band saw is a little safer and easier to operate, but unless its blade is wide, it has a tendency to wander. Most home workshops have a table saw, which will give you a nice, smooth cut if you are careful

You will be using power tools to machine the parts for your canoe, so it is wise to read and understand the safety information for each tool before you begin. In general, keep the following in mind while working with machines in your boat shop:

• Know where the danger is, and stay away from it. On a stationary power tool, the cutter is generally in a predictable place: to hurt yourself, you have to move into the cutter. That said, don't underestimate the unpredictable dangers.

• Be aware of the direction the cutter is rotating. Always feed into the cutter. Never feed in the same direction that the cutter is turning: the wood will climb the blade and try to catch up to the speed of the blade, turning the piece being cut into a missile. Instead, feel the resistance as the cutter cuts its way through the wood. Anticipate the forces the cutter puts on the piece being cut. If the back of your table saw is not protected by a guard or splitter, be careful re-turning boards on the saw: the piece could climb the back of the blade and take off in the direction of the operator.

• Try to achieve the optimum feed rate. If a piece is fed too slowly, the cutter can heat up and burn the wood. If a piece is fed too quickly, the machine can bog down, overheating the motor.

• Keep blades and cutters sharp. Use a blade that is sharp and of an appropriate design for the cut you are making. A sharp blade is safer to use, because it gives you more predictable control.

• Protect your hands. Wear gloves for handling splintery wood such as cedar. You may not pay much attention to slivers when you are having fun, but if you forget to dig them out, they may become infected as they grow out on their own. Keep a pair of tweezers handy for pulling slivers. If you pull a sliver right away, there may still be a bit sticking out to grab hold of. If not, dig it out with a sterilized needle.

• Protect your hearing. Machining planking is a noisy job, with one or more power tools running at the same time. Wear earmuffs or earplugs if the noise makes you feel at all uncomfortable.

• Protect your eyes. Always wear eye protection while operating

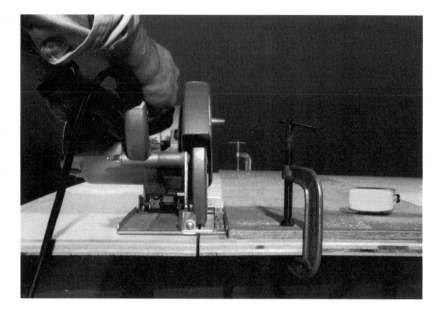

power tools. Protective goggles and full-face shields are inexpensive and available; use them.

• Control the dust. Ripping and machining the planking for your canoe will produce about three garbage bags of dust and shavings. Think about this when choosing a location for ripping. Cutting outside is a good idea if at all feasible. This will also solve the problem of finding a space 40 feet long (or double the length of the longest plank being cut) in which to do the job. Do what you can to control the dust at the source. At the very least, provide good cross-ventilation, and wear a dust mask. Watch for dust buildup on and around the motors; this will contribute to premature overheating.

• Clean up before leaving for the day. Yours would not be the first shop to burn down from a bad extension cord shorting out under a pile of tinder-dry shavings. ❯

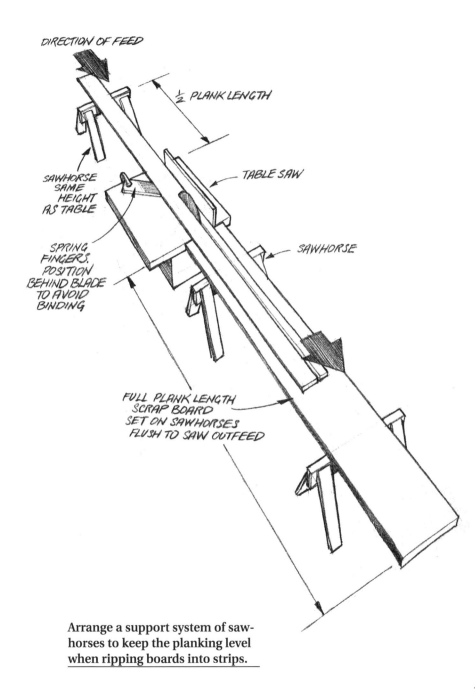

DIRECTION OF FEED

½ PLANK LENGTH

TABLE SAW

SAWHORSE SAME HEIGHT AS TABLE

SAWHORSE

SPRING FINGERS, POSITION BEHIND BLADE TO AVOID BINDING

FULL PLANK LENGTH SCRAP BOARD SET ON SAWHORSES FLUSH TO SAW OUTFEED

Arrange a support system of saw-horses to keep the planking level when ripping boards into strips.

and use a sharp, hollow-ground combination blade or a thin planer blade. The latter will give you better strips with less waste, but use it only if the wood is perfectly dry.

These long boards will sag and bind the blade unless they are supported. Still, it is safer and more accurate to make preparations to do the job alone than to try to work with (and against) a helper.

For a solo operation, set up a sawhorse the same height as the table, about 8 feet from the infeed side of the saw. On the opposite side, set up two more sawhorses, with a board or piece of plywood between them. Butt the board flush to the outfeed side of the table to support the plank as it leaves the blade (as shown, left). With this system, you should be able to control the plank and keep it level as you push it through the saw.

The ripping process will flow more smoothly if you clean the saw table and rub it with paraffin before you start. Set the blade slightly above the thickness of the wood (although a hollow-ground blade should be raised a little higher for extra clearance, as the blade is thinner near the center). Set the rip fence at ¼ inch, almost parallel to the blade but offset fractionally away from the back of the blade to prevent binding and kickback.

For consistent thickness, the plank must be pressed tightly against the fence. This is danger-ous work for human hands, espe-cially as the board gets thinner. Rather than lose fingers, and for greater control and safety, make a set of spring fingers, some-times called a "featherboard" (see Builder's Tip, page 80).

With spring fingers and lumber supports in place, begin to push the board through the saw blade. Proceed cautiously at an even rate, watching for gaps between the board and fence. If the plank wanders and causes a thin spot in the strip, break it out as soon as it is through the saw. Don't force the board: the blade may bind, or the motor may stall and overheat. Let the cutting of the blade set the speed.

When the end of the board reaches the table, use a push stick (see page 80) to guide it through the blade to the other side. This will give you the longest consistent strip possible. When they are all cut, store the strips where they will not be trampled.

Preparing the wood strips is an incredibly dusty operation, because for every two planks you rip, one is blown away in sawdust; so wear a mask at all times, and be sure the shop is well ventilated. It is also a good idea to wear safety goggles or glasses. Remember to keep them clean.

If you do not want to rip your own planking, you can buy it pre-cut or pay a local cabinetmaker to

Spring fingers clamped to a saw table will act like an extra hand, pressing the plank firmly against the fence while you feed the plank through the blade.

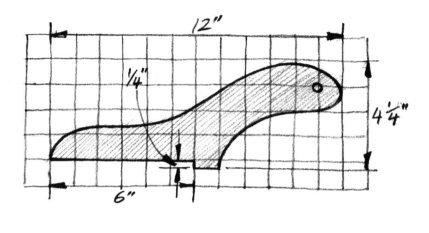

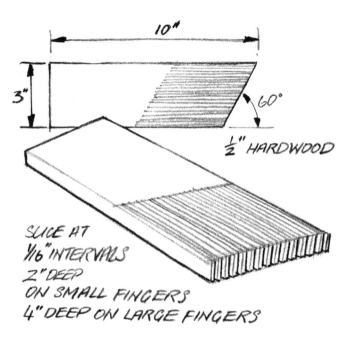

10"

3"

60°

½" HARDWOOD

SLICE AT
1/16" INTERVALS
2" DEEP
ON SMALL FINGERS
4" DEEP ON LARGE FINGERS

To make the spring fingers, choose a piece of hardwood 8 to 10 inches long and roughly 3 inches wide. Cut one end at an angle, as shown above. Then slice the angled end through at 1/16-inch intervals. These are the "fingers." Rub the tips of the fingers with paraffin to reduce friction.

To use the spring fingers, fasten them to the saw table with a large C-clamp, as shown on the right. Position it so that the fingers will exert pressure on the plank just before it meets the saw blade, holding the wood tightly against the fence.

A push stick, top right, provides a margin of safety when feeding wood through a table saw. It keeps your own fingers farther from the blade. Cut one from 1/4-inch plywood, in the dimensions shown.

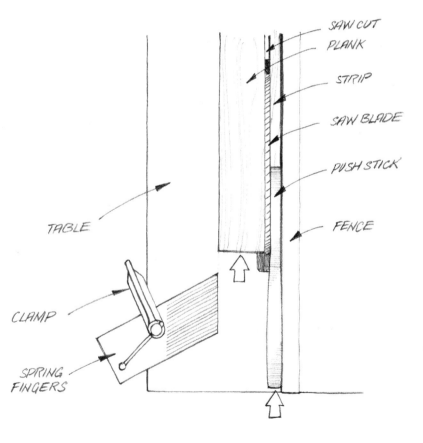

12"

1/4"

4 1/4"

6"

SAW CUT
PLANK

STRIP

SAW BLADE

PUSH STICK

FENCE

TABLE

CLAMP

SPRING
FINGERS

The three edges of planking; although it needs to be machined, bead-and-cove edging provides the ideal gluing surface.

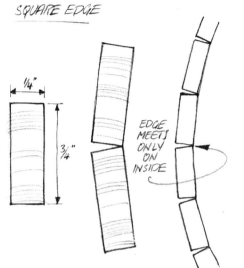

SQUARE EDGE

1/4"

3/4"

EDGE MEETS ONLY ON INSIDE

SHIPLAP EDGE (MILLED ON SAW OR ROUTER)

1/4"

1/8"

1/8"

3/4"

1/8"

1/8"

EDGE MEETS AT OVERLAP

BEAD & COVE EDGE (MILLED ON ROUTER OR SHAPER)

1/4"

3/4"

EDGE MEETS MOST SURFACE

rip the boards for you. Whichever route you take, be sure to end up with long, absolutely uniform 1/4-inch planks.

Nothing will contribute more to a good building experience and a fine boat than properly machined planking: its importance cannot be overemphasized. Once you have to start compensating for poorly machined planks, the extra work and confusion will persist until the hull is sanded and fiberglassed. There is enough to think about without having to deal with planks that don't fit together. Remember that if there is a 1/16-inch step between two planks on one side, there is another 1/16-inch step on the other. Cleaning up

the joint on both sides will take off 1/8 inch—fully half the thickness of the plank.

MACHINING THE PLANKING

Using this square-edge planking as is has serious drawbacks. Because the planks cannot be interlocked, it is hard to keep them in line when they are being laid across the molds. Even with a fortune in temporary staples punched between the stations, the strips will want to spring apart.

Because the hull is a continuous curve, the butting edges will not mate along their full width. This creates gaps, especially on sharp curves, and reduces gluing surface so much that planks

may pop apart when staples are pulled. For an idea of the problems that occur, hoist a butt-planked canoe over your head at midday; chances are, shafts of sunlight will pierce the hull.

The amount of gluing surface can be improved on square-edge planking if you bevel the edge of each strip to mate with the one below. This requires a fair amount of skill, because it is a rolling bevel and entails a great deal of trial-and-error fitting.

A better solution is the bead-and-cove edge. It will give you the smoothest, tightest joints with minimal fuss. Regardless of the angle at which they come together, the bead and cove lock the

strips together in both directions and provide maximum gluing surface. Although somewhat more fragile, bead-and-cove edging reduces stapling, frustration and fairing time. One builder, after working with butt planking, decided to switch to bead and cove for his next canoe. Using a molding cutterhead and knives on his table saw, he machined all the planking in half an hour, saving himself hours of fitting and fairing.

Today, bead and cove is best milled using router bits, available from mail-order tool catalogs. (See Sources, page 202.) These can be set up using two routers so that both edges are milled in the same pass. If you machine the two edges

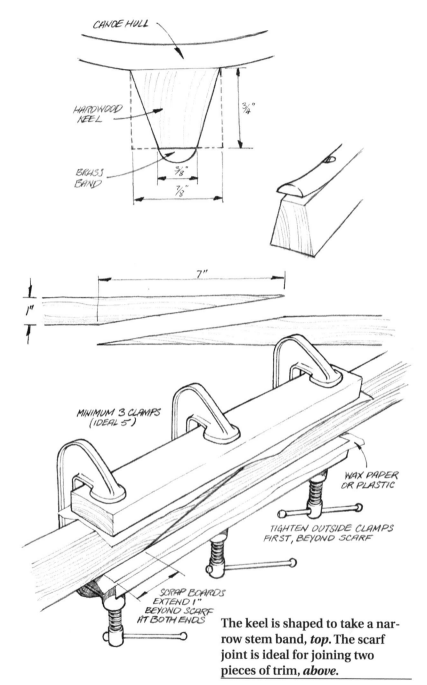

The keel is shaped to take a narrow stem band, *top.* The scarf joint is ideal for joining two pieces of trim, *above.*

separately, do the bead edge first and then the cove. The latter is fragile and should be handled as little as possible.

The Keel

Keels are generally made from hardwood, because this part of the canoe gets most of the hard knocks. There are many types and sizes of keels, but the method of machining and fastening is basically the same. The keel described here is appropriate for all the canoe designs in this book.

Choose the straightest and clearest hardwood plank you can find, and rip a ¾-by-⅞-inch piece, about a foot shorter than the overall length of the boat. This must be shaped into a triangular piece with a ⅞-inch base, where it attaches to the hull, and a ⅜-inch seat for the brass keel band.

To do this, draw the angles on the end of the keel (as shown, left). Set the saw to the same angle, and cut a piece of scrap lumber to test for accuracy. Cut the keel, then clean up the saw cuts with a block plane or cabinet scraper. Sand the angled sides with 120-grit sandpaper, keeping the edges of the keel sharp.

The Gunwales

On a canoe, gunwales have little to do with artillery but everything to do with structure—they tie the boat together end to end. Projecting beyond the hull both inside and out, they absorb and distribute stresses along their entire length.

Gunwales must be tough enough to withstand the flexion of a hull in rough water and strong enough to support the hanging seats, yet light and supple enough to take the long compound bend of the sheer-line. They can be as simple as square lengths of wood, or they can be carved and tapered to add an elegant touch of finesse to your boat.

The gunwale dimensions for each canoe can be scaled from the line drawings, though this is difficult. It is better to machine them after the hull is made and take the length from the finished body of the canoe.

Sometimes, it is difficult to find hardwood long enough for the job, but this can be solved by gluing two short pieces with a scarf joint, provided they are similar in color and grain. Mark both with an angle 7 inches long for every inch of thickness. Cut each roughly to size on the table saw, and dress to the line with a plane. Because the open grain absorbs a lot of glue, apply epoxy to both surfaces until no more will soak in, then clamp the joint together. By attaching the scarf joint to the hull so that one end lies on top of the other, it will be virtually invisible from above.

MACHINING THE INWALES

Inwales make up the inside half of the gunwales and can range from subtle slivers of trim

MAKING A PLANK FEATURE

You can add visual distinction to your canoe—and make use of short planks—by making a feature pattern on your canoe, installed either on both sides of the hull or on one side of the bow or stern.

Feature planks can be assembled right on the mold, but we find it works just as well or better to prepare the design feature before beginning to plank the hull. The planks that make up the design are glued together on a jig on the bench, then the feature piece is marked with reference lines so that it can be installed when the hull is planked.

Basswood and dark western cedar create high-contrast designs, but woods with less contrast produce equally interesting, if more subtle, effects. Whatever your color choice, choose a wood with similar density to the planking. This becomes important during the sanding stage. As the surface is smoothed, harder wood will sand more slowly, ending up higher than the surrounding surface. If you have to use a dense wood, you may have to finish it with a scraper to bring it level with the softwood.

Begin by drawing a full-size pattern, including the plank lines in the design. (The width of the plank lines must be the actual width of coverage, not the width of the plank.) The design will be made up of individual planks, but the end result will look like inlay.

Cut the parts, then lay them out on the pattern to be sure they fit together. If you don't have access to a power saw that makes accurate, repetitive cuts, you can cut them by hand. Make up a miter box that will give you a consistent angle and vertical cut. To compensate for the lack of precision, cut intersecting pieces at the same time. Lay the planks parallel and one on top of the other to make the cut.

The pieces are put together in a jig, which keeps them straight and facilitates clamping. To make the jig, staple a piece of planking along the front edge of the workbench, with the cove side facing out. This will act as a guide to line up the pieces and hold them in a straight line while the glue sets. Position the guide about two plank-widths in. This will accommodate the feature plank you are working on and another short clamping piece that will hold everything in place. Before proceeding any further, it might be a good idea to cover the area with plastic film or tape so that the feature plank doesn't become part of the bench.

Before gluing together the pieces that make up each feature plank, do a dry run. You don't want any surprises when there is wet glue on all the parts. When the two bevels are fitted together and the edges are parallel, draw a reference line across the joint.

Use a fast-setting carpenter's glue so that you don't have to wait long before assembling the next plank in the feature. Leave the pieces clamped long enough for the glue to grab, then take the glued plank out of the jig, check the joints, and clean up any glue that has squeezed out on the bead or cove. When the planks are all glued, arrange them in order and draw a reference line across all the planks. You will use this reference to position the feature on the mold. ◗

to elaborately carved handrails.

The lightest and simplest inwales are shaped from a solid piece of ⅜-by-¾-inch hardwood cut a few inches longer than the sheer-line. Although too narrow to hang seats from, they are ideal for small, one-man Nessmuk-style canoes, where the paddler sits in the bottom of the hull. After they are fitted, the edges are round so that water is not trapped inside the canoe when the hull is overturned.

Solid ¾-inch square inwales are the strongest, best suited for large, rugged canoes, but they are heavy and chunky-looking and prevent water from draining out of the boat when it is overturned.

Scuppered or slotted, inwales overcome the drainage problem, and we prefer them because they are reminiscent of those on traditional cedarstrips, where the narrow ribs create rhythmic spaces between the hull and inwale. Scuppered inwales have the strength of solid inwales but can reduce total canoe weight by as much as a pound each. The slots are useful to lash gear to.

If you choose the airy elegance of scuppered inwales, indulge your creative whims in the size and placement of the slots: elegant, long handrails or closely spaced eyelets. They can extend the full length of the sheer-line or stop before the decks (as shown, right). But draw the design first, making sure that there is solid wood where the seats and thwarts will hang.

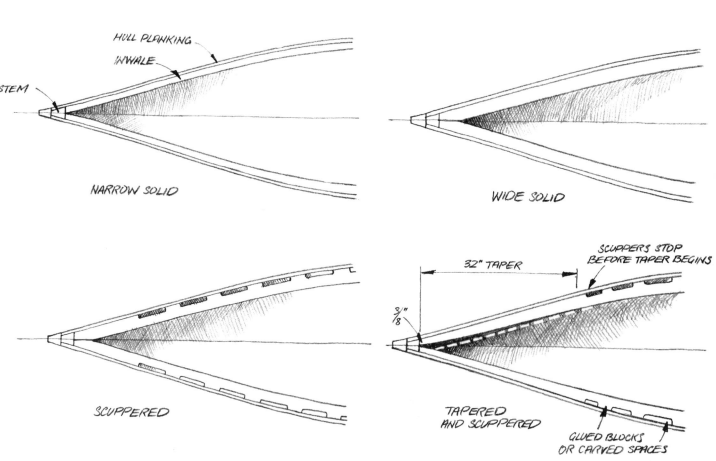

Solid inwales, *top,* are the easiest to make, but when wide, they are too heavy and when narrow will not hold a seat. Tapered and/or scuppered inwales, *above,* are more functional and look more elegant.

84

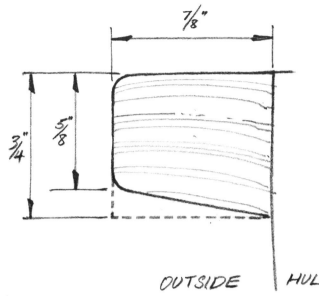

7/8"

3/4"   5/8"

OUTSIDE   HULLSIDE

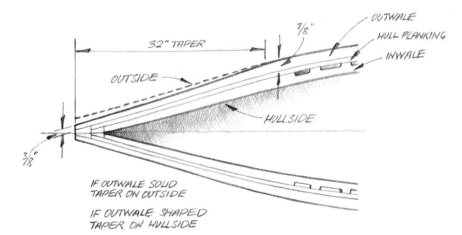

32" TAPER

7/8"

OUTSIDE

OUTWALE
HULL PLANKING
INWALE

HULLSIDE

3/8"

IF OUTWALE SOLID
TAPER ON OUTSIDE

IF OUTWALE SHAPED
TAPER ON HULLSIDE

Outwales can be tapered so that lines flow smoothly toward the ends of the canoe. Reduce weight by beveling the bottoms on a table saw.

The slots can be carved from a solid inwale, or if the inwale is narrow, they can be formed by gluing blocks between the inwale and the hull. Both methods are fiddly and time-consuming, but the final effect is worth it.

To produce a carved inwale, draw 1/4-inch-wide slots on a 3/4-by-7/8-inch piece of hardwood of the appropriate length. Cut out the holes using a dado blade on a table or a radial arm saw, a jigsaw, a router with a core box veiner bit or the edge of a large 1-to-1 1/2-inch Forstner or sawtooth machine bit.

Alternatively, cut blocks from 1/4-by-3/4-inch lumber. Use scrap planking, or for an interesting visual effect, use wood of a contrasting color. Using epoxy resin, glue and clamp the blocks to a 3/4-by-5/8-inch piece of hardwood a few inches longer than the sheer-line. When the glue is dry, remove the clamps and sand off any excess. Round the inside edges of the holes with a rasp, a scraper or sandpaper.

To complement the fine, graceful lines of the canoe, the inwales may be tapered toward the stems. To produce the taper, start about 32 inches from each end and shape the hull-side edge of the inwale from 7/8 inch to 3/8 inch. If you taper the inwales, you should stop the scuppers before the taper begins, as illustrated.

Note that if your design calls for a steep tumblehome, the inwales will have to be beveled so that the top of the gunwale sits level. Bevel the hull side before scuppers are cut.

MACHINING THE OUTWALES

Outwales (the other half of the gunwales) should be wide enough to turn aside waves but not so wide as to inhibit the paddler from reaching the water. Cut from 3/4-inch lumber, they can range in width from 3/4 inch to 1 1/8 inches, but 7/8 inch is a workable median.

Rip the outwales from a good, clear piece of hardwood (or spruce, if you want to reduce weight), slightly longer than the sheer of the canoe.

To give the outwale a finer line and to reduce weight without impeding function, bevel its bottom edge so that the final outside thickness is 5/8 inch (as shown, left). Shape it in the same manner as the keel, rough-cutting with the saw blade set to the angle drawn on the end of the stock and shaping the final edge with the plane and/or cabinet scraper.

For even more finesse, the outwales can be tapered toward the stems. The cut is made on the hull side if the outwale is beveled; otherwise, it is made on the outside. Beginning 32 inches from each end, taper from the full width to 3/8 inch at the stem. Cut the line roughly on the table saw, then clean up the cut with the plane or cabinet

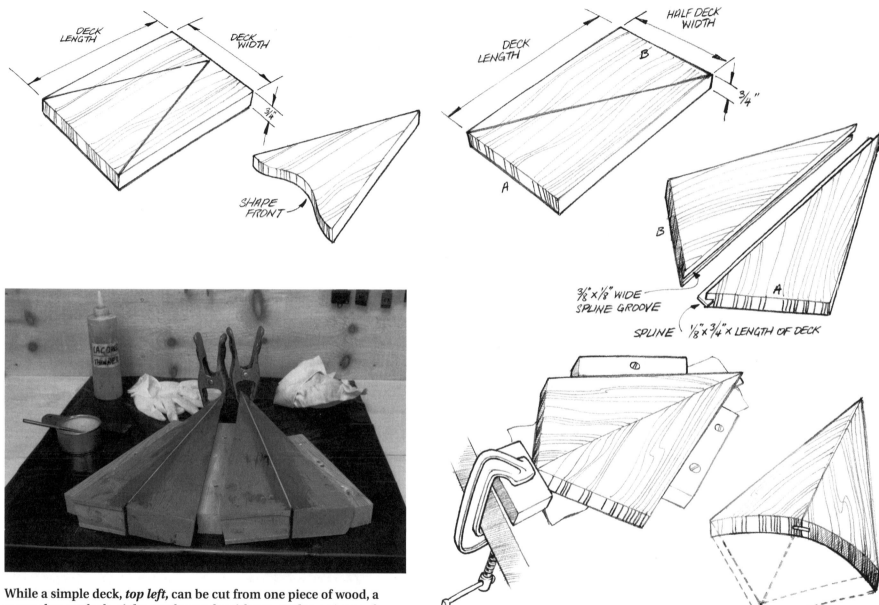

DECK LENGTH

DECK WIDTH

3/4"

SHAPE FRONT

HALF DECK WIDTH

DECK LENGTH

B

A

3/4"

B

A

3/8" x 1/8" WIDE SPLINE GROOVE

SPLINE 1/8" x 3/4" x LENGTH OF DECK

While a simple deck, ***top left,*** can be cut from one piece of wood, a more elegant deck, ***right,*** can be made with two or three pieces of wood joined with splines. After the parts are glued, they are left to dry in a jig. Clamps and wedges, ***above,*** keep the joint tight.

A well-designed deck draws the eye forward, toward the stem.

scraper. Edges may be rounded and sanded before or after the outwale is fastened to the hull.

THE DECKS

Decks tie the two sides of a canoe together at the stems, both structurally and aesthetically. They can be as short as a simple breasthook, or they can extend for almost the entire length of the canoe, leaving only an oval Rob Roy-style cockpit in the center. The decks shown in this book cover a range of styles and are completely interchangeable.

There are almost endless variations in deck design, depending on the time, money and effort you want to put into that part of your boat. It is here that you can let your imagination soar and make your canoe truly distinctive.

Begin by preparing a cardboard pattern of your own design, or take dimensions from the line drawings. When machining the decks, leave an extra ¼ inch of wood on all sides for fitting. Since they are glued to the inwales, they should end up the same thickness.

The simplest deck is shaped from a single piece of ¾-inch hardwood, although because of the deck's triangular shape, the length will be limited by the width of the board (see facing page). Cut it out, and shape the front edge so that it is visually pleasing and comfortably accommodates the shape of the hand, since you will probably use this as a grip to haul

your canoe out of the water.

If your lumber is too narrow to make a deck of the desired length, or if you want to explore a deck's visual possibilities, you can join two boards with a spline. Keep in mind that the grain should always follow the line of the inwales, keeping the short grain on the inside where it is tied together with the spline. Arranged this way, the grain lines will converge at the stem, complementing the overall symmetry of the canoe.

Make a diagonal cut in a ¾-inch board (as shown, facing page). Flop one triangle so that the acute points meet. Mark which side will be the top of the deck.

Set the saw blade at ⅜ inch, and cut a ⅜-inch-deep-by-⅛-inch-wide groove in the mating surfaces of the triangles, pressing the bottom side of each deck piece against the table to ensure that the spline grooves line up exactly. Cut a ⅛-by-¾-inch hardwood spline the length of the deck. Dry-fit the triangles and spline together.

Set the deck on your bench, which should be protected with plastic or wax paper. Make a clamping jig by screwing 1-by-2-inch blocks along the inwale sides of the deck, fastening one to the bench with two screws and one with a pivot screw in the center.

Remove the deck, separate the parts, and apply glue to all mating surfaces. Fit the deck together, and slide it into the jig, letting the pivot block find its own angle; then clamp a block at the front to keep the deck firmly in the jig. When the glue is set, remove the jig and shape the front edge, as shown.

With the basic technique of the spline joint, the design possibilities become endless. The two triangles can be separated by a straight or tapered piece of wood of contrasting color, fastened with two splines. By putting a slight angle on the mating edges of the triangles, you can create a cambered deck that complements the curving lines of your canoe.

For interesting texture, try a bookmatch deck: instead of cutting two triangles, cut one from a 1¾-inch board and slice it open it up so that the grain is mirrored on both sides, as shown.

To make a deck of alternating dark and light strips, glue together ¾-inch strips of the desired width and length of the deck. When you have a board half the width of the deck, cut it diagonally and flop one triangle to produce central converging stripes.

MACHINING THE COAMING

The type of wood you choose for your decks matters little as long as it has sufficient grain

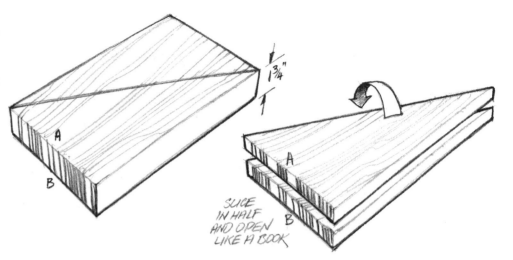

SLICE IN HALF AND OPEN LIKE A BOOK

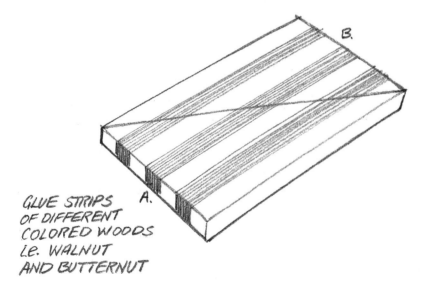

GLUE STRIPS OF DIFFERENT COLORED WOODS i.e. WALNUT AND BUTTERNUT

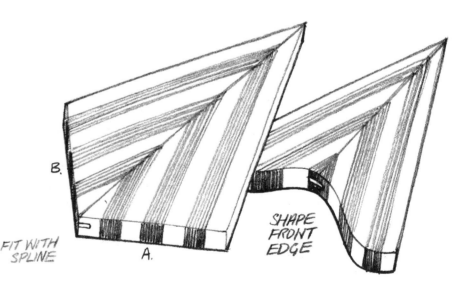

FIT WITH SPLINE

SHAPE FRONT EDGE

A bookmatch deck, which is cut from a thick board of highly figured wood such as bird's-eye maple, features a perfectly matched grain that radiates toward the stem of the canoe, *top right.* For an even more dramatic effect, contrasting woods can be laminated into a single plank, which is then cut and splined together, *bottom right.*

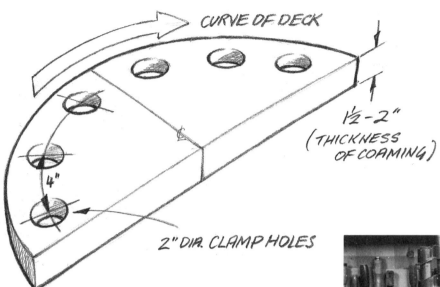

CURVE OF DECK

1½ - 2"
(THICKNESS
OF COAMING)

4"

2" DIA. CLAMP HOLES

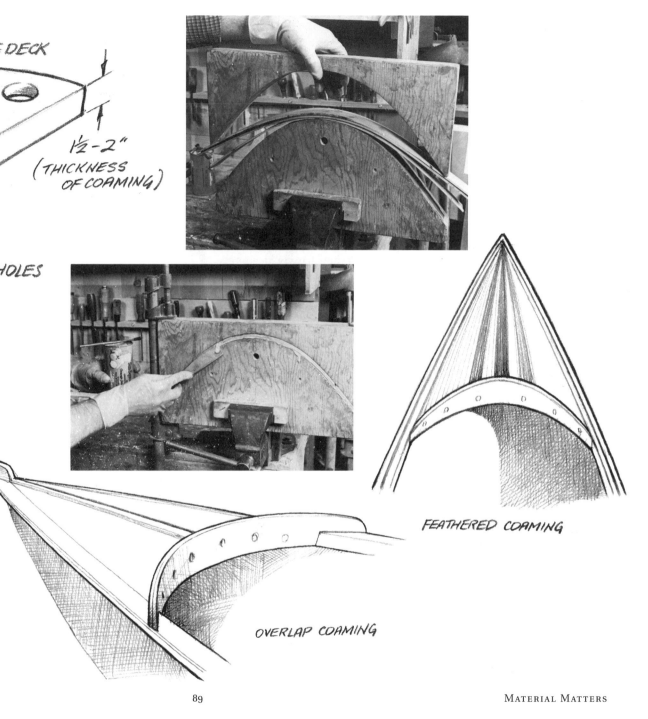

A traditional coaming can be added to decorate the edge of the deck. To reproduce the exact curve of the deck, the coaming is steam-bent on a mold, *above*, that has been drilled to accommodate C-clamps. Coaming can also be shaped on a two-part mold. First the strips are steamed and shaped in the mold, *top photo,* and later, after drying, they are glued together, *bottom photo.* The coaming ends can be feathered into the inwales, or its curving top can be half-lapped over the entire gunwale, as illustrated.

FEATHERED COAMING

OVERLAP COAMING

strength to hold the gunwales together. If you use a softer wood, such as butternut or cedar, you can tie the grain together with a coaming, a feature traditionally seen on vintage Peterborough canoes. Visually, it lends a luxurious air to your canoe, especially if highly figured, richly colored woods are used.

The coaming will also cover the exposed grain at the front edge of the deck. As the illustrations (facing page) indicate, the coaming can either feather into the inwale or extend over the gunwales. It is made by laminating together three 1½-by-⅛-inch strips of a good-looking hardwood that bends easily (cherry, oak or ash).

To reproduce the curve of the deck correctly, make a simple two-part mold. It must be the same thickness as the coaming and follow the line of the deck's front edge. Steam the hardwood strips, and then, with the bottom of the mold clamped securely in a bench vise, lay on the hot, damp strips and tightly clamp the top of the mold over them.

After 24 hours, remove the strips to dry, waiting another day before spreading epoxy glue on all inside surfaces. Clamp it again in the mold, but not so tightly that all the glue is squeezed out, starving the joints. Wipe the laminated joints clean. When the glue is set, remove the coaming from the mold and sand smooth.

The coaming can also be

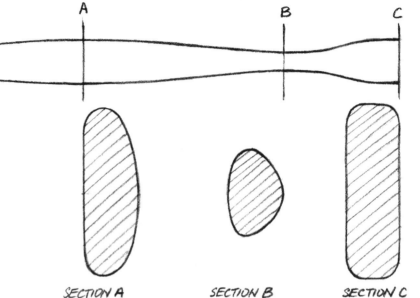

SECTION A   SECTION B   SECTION C

Hardwood thwarts need not add weight if they are well designed, *right*. Notice how the shallow arch on the wide central areas is attractively complemented by the rounded narrow parts on either side of the thwart.

formed on a one-piece mold (see facing page) that is similar to a stem mold in that the laminations are held in place with a succession of C-clamps secured through clamp holes. (For a full discussion of steaming and laminating techniques, see page 110.)

Dry-fit the coaming onto the deck, and screw with 1¼-inch #6 roundhead screws. After the deck is secured between the inwales, fasten the coaming permanently with glue and screws. Counter-boring the plugs is optional.

THE THWARTS

Thwarts tie the canoe together in the middle, sometimes doubling as seat rests and carrying handles, so they should be strong enough to support a person's weight and comfortable to the hand and shoulder if they are to be used for short portages.

Don't let their utilitarian function spoil the appearance of your canoe. Some builders have ruined the lines of their craft by inserting heavy-duty doweling that resembles a sausage; concentrate on making the canoe attractive, no matter how simple.

Thwarts can take any shape, and because they require little wood and their figured surfaces are highly visible, this is an excellent place to use those fancy hardwoods of your dreams.

With a little extra work, you can cut the board to a shape of your own design. Draw half the pattern, and repeat it for a consistent flow of lines, as shown above. Round off the edges, and sand it to a fine finish.

For a more unique thwart that releases the dynamic character of the wood and comfortably takes the curve of the hand, refine the flat cutout with a spokeshave so that the widest part is thinnest and the narrow areas a little thicker, with the lines flowing smoothly between.

Sculpting the thwart takes only a little extra effort, yet it will reduce weight and accentuate the grain dramatically. It should be finished by smoothing with a

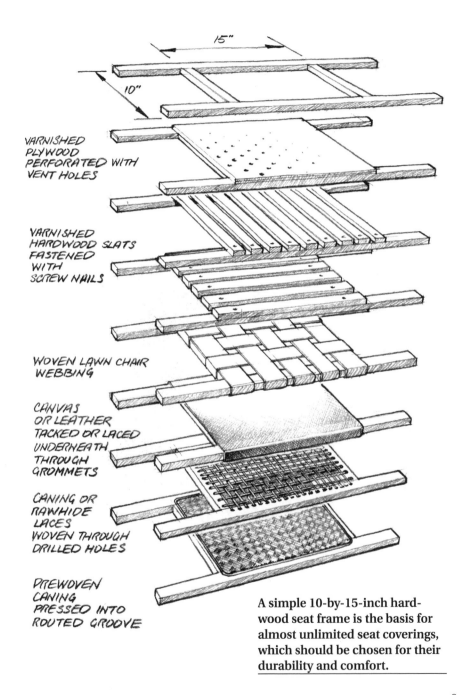

15"

10"

VARNISHED
PLYWOOD
PERFORATED WITH
VENT HOLES

VARNISHED
HARDWOOD SLATS
FASTENED
WITH
SCREW NAILS

WOVEN LAWN CHAIR
WEBBING

CANVAS
OR LEATHER
TACKED OR LACED
UNDERNEATH
THROUGH
GROMMETS

CANING OR
RAWHIDE
LACES
WOVEN THROUGH
DRILLED HOLES

PREWOVEN
CANING
PRESSED INTO
ROUTED GROOVE

A simple 10-by-15-inch hard-wood seat frame is the basis for almost unlimited seat coverings, which should be chosen for their durability and comfort.

cabinet scraper and/or sanding with 120-grit sandpaper. For a finer finish with hard grain, wet it down, then sand again with 220-grit sandpaper. Apply varnish (see page 175).

THE SEATS

Like decks, seats are infinitely variable and can reflect the whims of the builder. Whatever the covering, they all begin with the same basic frame, constructed from ¾-by-1½-inch hardwood. The 10-by-15-inch seat frame described below not only fits most canoes but accommodates most derrieres.

Begin by laying out the frame members on the workbench. Fasten them together with two 2-inch #6 screws at each joint, predrilled, countersunk and counterbored if plugs are desired (see page 171). Dismantle the frame, apply epoxy glue to all mating surfaces, then screw permanently into place.

These screws may get in the way if you are making a drilled or routed seat. In that case, join the seat frames with a simple dowel. Clamp the frame in position on the bench, and drill two ¼-inch holes through both frame parts at each joint. Plane two edges of a ¼-inch dowel slightly, and glue and press in place. Cut off flush. If you have the equipment and expertise, mortise-and-tenon or blind dowel joints are ideal.

When the joints are secure, round off the edges of the seat frame and sand with 120-grit

sandpaper. Finish-sand with 220-grit. Varnish with at least three coats over any exposed wood (as described on page 175).

When choosing a covering for your seat frames, your priorities should be comfort, durability and style. Most variations are within the capabilities of amateurs, though cane and rawhide may be exceptions. Good-quality models of both types are readily available at a reasonable price (see Sources, page 201), so it might be easier to buy a seat from professionals rather than spend the time to learn how to weave cane.

With seats, as with all the trim, there are two ways of approaching the machining process. On the one hand, you can hone your woodworking skills on these small projects without wasting a lot of materials as you build up your confidence for the hull. Or, if you are a purist in matters of color and line, you may want to wait until the hull takes shape before designing trim that will be its perfect complement.

CHAPTER 7

FUNCTIONAL FORM

Making the Mold

MY BOATS AND CANOES HAVE BEEN BUILT WITH AS MUCH REAL VALUE IN THEM AS TIME AND CARE AND SKILL AND THE WILL TO BUILD ON A QUALITY BASIS COULD MAKE POSSIBLE.

—Walter Dean

To build the perfect canoe, one must begin with the perfect mold. This may seem to state the obvious, but it is well worth whatever time and effort it takes to start from the very best mold possible, because every imperfect curve and twist that is part of the form will be reproduced exactly in your finished canoe.

So choose a good plan, and take your time setting it up. This part of the process requires systematic attention to detail and a healthy respect for accuracy. But it is also where the fun begins, where you begin to acquire some of the boatbuilder's skills and where you first catch a glimpse of the lovely craft you will one day paddle.

If you can beg, borrow or rent the forms for a canoe that suits your needs and desires, then by all means do so. But keep two things in mind. First of all, be aware that plans are copyrighted. Most plans are sold with the understanding that the builder is buying the right to produce one (and only one) boat for his or her own use. If the intention is to build many boats, if the canoebuilding is, in other words, for profit, then the cost of the plans—and/or the royalty— is adjusted upward accordingly. Therefore, before making a second canoe from a mold built from purchased plans, you must ask the permission of the owner of the design. This makes good moral as well as legal sense. The money you spend buying a plan supports and encourages the creation of more good-quality designs.

Second, since you will be devoting many hours of work to the hull you build, you want to be sure that the mold you borrow or rent is worth the time and money you are about to invest. Do not rely on someone else's preparatory work unless you are thoroughly familiar with the canoe which last came off that mold. If it cuts through the waves like an arrow and has all the design features you want, con- gratulate yourself on your good fortune. But if the canoe paddles like a barge and looks like a water- ing trough, then you would be wise to take the time to make a mold of your own. Trying to fair a sloppy mold is a frustrating under- taking and can end up being more work in the long run than starting fresh with a plan in which you have confidence.

It may be the most exacting part of the process, but building a mold is not really difficult, and it actually becomes exhilarating as you see, ever so gradually, the shape of things to come.

MAKING THE MOLD

Tools
2 C-clamps (about 2½-inch)
24-inch carpenter's square
fine-nib ballpoint
    pen/pencil/marker
utility knife
band saw or saber saw

wood or plastic batten (⅛-by-
  ⅜-by-32-inch)
pushpins, ¾-inch brads, finishing
  nails or weights

Materials
two 4-by-8 sheets ⅜- or ½-inch
  particleboard or plywood*
4 sheets carbon paper
1 roll 1-inch masking tape

*This is sufficient to cut out all the
molds for most canoes up to 16
feet, but measure from your plans
to be sure.

The first step in making the
mold is to transfer the station lines
from the body plan to the forms
that will determine the exact
shape of your canoe. This involves
tracing, very accurately, the contour of each station onto a sheet
of stable, inflexible material, such
as plywood or particleboard, then
cutting out the molds.

If the design you are building is
asymmetrical, each station mold
will be a different shape. However,
if the canoe is symmetrical, all the
stations except the center one are
duplicated to produce both a forward and an aft end of the canoe.

Line up the baseline of the plan
with the uncut edge of the mold
material, and mark the position
of the centerline on the board.
Remove the plan, and using a
square, draw the centerline perpendicular to the uncut edge. To
double-check that the centerline
is dead-on, flip the square over

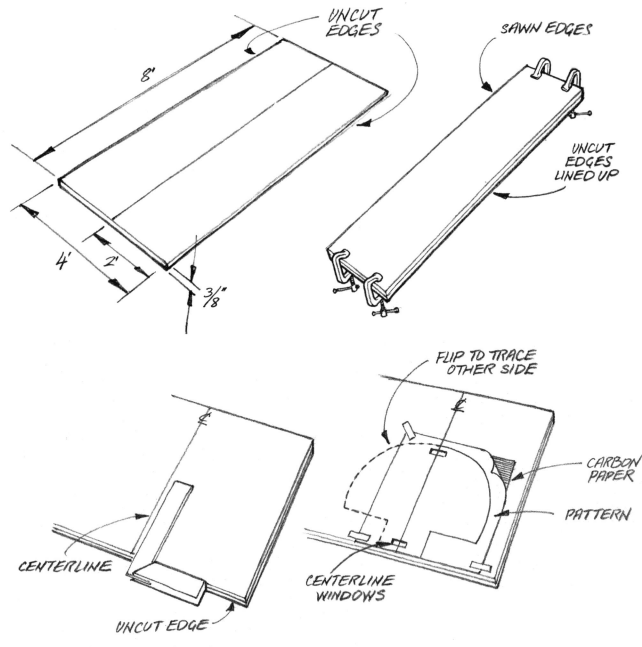

Transferring the pattern to plywood.

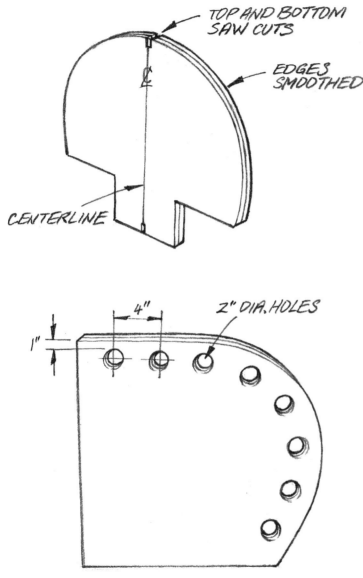

TOP AND BOTTOM SAW CUTS

EDGES SMOOTHED

CENTERLINE

2" DIA. HOLES

4"

1"

CUT OUT HOLES BEFORE SEPARATING STEM MOLDS

A stem mold

on the centerline and confirm the other side. This will be your primary guide when marking out and setting up the molds on the strongback.

On the paper plan, cut ¼-inch windows out of the top and the bottom of the centerline and at the baseline. Lay the plan on the board, and use the windows to match the centerline of the plan with the centerline you drew on the board. Also match the baseline with the edge of the mold. When they line up exactly, secure one or two edges of the plan to the board with masking tape.

Slide two sheets of carbon paper under the plan, one facedown and one faceup (as shown, facing page). As you trace the outline, the carbon paper will transfer the line to the board and, at the same time, onto the back side of the plan, where it will be clearly visible when you flip the plan to draw the second half (the mirror image) of the station. Mark the sheer-line, and trace the centerline so that these will also appear on the flip side of the plan.

You can, if you wish, trace the outline freehand, but you will achieve a cleaner line and a fairer curve if you use a batten to provide a guide. Any narrow strip of straight-grain, flexible wood (or plastic) will do. Drive pushpins or brads (small finishing nails) through the plan every 4 or 6 inches, positioning each pin so that one side is flush with the line

you want to trace. Then bend the batten so that it follows the line exactly. Secure it in place with

A batten produces a fair curve.

more nails or with weights while you trace your line.

When the first half of the station is traced, flip the plan to the other side, line up the centerline and the baseline again through the windows, tape the plan in place, slip a single sheet of carbon paper facedown under the plan, position the batten, and trace the other half. Remove the plan, and identify the mold with the number of that station.

The stem molds are handled a little differently. Since they are set perpendicular to the other stations, creating the bow and stern of the canoe, they look quite different from the station molds. The plan isn't flipped, so the stem molds look like half a station.

If the plans you are using do not provide for inside stems on the canoe, add them. This requires an adjustment to the plan: deduct the shape of the ¾-inch inside stems from the full-size draw-

FUNCTIONAL FORM

If you have a band saw and if your design is symmetrical, you can cut your time in half and improve your accuracy by marking and cutting both the identical station molds at once. Note: Check your plans first, as this is true only if none of the molds is higher than 24 inches.

Cut the 4-by-8-foot sheets of particleboard in half lengthwise, creating two 2-by-8-foot panels that are laid one on top of the other. Since a factory presumably can cut straighter than we can, line up the uncut edges of the 2-by-8-foot sheets and clamp them together. The method for transferring the lines of a station mold onto the board is the same as for a single sheet. Reproduce all the stations as duplicates except for the one at the center of the canoe: you'll need only one midpoint station mold.

Fasten the sheets together with two or three ³/₄-inch finishing nails inside each station. This will keep the two pieces lined up as you cut around the outline. (Try not to drive the nails through the bottom, because you may cut yourself on the exposed tips and may scratch the saw table.)

After you cut out the duplicates, remove the nails and separate the twin molds, marking the station number on the second one. Using the saw cuts, draw a centerline on each side of both molds.

If you are using a saber saw, we recommend that the molds be traced and cut one at a time, because it is difficult to maintain a perfectly vertical cut through the double thickness of material.

ings of the bow and stern molds.

When all the molds are traced, cut them out with a band saw or a saber saw. Avoid using a jigsaw, if possible. It will do a good job, but it is very slow.

Whichever saw you use, take great care to stay right beside the line. If the saw wanders outside, the edge can be dressed to the line later. If it wanders inside, however, it will be difficult to

tell how much has been cut away, and any dips and hollows will have to be repaired.

As each mold is cut out, make a shallow saw cut (¹/₈ inch) in the top and bottom of the centerline. This will project the centerline to the back of the board.

After you cut out the stem molds, drill clamping holes (1¹/₄ inches or larger) around the curved perimeter. Make sure the holes are large enough to fit your clamps. Space them about 1 inch in from the edge, on about 3-inch centers. When it is time to laminate the stems, the laminations will be clamped in place through these holes. For a good lamination, you'll want the holes as close together as possible. If you don't have enough clamps for 3-inch centers, drill as many holes as you have clamps.

BUILDING THE STRONGBACK

Tools
string for taut line
pencil
square
plane
crosscut saw
hammer
C-clamps (and bar clamps, if you have them)
drill/driver
screwdriver
wooden wedges for leveling

Materials
two 4-by-8-foot sheets ³/₄-inch plywood or particleboard

2 lbs. 1⁵/₈-inch drywall screws
1 lb. 1¹/₄-inch drywall screws

Specifications
Length of box beam: 16 feet
Depth of beam: 8 inches
Width of beam: 8 inches
Length of top: 16 feet
Width of top: 12 inches
Height of strongback: 28³/₄ inches (adjustable)

Cutting List
Top: 2 pieces 12 by 96 inches
Sides: 4 pieces 8 by 96 inches;
    2 pieces 8 by 48 inches
Gables: 8 pieces 8 by 8 inches;
    3 pieces 8 by about 6¹/₂ inches
Legs: 4 pieces 8 by 24 inches;
    2 pieces 8 by 20 inches
Feet: 4 pieces 4 by 24 inches;
    4 pieces 4 by 8 inches

The strongback is the foundation that supports the mold sections on which your canoe will be built. It must be straight and solid, level athwartships (across its width) and also reasonably level along its length. All the steps in making and setting up the molds relate back to the strongback, so accuracy at this stage is important. Later on, you will be able to double-check each step using a level and the strongback centerline.

There are many styles of strongbacks. Our own preference has changed in the years that we've been building boats. We used to recommend building strongbacks from dimensional lumber formed

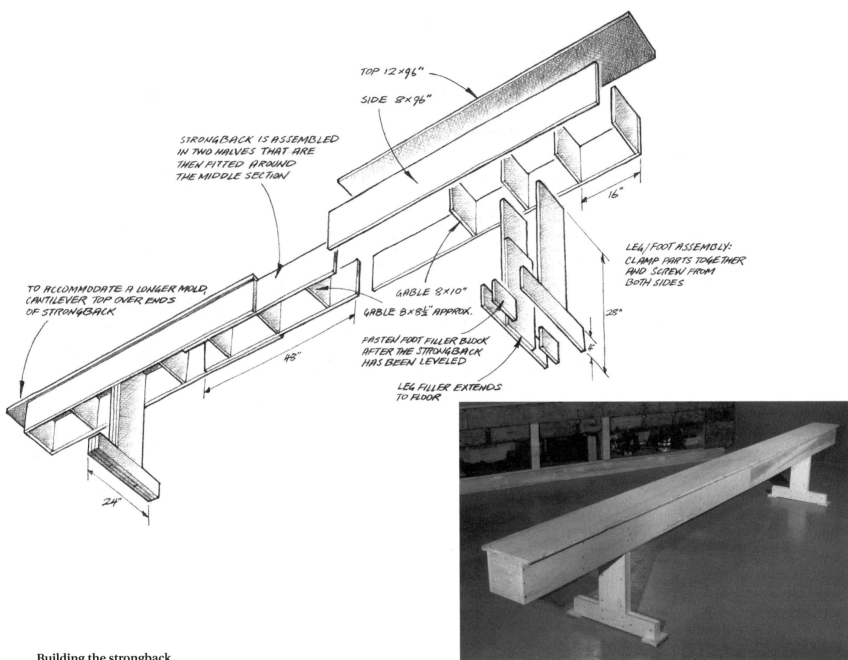

TOP 12×96"

SIDE 8×96"

STRONGBACK IS ASSEMBLED
IN TWO HALVES THAT ARE
THEN FITTED AROUND
THE MIDDLE SECTION

16"

LEG/FOOT ASSEMBLY:
CLAMP PARTS TOGETHER
AND SCREW FROM
BOTH SIDES

TO ACCOMMODATE A LONGER MOLD,
CANTILEVER TOP OVER ENDS
OF STRONGBACK

GABLE 8×10"

GABLE 8×8½" APPROX.

28"

48"

4"

FASTEN FOOT FILLER BLOCK
AFTER THE STRONGBACK
HAS BEEN LEVELED

LEG FILLER EXTENDS
TO FLOOR

24"

Building the strongback.

97

The strongback is assembled in the following order:

• Rip the boards to size.
• Assemble the two 8-foot sections of the box beam.
• Assemble the 4-foot inner section.
• Combine these three sections to make the 16-foot box beam.
• Assemble the legs around the gables; attach the feet.
• Level the beam, and attach the top.
• Stabilize the strongback by attaching it to the floor.

into a T-beam for rigidity. This is the method described in the first edition of *Canoecraft*. Since then, finding straight, dry 2-by-10 planks has become difficult. If you locate some, odds are that they'll be expensive and you won't want to waste them building a strongback.

For much less money, you can use plywood or particleboard to build a dimensionally stable support. This is the method that we now use ourselves and recommend to others. Built as illustrated, it will be a straight beam even if it's made from a slightly warped board, and it will remain true through moisture changes in the immediate environment.

Both plywood and particleboard are available and relatively inexpensive. The first choice for me is ¾-inch poplar plywood,

good one side. The wood is pleasant to work with, compared with spruce or fir plywood, though these are somewhat cheaper. Because of poplar's light color, pencil lines show up clearly, and the wood is soft enough that you won't be plagued with slivers.

Particleboard is a less expensive alternative and works very well. It is strong and durable enough to last you through the construction of several canoes. It is also smooth and light-colored, so pencil lines are obvious. The only caveat is that particleboard should be kept dry: if exposed to water, it can swell up and fall apart. To prevent this, you can seal the wood with varnish or paint, but the extra work and cost of doing this will probably make plywood more economical in the long run.

The strongback described here has evolved over many years of teaching canoebuilding classes in a variety of locations and environments. It is simple to make and exactly suits the needs of this style of construction, giving you predictable results even if your shop has an uneven floor. If you decide to build some other type of support for your molds, ensure that it will be a stable and predictable surface throughout the boatbuilding process.

STRONGBACK HEIGHT

The strongback determines the height at which you will be working for the next several weeks

or months as you assemble the molds and plank, sand and fiberglass the hull. For your comfort and good health, it is important to design it ergonomically, taking into account the particular needs of your body.

The specifications indicate a strongback height of 28¾ inches. This is comfortable for me, but you can choose your own best height. First, make a mark on the wall at your maximum comfortable working height. This will be about 6 to 8 inches below your shoulder level. Then, consult your building plans, and note the height of the center station.

Measuring down from your mark on the wall, subtract the height of the center station and make another mark. This will be the final height of the strongback. Try to imagine the mark as the lowest edge of the hull you'll be building. If it seems to be a comfortable working height, use that measurement for your strongback. Otherwise, adjust the mark up or down until it feels right.

STRONGBACK LENGTH

The ideal is to have a strongback the same length as the canoe you are building, but in practice, there is some flexibility. The material, the cutting lists and the illustration are for a 16-foot strongback. A deeper mold can be set lower on this strongback by hanging the bow below the surface of the strongback. To build a shorter

craft on this strongback, the molds must be raised above the strongback enough so that you can work

Stem mold overhangs strongback.

on the ends of the stems—about 2 inches is fine.

If you are building a canoe longer than 16 feet, you can extend the top of the strongback to overhang the box beam. Do this by adding the extra length to the middle of the beam, where the inner box section will span any joints. Cantilevered in this way, the strongback can accommodate a hull up to 17 feet 6 inches in length.

CUTTING THE PIECES

If the pieces you cut are straight and accurate, the strongback will go together smoothly. This is easily

The T-square jig pictured here is simple to make and will speed up your marking and crosscutting chores while guaranteeing true right-angle cuts when using a portable circular saw or a router.

Construct the jig from two pieces of 1-by-4-inch softwood or plywood. The length of the jig "arms" will depend on the length of the pieces to be cut. In most cases, one piece should be about 1½ feet and the other about 2 feet long. Clamp the arms together in a "T," and confirm the right angle with a square before fastening the screws.

Having to add or subtract the width of the machine base for each measurement can be confusing and is a potential source of cutting errors. To simplify the process, put the jig together so that the top of the T is longer than necessary. When you make the first cut, the T will be trimmed to a length that represents the exact distance from the edge of the machine base to the inside edge of the cutting blade.

From then on, if you take your measurement from the end of the board on your left and line up the end of the T-square jig with this mark, the cut will be exactly where you want it. If measuring to the right, add the width of the cut.

done if you have a fully equipped shop, but if you don't, it might be a good idea to have the strongback pieces cut at a lumberyard. Such places usually have a panel saw or a large table saw that can do a perfect job in hardly any time at all. In most cases, the charge will be minimal.

If you decide to cut the pieces yourself, bear in mind that the exact width of the cut pieces is not as important as keeping the width of the pieces consistent with one another. For instance, if you subtract the width of the saw kerf from all your 8-inch and 12-inch pieces (making them 7⅞ inches and 11⅞ inches), there will be very little waste from a standard 4-by-8-foot sheet of plywood.

Make the cuts as straight as possible and at true right angles so that the strongback will be straight and level and the pieces will fit together easily. The best tool for cuts along the length of the sheet material is a table saw fitted with an appropriate blade. It is important to support the board at both the infeed and the outfeed ends. It doesn't really work to have a helper. Instead, cobble the supports together from sawhorses, ladders, plywood off-cuts or whatever you have on hand. Not only is this the safest method, but you'll get the most accurate cut if you can focus on guiding the board rather than struggling to balance the 4-by-8 sheet.

You can get excellent results with a circular saw as well. To ensure a straight cut, use the factory edge of another sheet of plywood, clamped in place (see photo, page 78).

A radial arm saw or miter saw is good for making the crosscuts. You can also achieve consistent right angles using a portable circular saw or a router if you use the T-square jig described in the Builder's Tip, above.

As you prepare the pieces for the strongback, keep in mind the cardinal rule of building: measure twice, cut once. Double-check every measurement before you turn on the saw. You'll be glad you did.

BUILDING THE BOX BEAM

The strongback we use is essentially a box beam mounted on legs. The box beam is made in three parts: two 8-foot sections and a narrower 4-foot section that fits inside to tie the two longer sections together. Each box beam has two sides, a top and a series of crosspieces, or gables.

Expect to spend a good part of a day building the strongback. Like much in the canoebuilding process, this is an exercise in patient preparation, but the rewards are great. The time you spend paying attention to the details and working through each step will provide the groundwork for the next step and will become a big part of the success of what is to come.

Follow the cutting list carefully, except when it comes to cutting the gables. With these, you'll have to double-check the exact thickness of your material, since the board may be a metric equivalent and not exactly ¾ inch.

Begin by assembling the three box-beam sections. If the material is at all warped, lay out the opposite sides of each box so that any bends work against each other. In other words, have both sides bend out at the middle or bend in at the middle. That way, the forces will cancel each other out instead of producing a curved beam.

To lay out the position of the gables, clamp the long sides of each box together. Mark the gable positions at 16-inch centers, scribing the edges of both workpieces at once. Even if your numbers happen to be off, the parts will still go together square.

Take the pieces apart, and from your marks, project lines down the inside face of each board, using a square to make sure that the lines are perpendicular. Note on which side of the line you intend to position the gable. Finally, scribe a line down the outside of each board to indicate the center of the gable so that you'll know exactly where to place the screws.

Assemble the sides and gables of each box in turn. Clamp the pieces together tightly with a couple of bar clamps, and drill pilot holes for the screws. (If you don't, there is a good possibility that a screw will strip in the end grain of the gable before the parts are drawn together.) The clamps and pilot holes will keep the direction of the screw under control and prevent the end grain of the gables from splitting. Fasten everything together with 1⅝-inch drywall screws.

Set the two 8-foot sections on the floor, and slide the 4-foot

Short section joins two long ones.

inner section into position so that its midpoint is at the join, as shown, thus tying the two longer sections together. Roll the three-section beam onto its side, and shim it until it is level, end to end. Level it enough that the joints in the middle fit together tightly, then clamp it in this position. (The shims should raise the beam enough to get a few clamps on the bottom side of the beam.)

The box beam will remain flexible, side to side, until the top is

Spacers show top edge is straight.

secured and final straightening is done. Before fastening the components together, however, confirm that the top edge of the box is as straight, end to end, as you

With the box beam turned upside down, assemble each leg around the third gable from the end of the strongback.

can make it. This will become the baseline of your mold, so it must be as accurate as possible. Any problems with the top of the strongback will inevitably become problems with the mold.

Stretch a string line tightly along the top edge of the beam from one end to the other, placing a ¼-inch spacer under each end of the line. This will raise the line a measurable distance above the beam and allow you to use another ¼-inch piece of material to check that the space is uniform along the entire length of the beam.

When you are sure that the top edge of the beam is as straight

as it can be, fasten the two outer boxes to the inner box using 1¼-inch drywall screws.

THE STRONGBACK LEGS

The legs for the strongback attach to the third gable in from each end of the box beam.

The easiest way to build the legs is to set the box beam upside down on the same leveling blocks you've just used and then assemble each leg around the appropriate gable.

Each leg is made up of three pieces: two long and one short. Begin by fitting the two long pieces to the gable, one on either side, making sure that the tops of the leg pieces are flush with the top of the upturned box beam. Then slide the shorter leg piece between the other two until it touches the gable. (It will extend 4 inches past the other two pieces.) Clamp the three leg pieces together, and fasten with 1⅝-inch drywall screws.

Drive a couple of screws through the leg pieces into the gable to secure them until the strongback is turned over and the legs are finally fastened. The middle leg piece projecting from between the other two in effect creates a tenon. Each foot is made

With box right side up, fasten leg.

with four pieces (two long and two short) that are attached to this tenon.

Attach the two long foot pieces first, fastening one on either side of the tenon. This will leave a gap between the foot pieces at either side of the leg. The two short foot pieces (foot filler blocks) will be installed there, but leave them loose for now. After the strongback has been leveled, the foot filler

blocks will be positioned permanently and secured to accommodate any irregularity in the floor.

Note: If you are building on a dirt floor, you can substitute stakes driven into the ground for the foot filler blocks. After you level the mold, screw the feet to the stakes.

Turn the strongback over so that you can tightly clamp the leg pieces to the gable. Fasten them together with more screws through the sides of the box into the edges of the legs.

LEVELING THE BOX BEAM

Before you begin setting up the molds, there is one more critical step. You need to make sure the box beam is as level as you can get it across the width and reasonably close to level from end to end.

Level the beam by placing small wedges or cedar shims (if you have them handy) under the feet. Using

Level beam before attaching top.

a spirit level, check for level in both directions directly over the legs. When the beam is as level as you can make it in both

directions, stabilize the beam by fastening the filler blocks in the gap between the foot pieces. Make sure they touch the floor and not the tops of the leveling wedges. Secure the filler blocks to the foot pieces by driving drywall screws in from both sides.

ATTACHING THE STRONGBACK TOP

The box beam is now sitting level in its intended place in your shop, but it is still flexible from one end to the other. To straighten and stabilize it, use the edge of the top as a guide.

The top is designed to be a little wider than the beam (usually about an inch on either side). Fig-

To produce a consistent overhang, clamp blocks to the underside of the top before fastening it to the box beam.

ure out how much the top actually overhangs each side of your box beam, and cut several small blocks to this width. Clamp the blocks to the underside of the top, along one edge (as shown, above).

Put the top on the box, push the beam snug against the blocks, then clamp the top to the beam, as shown, with C-clamps or bar clamps. Fasten the top with drywall screws spaced every 8 to 10 inches.

Now make one final, careful check with the spirit level. The top of the strongback is the first reference for everything else that will follow, so you'll want to ensure that it is true, side to side and end to end. You've been

To keep the strongback perfectly stationary, secure it to the floor with a blob of glue under each foot or with a cleat, as shown.

controlling all the variables carefully, but there still may be small waves on the strongback top. Discrepancies of up to 1/16 inch are tolerable. They can be compensated for when the mold is set up. Anything greater than that, however, should be identified now and corrected.

To keep the strongback stationary, fasten it to the floor, if at all possible. There will be a certain amount of pushing and pulling as the hull is built, and you'll want to be sure that the strongback isn't inadvertently moved out of level.

If the floor is concrete, dab a blob of thickened epoxy glue under each foot. But be fore-warned: you may lose a chunk of concrete when it comes time to break the strongback loose. On a wooden floor, you can fasten a cleat around the foot and screw it to the floor.

If, for some reason, neither of these options is workable, the least you can do is mark the position of the strongback on the floor with marker or masking tape. Then if the strongback shifts during construction, you'll be able to put it back where it's supposed to be. You can also try gluing sandpaper to the bottom of the feet and pile sandbags or some equivalent weight on the feet to provide extra stability.

If all the cuts were straight and you've assembled everything with care, you'll now have before you a solid, level and true foundation for your mold, a good, predictable work surface that will get your project off to the right start.

SETTING UP THE MOLD

Tools
string for taut line
straightedge
level
pencil/pen
small square
drill/driver
countersink bit
six 2½-inch clamps

Materials
1½-by-1½-by-12-inch station
  blocks, 1 per mold
1⅝-inch drywall screws
two ¾-by-¾-by-16-inch square
  corner blocks
paraffin or packaging tape

While building your canoe, you'll find that some steps sound simple but seem to take forever and that others look complicated or monotonous but in fact evolve like magic before your eyes. Setting up the mold is one of the latter. It is one of the most exciting steps in the process, because it will provide you with the first three-dimensional glimpse of your boat.

If the pieces have all been prepared with care, you can expect to spend three or four hours setting up and checking the mold. Although it is significant, the work itself is not difficult: it involves

BUILDER'S TIP: STRING LINES

String lines are used throughout the early stages of boatbuilding, while leveling the strongback and setting up the molds.

Choose a thin string that can be pulled tight without stretching or breaking. Braided cotton line works well, as does fishing line, though it is wise to avoid the light monofilament that is designed to be invisible to fish. It is hard

to see in the workshop too!

Note that the line produced by a snapped chalk line is too wide to be accurate for most boatbuilding purposes.

There are various ways of tying off a string line, but to make it easy to adjust, anchor it with a clamp, as shown.

simply lining up the centerline on each station mold between an upper and lower centerline, then fastening the mold to its station block. The trick is to get started right and do the steps in logical order. If you have confidence in the accuracy of each step, when something looks wrong, you won't have to backtrack through all the steps to find the problem.

LAYING OUT THE STRONG-BACK CENTERLINE

The first step in setting up the mold is establishing a centerline on the strongback. At both ends, measure the midpoint of the top, then join these points with a string clamped in place and pulled taut. Mark the string's position at intervals along the length of the strongback, close enough that you can join the marks with a straightedge.

With a good-quality straightedge, connect the marks, pressing hard enough to dent the surface of the wood. (A fine ballpoint pen makes a good, strong, indelible impression.) Finally, double-check for straightness by standing at each end of the strongback and sighting along the line. Your eye should be lined up with the centerline and slightly above the strongback. Close the other eye and squint. This will filter out distracting images and allow you to concentrate on the line.

LAYING OUT THE STATION LINES

The station lines are drawn perpendicular to the centerline at predetermined intervals. These intervals can vary from one plan to the next, depending on who

Use a string line and straightedge to draw an accurate centerline.

Locate the centerline midpoint, and draw the center station line.

designs the canoes or prepares the drawings.

We have tried a variety of spacing, from 10 inches to 18 inches, and found that 12 inches is just right. Less than 12 inches is overkill: you just don't need that many supports to produce fair lines. As the distance increases over 12 inches, you'll need extra staples to tie the plank joints together between station molds.

Consult your boat plan for the exact spacing of your stations. If it is more than 14 inches, watch that the plank doesn't develop a flat curve between the station molds.

Begin the process of laying out the stations by locating the midpoint of the centerline you drew

FUNCTIONAL FORM

on the strongback. With a square, draw a line perpendicular to the centerline at the midpoint.

The center station mold will be centered over this line. Measure out from the midpoint toward the bow end and the stern, using a tape measure to mark the correct intervals. To prevent the tape from shifting, tape it to the strongback or weight it down.

(If you use a ruler to measure from point to point, the accumulated error can be significant.)

Draw the station lines at each interval, perpendicular to the centerline. Set your square against the centerline: it is a more reliable reference than the outside edge of the strongback.

Finally, draw the position of the

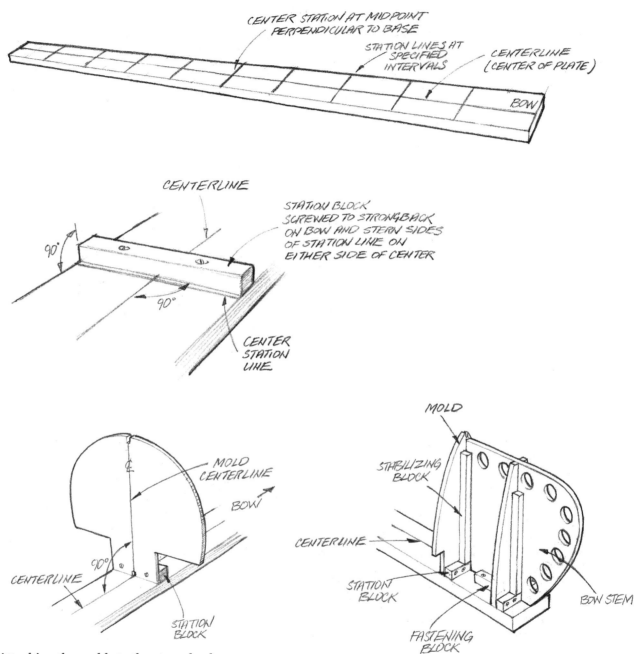

Stem mold sits on the centerline.

Attaching the molds to the strongback.

stem mold over the centerline. Pick up the proper width from your stem-mold material.

ATTACHING THE STATION BLOCKS

The center station mold will be positioned directly over the midpoint line. The other blocks

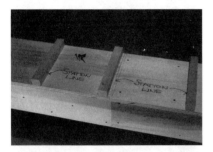

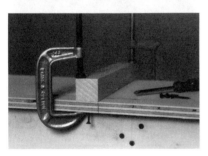

Clamp station blocks to the stem side of line, and screw in place.

will be secured on the side of the station line closest to the bow and the stern. All the molds will be held in place with station blocks fastened to the strongback, on the opposite side of the line.

To make the station blocks, cut as many pieces of dry softwood (1½ by 1½ by 12 inches) as you have station lines. The

blocks must be square so that the molds you attach to them will stand up straight at 90 degrees to the strongback.

Before screwing each station block to the strongback, clamp it in place to keep it from shifting out of position. If you are fastening the blocks from the top, drill pilot holes in the block so that the screw will draw the block tight to the strongback. (Use an 1¹⁄₆₄-inch drill for 2-inch #8 screws.)

Alternatively, you can attach the blocks by fastening them from the bottom with 1⁵⁄₈-inch screws. If you are using a power driver, drywall screws will have a good bite without requiring a pilot hole.

SETTING UP THE BOW AND STERN ASSEMBLIES

Note that if you plan to laminate the stems for your canoe on the stem mold, you'll find it best to do so now, before starting this next step (see page 109 for instructions). After the stems are laminated, proceed with setting up the mold.

In setting up the mold, the bow and stern assemblies are set up first. These usually consist of two parts: the stem mold and the first full-width station mold, which are fastened together in a T. (Some bow/stern assemblies consist of the stem mold and the first two station molds. This procedure is discussed at the end of the section.)

The bow and stern assemblies are self-supporting and become the reference for setting up all the station molds in between. As a result, you can expect them to take longer to set up than the others.

Begin by setting up the station that butts against the stem mold in a T. You will find the station-mold number on your plans.

Position the station mold against its block so that the centerline on the mold is lined up with the strongback centerline. Clamp the mold to the block, and

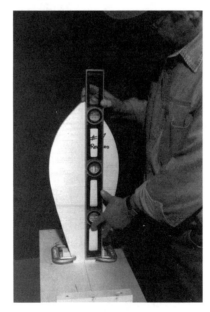

Use level to plumb the mold.

check that the mold is perfectly plumb. If it's not, lift a corner, shim, clamp and check again. Take special care with this first sta-

tion. If its centerline is off, you'll have to deal with a lot of annoying problems later on.

Fasten the mold to the station block with two screws. If you are using wood screws, drill pilot holes: you want the parts drawn so tightly together that they won't shift out of position. If you clamp the pieces firmly, drywall screws will work and the holes won't need to be predrilled.

Butt the stem mold tightly against the first station mold at its centerline, and clamp them together. If you don't have a clamp deep enough to fit through the clamp holes you drilled in the stem mold, try clamping a small corner block to the station mold (see page 107). This will act as a guide for the stem mold and will accommodate a small clamp.

Position the outboard end (the curving end) of the stem mold over the centerline on the strongback, and clamp to the strongback (see page 106). Do not fasten it with screws just yet. Wait until after both stem-mold assemblies are completed and checked for alignment before attaching it permanently to the strongback.

Before fastening the stem mold to the station mold, check for plumb at both ends of the stem mold.

Sometimes, the mold material will have a twist in it so that even though the curving tip of the stem mold is plumb, it isn't plumb at

Clamp the outboard end of the stem mold to the strongback. Before fastening, check for plumb.

This simple jig anchors the string line to the stem mold at the bow and stern and holds it directly over the strongback centerline. With the string line thus raised and secured, it is a simple matter to line up the station-mold centerlines between the centerline on the strongback and the upper reference line, as shown.

The jig is an L-shaped piece of wood. It can be cut from any scrap wood, though the piece should be sufficiently long that when you attach it near the ends of the stem molds, it holds the string high enough to clear the center station.

The critical dimension is the length of the short arm of the L. It must be exactly half the width of the stem-mold material. With the jig attached to the side of the stem mold, a string clamped onto the end face of that little arm will be held over the center of the stem mold.

the other end, where it meets the station mold. If that's the case, don't worry. Plumb the outboard end, since this will be the reference for positioning the stem; let the other end (within reason) fall where it may.

Drill pilot holes, and fasten the two mold pieces together with screws driven through the station mold into the vertical edge of the stem mold. If you need to control the end of the stem mold, you can reinforce this connection with vertical corner blocks to provide something to wedge against.

Note: If a stem mold falls too far out of alignment, you can make significant correction with a right-angled corner brace of the kind shown on page 107.

Some bow/stern assemblies consist of the first *two* station molds and the stem mold. This is a function of the overall length of the hull, the length of the stems and the fineness of the ends.

If such is the case on your plans, set up the stem mold to the second station mold using the same procedure as above. Cut the first station mold in half (with the width of the stem mold removed), then mount the halves on either side of the stem mold at the vertical station lines you traced from the plans.

Fasten a block to the stem mold on the same side as the station blocks. (These are, essentially, vertical station blocks.) Line up the half-molds against their blocks, then clamp them and drill pilot holes before fastening each with two screws.

Check the outboard edge of the

Create an upper centerline with a string-line jig.

stem molds with a level to make sure they are still plumb. If not, make the appropriate adjustments.

THE UPPER CENTERLINE

You now have a sense of the bow and stern of your canoe. The next step is to stretch a string line between the stem molds to create an upper centerline. This will be a critical reference point for elevation and straightness; it will confirm the position of the stem molds and will guide the installation of the remaining station molds. You can line up the station molds just using the strongback centerline and plumbing each mold with the level, but this leaves

room for some discrepancies. An upper centerline will eliminate most of these and will also be used to check the rocker when the mold is in place.

The string must be centered on the stem mold and positioned directly above the centerline drawn on the strongback. Getting it aligned perfectly may take some adjustments, which will be easy to do if the string is attached with the string-line jig shown on the facing page.

To establish the height of the string, add ¾ inch to the height of the center station (on every canoe design, this will be the tallest station). This represents the distance

from the top of the strongback to the top of the jig.

Clamping the string line ½ inch down from the top of the jig will position it ¼ inch above the center station and parallel to the strongback. Clamping the string line to the jig is easier than tying it with a knot and will simplify future adjustments.

After rigging the line, confirm that the string is centered on the stem mold. To do this, lay a straightedge alongside the stem mold and extending up past the string line. Measure the distance between the string and the straightedge: it should be half the width of the mold material. If it isn't, shim the jig until it is centered.

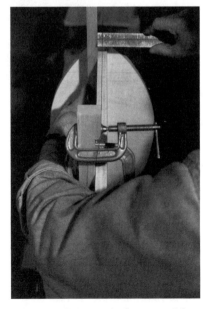

Center string precisely on mold.

With the position of the string line confirmed over the center of the stem mold, you can, with confidence, move on to the next step of centering the string line over the strongback centerline.

Check one end at a time. Position your eye directly over the string line at the station mold, and sight down the centerline on the station mold. If the line is where you want it to be, it will be superimposed over the station mold and strongback centerlines. If the lines don't match up, loosen the clamp on the end of the stem mold and shift it enough to reposition the line over the centerline.

Now check the other end, and confirm the position in the same manner. Note that getting one end positioned could throw the other end off slightly, so wait until both ends are lined up before attaching the end of the stem mold to the strongback. When you are satisfied, fasten each stem mold to the strongback with a ¾-by-¾-inch corner block cut to an appropriate length.

SETTING UP THE REST OF THE STATIONS

With the stem sections secure and the upper centerline in place, you can now set up the rest of the molds at their stations. Begin setting up from the ends, and work toward the middle so that you won't be confined to the 12-inch working space.

At each station, line up the centerline on the mold so that it is directly over the centerline drawn on the strongback and directly under the upper centerline. (The notch you made in the mold should be directly below the string.) Clamp the mold in place against its station block, then stand on something and sight down from above. You should see only one line: the string superimposed over the centerlines of both the strongback and the mold.

If you need to adjust the mold, lift the low corner to shim it, then retighten the clamp. The shim will help hold the mold steady and plumb. When you are happy with the position, screw the mold to the block.

Install the rest of the molds in the same way. Be sure to check that they are always on the correct side of the station blocks.

Glue and clamp mold plugs.

When all the molds are in place, stand at the bow or stern and take a sighting down the entire length of the hull. If you squint just so, you

Sight down to align centerlines.

should be able to superimpose all the centerlines over one another and pick out any that may be off. If any mold is out of line, take the time now to align it precisely.

Before removing the string line, note the relationship between the horizontal upper reference line and the space to the top of the molds. This will give you a preliminary check on the rocker in relation to a straight line.

If you used cheap plywood for your station molds, you may notice voids at the exposed edges of the board. (These are caused by gaps in the inner plies.) If a void is large enough to interfere with stapling the planks to the mold, take the time to fill it now. Whittle a softwood plug to fit the hole, then glue and clamp it in place. When the glue has set, trim it flush to the edge of the mold.

STABILIZING AND FAIRING THE MOLD

You'll notice that the molds are still a little wobbly at the top. You need to stabilize them vertically with a batten, a piece of scrap

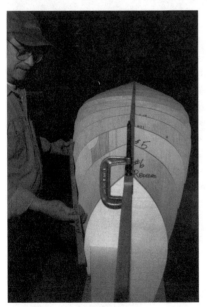

Stabilize the tops of the molds with a batten, *top*. Check all curves for fairness, *above*.

planking that you lay down the keel-line. Tack or clamp it to the end station molds, then use a small square or your level to plumb each station to the strongback. Fasten the batten at each mold with a 1-inch finishing nail (or staple), leaving the head exposed about ⅛ inch so that it can be pulled out later.

With the molds stabilized in all directions, check the fairness of the curves from one end to the other. If you had a good plan and were careful in tracing and cutting the molds, this stage should be little more than a pleasant formality.

First, check the rocker. Sight down the stabilizing batten at the keel-line, looking for a fair curve from one end to the other. You will need to check this out from several different angles to be sure.

To confirm that the mold is fair, bend a strip of planking (6 to 8 feet long) around the molds, parallel to the anticipated line of planking. Hold your hands as wide apart as possible, and start at the sheerline, slowly working your way up to the keel. The batten should just touch the edge of each mold, with little or no space between the station mold and the planking.

Tolerate irregularities up to $\frac{1}{16}$ inch on the sides and bottom. In these flatter areas, planking springs back, finding its own fair curve once the staples are pulled out. On hard curves, such as the turn of the bilge, be accurate within $\frac{1}{32}$ inch. If an unfair curve is molded in, there will be little change in the shape after the staples are removed.

Shave down high spots on the molds with a plane, spokeshave, sanding block or rasp. Be careful not to remove too much. If there is a serious dip in the mold, you'll have to glue in a piece of wood to fit. If a mold is extremely out of fair, move it back or forth, up or down, as necessary.

This step will produce the smoothest possible lines in your canoe. Ultimately, you have to live with the bumps and hollows in the hull, so fair the mold to your own standard of perfection.

PROTECTING THE MOLDS

At this stage of the operation—the last time that the molds are fully exposed—take some time to rub paraffin wax on the edges or to wrap them with plastic packaging tape. This will prevent glue from bonding the planking to the mold, which can make it difficult to release the hull from the mold.

For easy release, tape mold edges.

Packaging tape has some advantages over wax. It is a little more time-consuming to apply, but it creates a very reliable barrier and you don't have to worry about wax contaminating the edge of the planking or the inside edge of the stem.

LAMINATING THE STEMS

Tools
steaming/soaking equipment
C-clamps
block plane

spokeshave
fairing batten

Materials
six or twelve $\frac{1}{4}$-by-$\frac{7}{8}$-inch-by-40-
  to-50-inch hardwood strips
string
plastic sheeting
epoxy glue
epoxy solvent
sandpaper (#120)

Safety
gloves
ventilation
Note: Read safety instructions
for epoxy glue and solvent on
page 144.

This step is most easily done
with the stem mold clamped
in a bench vise or on the side of
your workbench. If you choose
to laminate the stems with this
method, the bending will be done
before the molds are set up on
the strongback.

You can also choose to set up
all the molds first and bend the
stems onto the mold after it is fastened to the strongback. In this
case, cut the stem stock closer to
the finished length, because the
length will be restricted by the top
of the strongback.

The inside and outside stems,
together with the keel and gunwales, are a vital link in the skeleton of a canoe, absorbing and
distributing impacts to the bow.
Structurally, the outside stems
tie the sides of the hull together,

making any other reinforcement
unnecessary. Inside stems support
the ends of the strips, giving you
more control during planking and
providing an accurate reference
for trimming the planks to the correct angle and length.

The purpose of outside stems
on original cedarstrips was to seal
the exposed end grain of the cedar
planking, but with epoxy construction, they add a traditional
finishing touch to the canoe, defin-
ing the profile of the canoe. Stems
serve an important aesthetic as
well as structural function, giving
the canoe a crisp, finished look.
When the outside stems are made
of contrasting wood, the effect is
even more dramatic.

Traditionally, stems are steam-
bent from solid hardwood. The
heat and moisture soften the
wood fibers. When pliable, the
wood is very slowly but firmly
bent around a form, clamped
and allowed to cool. After the
moisture content has stabilized,
the bent wood will hold its new
shape, although there is always
some springback.

Steam-bending a solid piece
of wood requires not only good,
straight-grained, air-dried stock
but also special equipment that
can exert considerable tension
and compression on the wood
fibers. It can be a quirky business,
with success depending on species
and quality of wood as well as on
bending technique and speed.
(Steam-bending is a science to be

Use a kettle and plastic pipe to steam-bend wood strips for stems.

mastered on its own. If you are interested in pursuing this, consult *Building Small Boats* (see Sources, page 203).

Since our objective, however, is to build a professional-quality canoe with low-tech equipment and layperson skills, we recommend laminated rather than solid-wood stems. The stem is ripped into thin pieces, which are steamed and bent on a form, then glued together. The result is as strong as or stronger than a solid stem of the same wood and is well suited to the home boatbuilder's arsenal of makeshift steamer and bending jigs. It also makes the need for ideal materials less imperative.

You will need three strips of wood for each inside and outside stem (a total of 12 pieces). Each strip should be 1/4 inch thick by 7/8 inch wide by the length specified by your design. The strips will be bent hot over the stem mold and allowed to dry before being glued together. The outside stems will be bent at the same time as the inside stems so that when they are finished, the pairs will fit perfectly together.

I suggest using a good, bendable softwood such as white cedar or pine for inside stems. These softwoods are strong enough, yet they are lighter, more bendable and easier to shape with a block plane and spokeshave than hardwood is. They also accept staples more readily. For the outside

stems, choose ash or cherry, because the denser hardwoods are more durable.

Laminating will allow you to get away with less than ideal bending stock, but even so, choose stock with the straightest grain you can find. It not only bends better but will be easier to shape with hand tools.

If you can, buy wood that is only partially air-dried. It will bend most consistently. If the wood you are using is very dry (or has been kiln-dried), get some moisture into the wood before steaming it. Soak it in the bathtub overnight, or wrap it in a wet towel and plastic film.

BENDING THE STEMS

A steam box can be anything that produces wet steam and includes some means for directing and containing the steam around the wood. Steam burns are swift and painful, so whatever system you set up, make sure it is safe. Always wear gloves, and be careful that other body parts aren't inadvertently exposed to escaping steam.

The electric-kettle steamer described here is about as simple as a steamer can get. All you need is a kettle, a piece of 2-inch plastic pipe several inches longer than the stems and several rags. We have a big steamer in the shop, but for bending a single pair of stems, this system is fast to set up and does the same job. If the kettle

is the type that has an automatic shutoff once the water reaches a boil, modify it by disabling or bypassing the thermostat. You can use the kitchen kettle, since the

Steam strips about 15 minutes.

process does no harm, but rinse it out before returning it to household use.

As a general rule, wood is steamed for one hour per inch of thickness. For our 1/4-inch laminations, 15 minutes should be long enough for most bends under most circumstances. But species and moisture content can vary dramatically. If the wood feels stiff and under extreme tension when you start to bend it, stop before the fibers break and put the strips back in the steamer

for another 5 or 10 minutes.

Because they are thin, the strips of wood not only heat up but cool down quickly. Once you take the wood out of the pipe, your optimal bending time is only about 45 seconds. That doesn't leave much time to get the pieces out of the steamer, arrange them on the mold, place the first clamp and start the bending.

It is essential, therefore, that you are well prepared in advance. Organization is everything here. Before steaming the wood, stack the strips for the inside and outside stems in the proper order and use plastic electrical tape to secure the ends together. Have your clamps ready, six for each stem mold, adjusted to size. It will also help a lot to solicit an extra pair of hands— one person to bend the wood, the other to clamp. Do a quick rehearsal beforehand so that everyone knows his or her job and when to do it.

Fill an electric kettle with water, and set the pipe over the spout, propping it against the workbench. Wrap a clean rag around the spout and the bottom of the pipe so that steam doesn't leak out but is directed upward. Stuff a rag in the top to contain the steam. Bring the water to a boil. When the pipe feels hot, insert the stem strips in the pipe and replug the top tightly with the rag. Steam the wood for about 15 minutes, or until it is flexible.

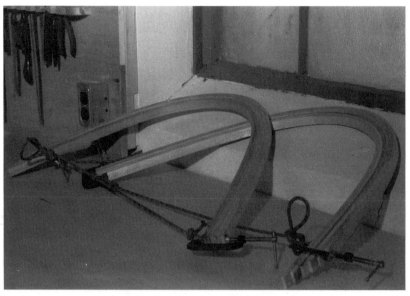

After removing from mold, tie strip ends together and dry 24 hours.

Bend and clamp steamed wood strips to stem mold, secured in a vise.

Take care not to boil the kettle dry.

When the strips are pliable, remove them from the steam box. Position them on top of the stem mold. If your stem mold is already on the strongback, butt the strips squarely against the station mold. If not, let the ends of the strips extend slightly past the end of the mold. You can trim them off neatly after they are glued.

While one person holds the wood and begins the bending, the other should clamp the laminations lightly at the first hole in the stem mold (the end that will be down inside the canoe). Continue around the stem curve, bending the laminations with a steady, firm motion. Move slowly enough that the outer edge of the strip has time to stretch but briskly enough to prevent the wood from cooling and stiffening. Keep that 45-second time limit in mind.

Keep up to the bend by adding a few clamps in strategic places. You don't have to clamp in every hole: four or five should be sufficient at this stage. Be careful not to overtighten the clamp so that it distorts or compresses the softened wood fibers. If you can't resist reefing down on the clamps, use clamping pads to protect the wood. But I find it easier just to go easy on the pressure, because the pads add one more element to a process that needs to be speedy and streamlined to be successful.

Brush a thin coat of epoxy glue on mating surfaces, and press together.

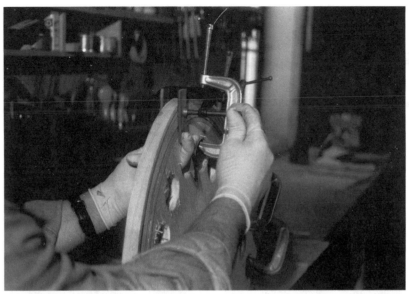

Use pieces of scrap wood to draw stacked laminations into alignment.

Wait overnight, or until the wood feels dry, before removing the stems from the mold. The softened fibers need time to harden up again so that the wood will hold its new shape. Also, for a good structural join, the epoxy glue has to penetrate the surface, and glue won't displace moisture.

Leave the stems on the mold overnight, then unclamp them and give them another 24 hours to continue drying. Tie a string from one end of each stem bundle to the other so that the wood retains its curve, and hang them up so that air circulates fully around the wood. If you had to soak the wood before you steamed it, the strips may take a little longer to dry.

Note: As a last resort, for those without an electric kettle, wood strips can also be bent by soaking them overnight in a bathtub of hot water. In the morning, drain the tub, refill it with the hottest water possible, and soak the strips for another half-hour before bending. The hotter and wetter the wood, the more flexible it will be, allowing the wood fibers to compress along the inside of the curve and to stretch on the outside of the curve without tearing. Strips bent after soaking in water should hang for two or three days before they are glued.

GLUING THE STEM STRIPS

Because the stems are a major structural member of the canoe and because they need to be waterproof, the strips should be laminated with epoxy glue. Use the same epoxy you'll use to lay up the fiberglass cloth. Make it into a glue by thickening it with a cotton-fiber filler such as #403 Microfibers or fine sanding dust. (Avoid silica-based thickeners, as they will dull your edge tools.)

Work clean and work safely. Read and understand the technical and safety information relevant to the epoxy system you are using, and review the safety precautions outlined on page 144. Be as clean as you possibly can with the epoxy. If you get glue on your gloves, wipe it off with a dry rag (lacquer thinner will dissolve most plastic gloves). Wipe up a mess when you make it, or the epoxy will get on your tools and your bench, and when you touch these with your bare hands, it will be on your skin.

When the strips are ready to glue, protect your work surface with a sheet of plastic. Lay out, in order, the strips for the inside and outside stems at the stern and at the bow. Before you proceed any further, put a layer of plastic packaging tape on the outside surface of both inner stems so that you don't accidentally glue the inner and outer stems to each another.

Brush a thin, even coat of epoxy glue on each of the mating surfaces, and press together. (Remember not to glue the inside stem to the outside stem.)

Clamp each pair of laminated stems firmly to its stem mold, this

Clamp on alternate sides of the mold to prevent distortion.

time using a clamp in every hole. The clamps should be as close together as possible to get even pressure over the full length of the stem. A little glue will likely ooze from the sides, but do not tighten the clamp so much that all the glue squeezes out, starving the joint.

Begin clamping at the end of the stem mold where it connects to the first station mold. After you have set the first clamp, place two pieces of scrap wood (or two short pieces of planking) on either side of the stacked laminations and draw these together with another clamp to force the strips into perfect alignment. Then clamp the stems down to the mold at the next hole. Work along the stem, repositioning the aligning jig, then setting the clamp at the next hole.

As you proceed, it is a good idea to set the clamps on alternate sides of the mold. This will give you more working room and ensure that the stems won't be rolled to one side by the tightening action. For the same reason, be careful to position each clamp squarely over top of the stack of strips.

When all the clamps are in place, clean away any excess glue with a putty knife and wipe the stems with a rag dampened with lacquer thinner. This will make it easier to separate the inner and outer stems and save the effort of sanding off excess glue later.

Spread out the rag to dry before discarding. This is an important safety precaution: a solvent-soaked rag can spontaneously combust if wadded in a ball at the bottom of a garbage can.

When the glue is thoroughly set (wait overnight), remove all the clamps and separate the stems. Before removing the stems from the mold, mark where the ends should be trimmed. Using a block plane, round off the end of the inside stem at the keel-line, where it will be visible inside the boat. It looks neater this way, and the epoxy and the varnish will adhere better to the rounded edge.

If you bent the stems with the stem mold fastened in a vise, set aside the stems now and return to page 105 to continue setting up the mold. When the mold is assembled, confirm that the end of each stem fits squarely against the first full-width station mold.

SHAPING THE STEMS

Shaping the stems is one of those steps which might look complicated and even intimidating at first but which, in practice, is quite straightforward. It is a matter of removing from the side of the stem any wood interfering with a fair line that extends from the ⅛-inch leading edge of the stem back to the edge of the station molds. Once the square inside stem has been shaped with a rolling bevel from the sheer-line to the keel-line, the hull planking will lie flat all along that curving edge.

To do this, you'll use a fairing batten, one of the most ancient of

114

After the mold is set up, clamp the inside stem in place.

boatbuilding tools. While pleasant, the job can take longer than you might expect, especially if you are still getting to know your tools and wood-shaping techniques.

Set aside the outside stems, and clamp the inside stems back on the molds. Get your block plane and spokeshave ready: sharp tools will make this job a pleasure.

For a guide as you do the actual shaping, draw a centerline on the leading edge of the stem using either a marking gauge or a combination square set to half the width of the stem.

Now draw two parallel lines, one on either side of the centerline, to show the ⅛-inch width of the leading edge. (Mark the centerline in red and the parallel lines in a contrasting color.) This leading edge will narrow down to the centerline, where the stem begins to flatten out as it turns into the bottom of the boat. Exactly where this occurs will be obvious as the stem is shaped and confirmed with the fairing batten.

To get the correct bevel at any given point along the length of the stem, hold a batten (a 6-to-8-foot cedar strip) parallel to the direction of the finish planking. Bend it around the station molds. Note the material that must be removed in order for the batten to touch the ⅛-inch line and flow back into the body of the canoe.

Remove unwanted material from the stem with the spokeshave and block plane. There is a

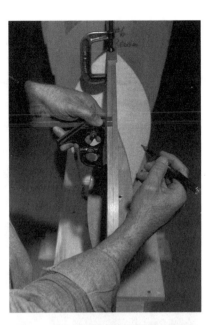

Draw centerline on inside stem, *top*, then parallel lines to create ⅛-inch leading edge, *above*.

115

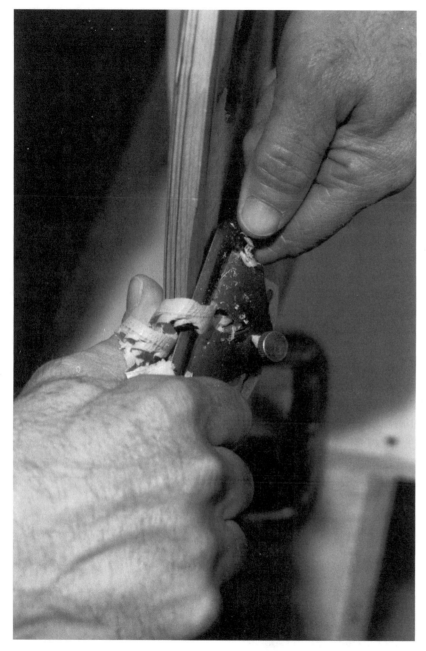

Starting at bottom, bevel stem in small sections.

BUILDER'S TIP: WAXING THE SOLE

A sharp tool is easier to control and safer to use than a dull one that is fighting you. Furthermore, a tool that is doing what you want it to makes jobs like shaping stems a pleasure. (If you want to know more about sharpening, check the references in Sources, page 203.)

For ultimate control of a sharpened tool, wax the bottom so that all the resistance you feel is the blade as it slices cleanly through the wood. Without the confusion of the friction between the sole and the wood, it is easier to concentrate on where the blade is and what it is doing.

Bevel stem so batten lies flat.

tendency for an unwanted crown to develop in the middle of the stem, but if you work the middle first, the sides will take care of themselves.

The hardest part of shaping the stems is hanging on to the stem

while you work it with the spokeshave and block plane. We've found we get the best control by starting at the lower portion of the stem and shaping just enough that the first four or five pairs of planks can be installed. Once these planks are in place, they help secure the stem and make it easier to relate the plank line to the rolling bevel you are creating.

With the first few planks holding the stem stable, prepare the next section of stem before laying on more planks. Keep at least 2 inches of stem prepared ahead of the planks so that the edges of the planks don't get damaged as you shape the next section of stem.

As planking progresses, keep shaping the stem ahead of the planks, checking often with the batten. Be careful to hold the batten parallel to the plank line; don't force it to fit the shape you've just cut. The purpose of the batten is to give you information, not to be forced into the shape you want.

In this manner, work your way

The laminated ¾-by-⅞-inch stem must be shaped in a rolling bevel so that each plank will lie flat against it. The stem's leading edge must be ⅛ inch wide down the center, but its shaped sides will range from a deep vee (at point E) to a shallow cut (point A). A batten indicates the appropriate angles to cut. Since the leading edge will be delicate, protect it with small blocks when clamping it in place.

up the entire length of the stem, from sheer-line to keel, one section at a time, shaping both sides of the stem evenly.

When you have shaped enough stem to get started and are sure it will not have to be removed again, fasten it to the end station mold with a 1¼-inch #6 wood screw and washer. Drive the screw through the station mold into the end of the stem, drilling pilot holes first to prevent the laminations from

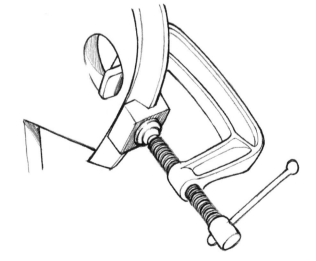

USE BATTEN STRIP TACKED AT ANTICIPATED ANGLE OF PLANKING TO BEVEL STEM

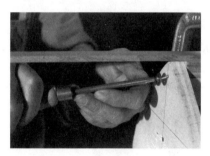

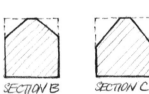

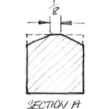

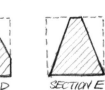

Temporarily secure stem to mold.

splitting and to ensure that the parts draw together properly. Keep in mind that these two screws (one on each inside stem) will have to come out when you remove the hull from the mold.

SECTION A SECTION B SECTION C

SECTION D SECTION E

FUNCTIONAL FORM

The laminated ¾-by-⅞-inch stem must be shaped in a rolling bevel so that each plank will lie flat against it. The stem's leading edge must be ⅛ inch wide down the center, but its shaped sides will range from a deep vee (at point E) to a shallow cut (point A). A batten indicates the appropriate angles to cut. Since the leading edge will be delicate, protect it with small blocks when clamping it in place.

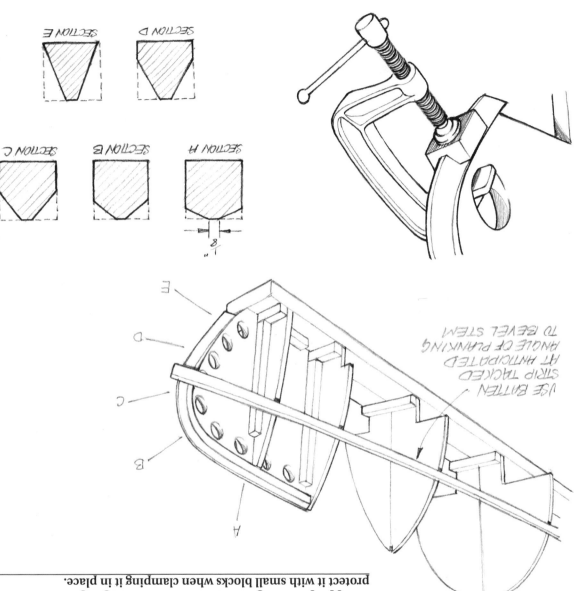

USE BATTEN STRIP TACKED AT ANTICIPATED ANGLE OF PLANKING TO BEVEL STEM

SECTION A
SECTION B
SECTION C
SECTION D
SECTION E

⅛"

up the entire length of the stem, from sheer-line to keel, one section at a time, shaping both sides of the stem evenly.

When you have shaped enough stem to get started and are sure it will not have to be removed again, fasten it to the end station mold with a 1¼-inch #6 wood screw and washer. Drive the screw through the station mold into the end of the stem, drilling pilot holes first to prevent the laminations from

Temporarily secure stem to mold.

splitting and to ensure that the parts draw together properly. Keep in mind that these two screws (one on each inside stem) will have to come out when you remove the hull from the mold.

CHAPTER 8

THE STRIPPER'S ART

Building the Hull

THE CANOE IMPLIES A LONG ANTIQUITY IN WHICH ITS MANU-
FACTURE HAS BEEN GRADUALLY PERFECTED. IT WILL, ERE LONG,
PERHAPS BE RANKED AMONG THE LOST ARTS.

—*Henry David Thoreau*

A Pacific Ocean hurricane may not be in your immediate future, but it is reassuring to know that your canoe will be tough enough to survive that kind of abuse. In 1977, Canadians Dennis Bilodeau and Jerry LaChapelle paddled a 19-foot Wanicott woodstrip/epoxy canoe from San Francisco to Panama in the first leg of a planned circumnavigation of North and South America. Off the coast of El Salvador, they were caught in a hurricane, standard fare for an ocean liner perhaps, but with winds gouging 20-foot troughs in the waves, it proved a real test for their canoe. With 1,000 pounds of gear and its occupants strapped inside, the canoe turned end over end in a manner that Bilodeau

claims would have torn other canoes to pieces. Incredibly, at least for those unfamiliar with the woodstrip/epoxy construction, the canoe (and paddlers) survived unscathed.

The woodstrip/epoxy canoe's strength and beauty come from the way the materials are combined to make a self-supporting monocoque structure, a technique borrowed from aviation, where the outer skins carry all or most of the stress. In the canoe, a sheath of fiberglass/resin covers a wooden core inside and outside, compounding the strength and stiffness of the individual components on much the same principle as an I-beam.

The core is constructed first by edge-gluing ¼-inch wooden strips over a series of station molds that define the shape of the canoe. After sanding, the wooden hull is covered on both sides with transparent fiberglass cloth sealed in a matrix of epoxy resin. Even in the face of advanced composite fiberglass and aluminum canoes, the woodstrip/epoxy technique compares favorably in terms of strength-to-weight ratio and stiffness.

Added to these desirable characteristics is the inherent beauty

of longitudinal strip planking and the accessibility of the method to the amateur builder. As you are about to discover, planking the hull is a straightforward task that is easily accomplished in roughly two weeks of evenings.

PLANKING THE HULL

Tools
utility knife
staple gun
level
¼-inch and 1¼-inch chisel
coping saw or dozuki razor saw
sharp pencil or .05 technical
    pencil
glue syringe
block plane
rabbet plane (optional)
spokeshave
staple puller
string line
straightedge
dividers

Staple the first plank flush to the sheer-line on the center molds.

At the stems, allow the first plank to follow its natural curve.

lumber marker (crayon)
2-inch C-clamps or small
　spring clamps
rags
homemade miter box

Materials
paraffin and/or plastic
　packaging tape
planking
⁹/₁₆-inch staples
1 quart yellow carpenter's glue
two 1¼-inch #6 screws

COLOR AND BEAUTY

If you cut the wood planks yourself, you most likely used more than one board. If so, there are bound to be surprising color variations among the planks. (If you bought the wood strips already machined, they could be even more varied.) One board may have a reddish tone and a coarse grain, while the others are pink and tan with a fine grain. As a result, a builder who does not color-match his planking could end up with a canoe that has large sections of hull which are all one color or another.

To some extent, this is a matter of personal preference, but a builder should be aware of color variation so that the end effect is not accidental. The least you can get away with is choosing a pair of planks that look similar, installing one on either side of the hull. The results will have an informal yet balanced appearance with a minimum of color-match-ing. Unbalanced color won't detract from the function of the canoe, but with a little planning, color variation can work for you and produce a boat that is distinctly yours.

For maximum control, lay the planks out on the floor to get a sense of the color range you have to work with. You can use the varying tones and textures to add dark accent stripes just above the waterline or below the gunwales. Or you can alternate dark and light planks so that the up-turned hull resembles an elongated bull's-eye. Or you can use some of the more interesting planks to create a feature pattern (see page 83). The possibilities are almost endless.

If you decide on a definite pattern, number the planks with a lumber marker.

THE FIRST PLANK

Planking begins at the sheer-line and proceeds evenly up both sides a few planks at a time so that the stems are not forced out of line. It is most convenient to attach the planks with the concave cove side up. This shallow trough will hold the glue and guide the syringe as the glue is being applied.

To locate the first plank (the sheer plank), staple the middle of a full-length plank to the center mold, flush with the sheer-line of the hull. Staple the plank flush with the sheer-line of every sec-

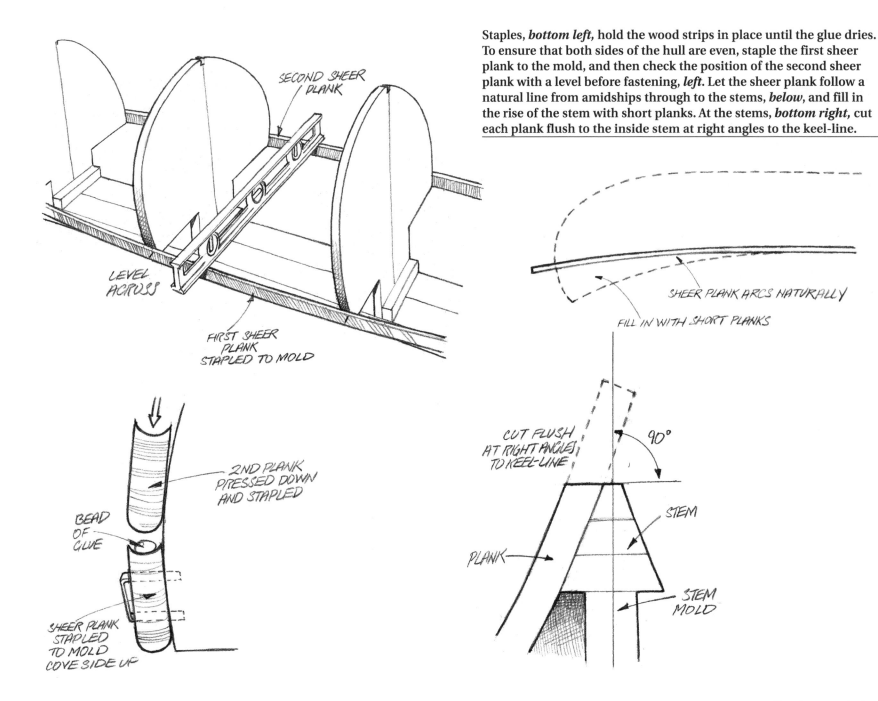

Staples, ***bottom left,*** hold the wood strips in place until the glue dries. To ensure that both sides of the hull are even, staple the first sheer plank to the mold, and then check the position of the second sheer plank with a level before fastening, ***left.*** Let the sheer plank follow a natural line from amidships through to the stems, ***below,*** and fill in the rise of the stem with short planks. At the stems, ***bottom right,*** cut each plank flush to the inside stem at right angles to the keel-line.

SECOND SHEER PLANK

LEVEL ACROSS

FIRST SHEER PLANK STAPLED TO MOLD

SHEER PLANK ARCS NATURALLY

FILL IN WITH SHORT PLANKS

2ND PLANK PRESSED DOWN AND STAPLED

BEAD OF GLUE

SHEER PLANK STAPLED TO MOLD COVE SIDE UP

CUT FLUSH AT RIGHT ANGLES TO KEEL-LINE

90°

STEM

PLANK

STEM MOLD

You may notice that your stapler is burying the crowns of the staples in the surface of the plank, bruising the wood and sometimes even breaking the fibers. While the bruise may swell out again after the surface is wetted down, any broken fibers will remain a dark scar on the hull of your canoe.

To prevent this, you can modify your stapler by building up a pad of tape directly behind where the staples exit, as shown. This will hold the stapler above the wood surface, creating a small space in which to wiggle the stapler without damaging the planking.

ond station mold along the center two-thirds of the mold. (These staples are temporary and will be removed once the hull is glued and ready to be sanded.)

In most cases, the sheer-line at the bow and stern rise too sharply for the sheer plank to follow comfortably, so let the plank follow the sheer-line through amidships, and continue this shallow arc to the stems. At the bow and stern, the space between the sheer plank and the actual sheer-line will be filled in later with shorter planks. This was the solution for the sharply curving sheer on the original cedarstrip boats of the early Peterborough builders, and it still works well. If you force the sheer plank into an exaggerated curve, your canoe will look awkward, whereas if the planks run parallel to the waterline, the eye will move forward, giving your craft a sleek, fast appearance.

There are practical as well as visual considerations in making the first plank follow the sheer-line for the entire length of the canoe. If you don't, as the planks approach the centerline on the bottom of the hull, they will be forced into a highly stressed compound bend. The tension thus produced can pull the planks away from the mold. Most of this tension will be avoided by allowing the sheer plank to run parallel to the waterline.

With the first plank in place, stand first at one stem and then at the other, and examine the curve. The sheer plank should present a continuous, fair curve without any hooks or waves. If a plank appears high or low on a station, pull the staple and allow the plank to find its own curve. It is important for the first plank to be fair, as it is the foundation for all the rest. Any problems with this first one will be repeated on subsequent planks.

When you are satisfied, staple the plank to the remaining molds. At the bow and stern, spread carpenter's glue on the stems before stapling the plank in place. Then carefully cut the plank flush with the stems at right angles to the keel-line.

Now set up the sheer plank on the other side, making sure that it, too, follows a fair curve. With a spirit level, check from one plank to the other to confirm that the planks are level along the entire length of the hull. If it comes down to splitting hairs, go with a fair curve.

When you are happy with the position, staple the plank to the remaining molds, glue and staple the plank at both stems, then trim carefully to length.

PLANKING THE HULL

From this point on, you'll make rapid progress, seeing dramatic changes hour by hour, a welcome payoff for all the preparatory work you've done.

The routine for gluing is simple and, if done as described, will not only get the job done efficiently but will ensure that you don't forget to put glue on the stems.

Fill up a glue syringe, and begin

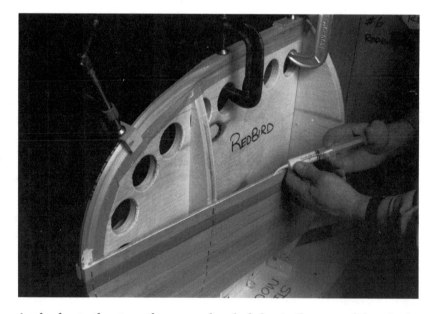

Apply glue to the stem, then run a bead of glue in the cove of the plank.

The syringe (available from epoxy or dental suppliers) holds enough glue for about 18 feet of plank, so you can judge how much glue you are using. If you run out halfway down the plank, you are applying too much. If the syringe is still almost full when you reach the far end, you are applying too little.

Applying the right amount of glue is a knack that you will develop as you become comfortable with the process. In principle, there should be just enough to bond the joint, with only a small amount squeezing out when the next plank is stapled in place. In practice, it is better to use too much and wipe off the extra than to use too little and worry about the planks coming apart when the staples are pulled out.

When filling the glue syringe, use this trick to keep glue from dripping all over your shoes. Place your little finger over the tip of the syringe, and slowly pour in the glue. Stop pouring before the glue reaches the top so that the plunger will fit in without making a mess. Holding the tip of the syringe over the mouth of the glue container, start the plunger, squeezing out enough glue to lodge the plunger. Then pull back on the plunger slightly to create enough suction to prevent the glue from weeping out. Wipe off excess glue as you go with a water-dampened cloth. Glue comes off a lot more easily when it is still wet.

by putting a thin film of glue on one stem, just enough to cover the width of the next plank. Then set the tip of the syringe in the cove of the sheer plank, and run a bead of glue from one end of the canoe to the other. Finally, spread a plank's width of glue on the other

Avoid damage to cove by using scrap planking to seat wood strips.

stem. The same procedure—stem, plank, stem—is repeated as you glue all the planking.

Begin installing each new plank at the "0," or center, station mold, and work out toward the stems. To avoid running out of plank at one end, locate the middle of the wood strip by balancing it on your finger. If you are working alone and the ends of the plank are unwieldy, try spring clamps to support the ends.

Do whatever you must to ensure that the beaded edge of each plank fits snugly in the cove of the previous plank. To help seat the bead, rock the plank slightly in the cove or use the bottom of your stapler to tap on the plank between the stations. Be careful not to damage the fragile edge of the cove as you press the plank into position. If there is a problem with edges breaking, try pressing with a short piece of scrap planking.

Pay special attention to fitting planks in the area where the sides meet the bottom, at the bilge. Making sure the bead fits into the cove here will save a lot of filling later: the joint will look cleaner, and the boat will be stronger. In this tricky spot, try rocking the plank gently back and forth to get it seated properly.

Continue up the hull, fitting each plank firmly into the one below, then stapling it to the mold at every station. On the first three or four rows of planks, squeeze the planks together (rather than bearing down) to avoid pushing the sheer plank out of position. Line up the staples on each mold

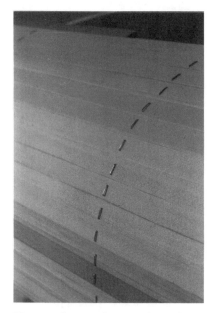

Line up the staples consistently.

so that the holes which are left behind after the staples are pulled out will become a subtle element of the visual design.

After each plank has been stapled in place, it is a good idea to wipe off any excess glue with a water-dampened cloth. Reach inside the hull, and wipe away any drips you find there as well. Avoid soaking the surface, as this may cause a black stain around the staples.

As you proceed with the planking, you'll have to stop periodically to shape the next section of the in-side stems. Always shape ahead of the planking, and keep a couple of inches clear in front of the wood strips. If you get too close, the plank edge could get mashed during the shaping process.

Watch how the planks are landing on the shaped edge of the stem. Trim each end so that it is flush with the leading edge of the inner stem. Use the leading edge of the stem as your guide, making the cut perpendicular to the centerline and just a hair longer than the stem. When you are making these cuts, remember that the object is to end up with a crisp line between the outside stem and the plank ends, with a minimum of preparation.

It is a good idea to trim the planks one at a time rather than wait until several planks are in place. If you leave an individual plank sticking out, it is bound to catch on a shirtsleeve and tear out a chunk of hull. Also, it is easier to make an accurate cut if other planks aren't in the way. The time you might save by trimming in a haphazard manner is not worth the frustration of having to work the end grain of the planks down to a crisp curve later.

JOINING SHORT PIECES

The first few planks should run the full length of the hull, but you may eventually have to use some shorter planks.

Join them on the hull using a simple glued butt joint. Make this

Butt-join short planks between molds; clamp with scrap wood strips.

joint between two station molds so that you avoid a concentration of holes at the station line. Stagger joints to avoid a structural and visual weak point in any one area of the hull.

The next plank will serve to hold the two joined pieces in line as the glue sets, but don't leave the butt ends unsupported while you prepare that next plank, especially if they are not lining up well. Staple a short length of planking across the joint so that it spans several station molds. Alternatively, clamp two short pieces on either side of the joint to keep the planks in line.

If the joint falls in an area where there is a lot of twist in the planks, you may have to use both techniques in order to keep the joint under control.

THE TURN AT THE BILGE

Once you have planked up the sides of the hull, you will come to the somewhat sharper turn at the bilge, where the sides become the bottom of the boat. In these places, the tension on the planks increases, and the usual number of staples may not be sufficient to hold the planks in place.

The stapleless system (see facing page) takes advantage of jigs that can be used to secure

Continued on page 128

It is possible to build an entire canoe without using any staples at all. It takes a bit more time and requires a bit more attention, but it is quite satisfying if you want the most traditional-looking boat possible. What's more, the techniques we have developed for building in this way have proved useful even if staples are being used to plank the hull. The clamping tricks and jigs come in handy for situations (such as the compound curve at the turn of the bilge) where a single staple isn't enough and two staples are too many.

We began developing this system in the early 1980s, at about the time we built a canoe for The Right Honourable Pierre Elliott Trudeau, then Prime Minister of Canada, as his personal wedding gift to His Royal Highness Prince Charles and Lady Diana. Since that time, we have built all our Bear Mountain recreational canoes without stapling the planks to the molds. Experienced builders, in particular, find this an interesting method. We find that most people, after building one canoe, are challenged by the prospect of avoiding the holes altogether in their second hull.

Building this way is a matter of both aesthetics and structure. An unperforated hull is, of course, that much closer to visual perfection. After all, which question would you rather answer: "What are all those little holes for?" or "How on earth did you hold all those pieces together at once?"

In theory, the stapleless system should also produce a stronger hull. Jigs and clamps can secure the planks much more tightly to one another than staples can. This should reduce the chance of improperly fitted bead-and-cove joints and eliminate the possibility of voids between the planks. Controlling the planking in both directions makes for a tighter-fitting, more complete and solid core.

This is not to say, of course, that building with staples will produce an inferior boat. The staple holes do not compromise the integrity of the hull, and as a system for a first-time builder, it is reliable and admirable in its simplicity and effectiveness. But for someone looking for a challenge, stapleless hulls are worth investigating.

Admittedly, building without staples does take a little longer. The jigs we use can handle three new planks at a time. This shouldn't matter, however, to those building in their spare time, since installing three planks on each side of the hull is a good evening's work. At this rate, most hulls can be completed in about 10 sessions.

If you study the photograph above carefully, you can see exactly how the basic clamping jig works. This device does two things: it pushes the plank tight against the last one installed, and it simultaneously holds the planks firmly against the molds. Notice that, while the flat wedge on the outside that holds the plank against the mold is simply a wedge, the one pushing the plank down against the previous one (the edge wedge) was cut from a piece of planking, with the bead edge preserved to fit into the cove of the wood strip it is pushing against.

In the bilge area and when you are finishing up the bottom of the hull, you may need to reduce the number of planks that you set each time you reposition the jigs. Let the time it takes to position and secure the planks be your guide. Do only as many planks as you can comfortably fit and position before the glue begins to set. Whenever you are unsure how long it will take to position everything, try dry-fitting the pieces first without glue.

THE FIRST PLANK

The first plank must be fixed firmly to the molds before you begin. Because this plank will be covered by the gunwale and won't show, you can use 1¼-inch finishing nails to secure it in place. If additional planks will later be used to build up the sheer-line at the bow and stern and

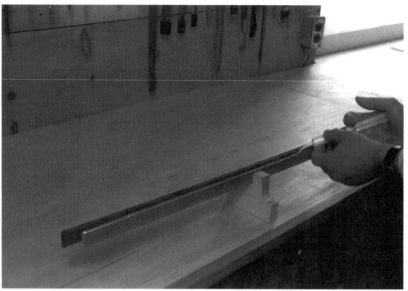

if the starter plank will therefore be visible in those areas, use an L-shaped cleat to secure the plank to the end molds. Glue this first plank to the stems before you continue.

INSTALLING THREE PLANKS AT A TIME

Begin by placing the third plank in the jig and wedging it up out of the way. This piece requires no glue and must go in first, because you won't be able to get it past the other two pieces once they are installed.

Next, apply glue to the cove of the last plank installed on the mold and also to the coves of the other two planks yet to be attached. You'll

need something to hold these planks on edge as you apply the glue, so prepare and fasten to the bench three or four simple fixtures that will hold two planks on edge as the glue is applied, as shown above.

Starting at the center mold, slide the two planks up under the clamping jig at each mold. Fit these planks together, and then bring down the third plank that you have already positioned in the jig.

Snug them all in place with a couple of softwood wedges. Push in the edge wedge to bring all three new planks tight against the last plank and each other. Use the flat wedge to push them against the molds. Note that it doesn't take much pressure to hold the

planks against the mold: there will be more pressure bearing down to hold the planks against each other.

Move on to the next station, working systematically but quickly toward each end, then clamp the planks to the stems, left. When this is done, go back over all the other wedges, checking for fit and tightening where necessary.

CLAMPING THE STEMS

There is a secret to clamping planks to the stem: glue sandpaper to the bottom of each of the beveled clamping pads. The clamps will now hold the plank tight against the face of the stem without sliding off.

CUSTOM JIGS

When fitting planks at the centerline, you will need something smaller and more flexible than the large jig that accommodates three planks at a time. In these cases, as at the stem, you can simply screw a small block to one of the station molds and brace a wedge against that. Notice in the photograph, top right, that the block pivots on the screw to match the angle of the wedge. Once again, the bead edge is preserved on the wedge so that the plank is also held down to the mold.

In situations where there is not enough room for the large C-shaped jig and yet you need extra help to push the plank firmly against the molds, you can build a frame right over the hull, with two vertical members attached to the strongback and a horizontal crosspiece, bottom left.

The horizontal member straddling the hull permits you to clamp another length of board directly above any point on the hull that requires a little pressure. If you need to push down with any force against one side of the hull, you may have to set up another lever on the opposite side of the hull to balance the forces at work and to prevent the frame from wracking.

CUSTOM SOLUTIONS

No two hulls are exactly alike, and no two planking jobs will proceed in the same manner. With or

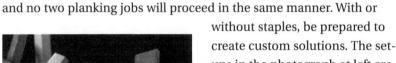

without staples, be prepared to create custom solutions. The set-ups in the photograph at left are good examples of how numerous jigs may be necessary to hold everything in place. Trust your own ingenuity.

At the keel-line (and, if all else fails, anywhere on the hull), use plastic packaging tape. If the tape is stretched as it is applied, its natural elasticity will create significant clamping pressure, holding the planks together as the glue sets. The tape works particularly well when the bottom of the hull is being closed. ❱

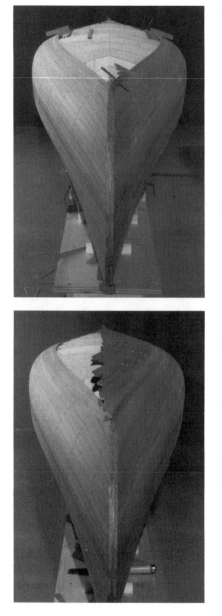

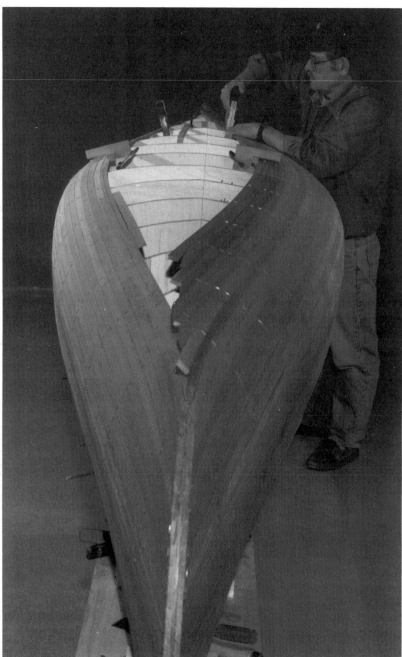

Remove keel batten, *top*; continue planking one side only, *above*, using short pieces, *right*.

Continued from page 124
planking at such tricky junctures. First, try adding an extra staple. The first staple will straddle the join, stitching the plank to the one

Secure plank at bilge with jig.

below, while the second holds the plank tight against the mold. This is usually enough to tie the planks together around the bilge.

If this doesn't give you enough control, use the stapleless jig shown above. At the Bear Mountain Boat Shop, we no longer use staples to plank recreational canoes. Instead, we use the stapleless system, developed in the early 1980s as a way of eliminating staple holes but equally useful as a way of coping with hard turns.

PLANKING THE HULL BOTTOM

Continue planking both sides of the hull up to the top of the stems. When you reach this stage, you will have to remove the last of the C-clamps holding the stems onto the stem molds.

When the planking on both sides of the hull is running almost parallel with the tops of the stems,

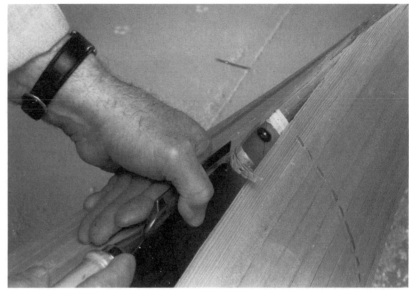

Mark a rough centerline an inch or so past the true center.

remove the keel batten and continue planking one side only. You can use shorter planks now, but be sure that the ends extend past the centerline of the hull.

If you didn't deliberately arrange the planks for your canoe into some sort of pattern, you should at least bookmatch the bottom. Choose the planks in pairs, and number them clearly. Put one set aside for planking the final half of the hull. Use the other set now, continuing to add planks to one side until the keel-line is covered.

THE CENTERLINE

Once the glue has set, prepare to mark and cut the centerline and to fill in the remainder of the bottom planking.

First, pull out any staples along the centerline that might interfere with your straightedge. Then mark a rough centerline that is a safe distance beyond the true center of the bottom of the hull (about ½ to 1 inch). Working from amidships toward each end, use a sharp chisel to trim the planking roughly to this line.

Work carefully. Following the line isn't that important, but it is good practice for what's to come. Hold the chisel firmly with both hands, and push it into the planks. Apply a gentle twisting motion to split off the excess wood.

To find the position of the true centerline, cut back the planking to the centerline where the stem molds meet the first full-width sta-

tion molds. Remove just enough material that you can sight down the centerline marked on the station mold. A consistent cut is more predictable to fit to, so try to keep this cut plumb. Be careful not to cross the centerline.

A utility knife works well for trimming the planks back to the centerline on the stems. Hold it in both hands, begin with light passes, and cut gradually deeper and deeper. Be aware of the grain in the wood and how it attempts to steer the blade.

The position of the centerline is so important and so visible that it is a good idea to mark it in two different ways. One method will serve to confirm the position of the other. First, project the centerline marks on each station mold to the outside of the hull. You can do

Trim planking to rough centerline, *above*, holding chisel firmly with both hands, *top*.

this by measuring from the mold centerlines to the edge of the planking and transferring this distance to the outside of the hull, or you can use the measuring jig shown at right.

To confirm the marks you've just drawn, drive a 1-inch finishing nail into the centerlines of the two stems and stretch a string line taut

Check centerline with string line.

between them. Place a small block under each end of the line to raise it up off the hull, making sure it is centered and not snagged on anything. Sight along the string down the length of the canoe to confirm that it is straight. Ideally, all the marks you made with the measuring jig will line up directly under the string.

It is more likely, however, that a few will be off, some to the right and some to the left. If the string line and the marks are seriously out of whack, track down the source of the problem and fix it. If only minor variations are evident, transfer the position of the string onto the hull by making a mark at each station mold. (The string has

a better chance of being straight, so go by it.) Use a different color for this second set of marks: you don't want to mix them up.

Join the second set of marks using your best straightedge and a fine ballpoint pen. (Do not use a marker: the ink will bleed.) Stand at one end of the hull, and squint along the line. If it looks good, check again from the other end, and if it looks straight from that end too, then trust your eye. You probably have an accurate centerline.

CUTTING THE LINE

You are now ready to cut the true centerline into the bottom of the hull. As you did when cutting the rough centerline, begin work amidships so that you are cutting across the grain, splitting the waste away from the centerline.

Stand on something stable so that you can work comfortably from directly above the cutting line. You need to be behind the chisel and high enough so that you can see exactly where you are cutting.

Plane centerline smooth.

BUILDER'S TIP: MEASURING JIG

This little jig can be made from either boxboard (the material cereal boxes are made from) or thin plywood. It can be any shape

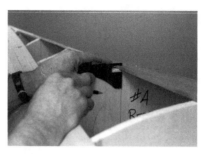

that fits, but it must have one straight side about 4 inches long; ½ inch from the other side, cut a ½-inch-wide slot about 2 inches long, as shown.

To use the jig, position it with the edge of the planking in the slot and the vertical edge of the jig lined up with the station-mold centerline. The end of the jig on the outside of the hull will indicate the position of the centerline.

Use your widest, sharpest chisel. Once the line is established, keep the back of the chisel against the cut surface to guide your progress. Be sure to keep the chisel plumb so that you create a plumb cut.

After roughing out the centerline, clean up the cut with a plane. A rabbet plane is ideal, because it can trim the plank edge right next to the station molds. A block plane will also work, provided you wedge the hull up off the molds. (Note that if you raise the hull in this way, you will have to compensate so that the cut is plumb after the hull is let back down into place.)

Ideally, you will split the centerline with your cut. You don't want to cut away the centerline itself, however, or you will be working

without a guideline. Once you have created as straight a centerline as possible, staple the hull back to the station molds and have a look. It's still not too late to make adjustments. If you see problems, take the time to fix them, because the better the centerline cut, the easier your work will be at the next stage.

FITTING THE REMAINING PLANKS

Fitting the rest of the planks into the remaining half-oval requires patience and some precise marking and cutting. Lay the first plank in position so that the ends extend over the centerline. Mark the cut for one end, and clamp the workpiece into the miter-box clamping jig, shown on facing page.

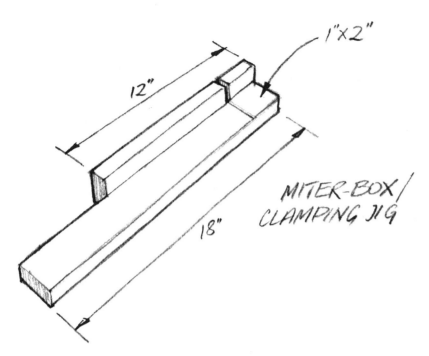

MITER-BOX/
CLAMPING JIG

Prepare last two planks as a unit in advance, clamping temporarily.

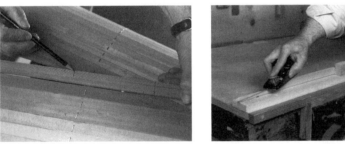

Extend plank past centerline and mark cutting line, *left*. Clamp plank in jig, *top*, chisel to line, then smooth with block plane, *right*.

Chisel down to the cutting line, then smooth the edge with a block plane. Depending on the design of the canoe and where a given plank falls along the centerline, you will also have to bevel it slightly to meet the plank on the opposite side.

Return to the hull, fit this end in place, and make a benchmark about a foot down the plank. Bend the plank into position along the rest of the span, and make another benchmark about a foot from where the uncut end crosses the centerline.

Using this second benchmark as a reference, mark both edges of the uncut end about $5/8$ inch past the centerline (i.e., mark the piece a little longer than would appear to be correct). The reason for this is that the bead slips back into the cove; to fill up the space, the length must be longer than it first appears.

Connect the marks with your straightedge, and using the miter-box clamping jig again, chisel down to the line, then plane the end of the plank smooth. When you fit this plank into place, use benchmarks at the end that you are fitting.

You will discover that the "extra" length disappears, because the beaded edge can now fit down into the cove of the previous piece where it belongs. Expect to make several trial fits, adjusting the plank with your block plane.

Remove the plank, add glue, and staple it in place. Continue planking the bottom until you have only three more planks to install.

PREPARING THE LAST PLANK(S)

It is easiest to install the last two planks as a single unit, made by gluing the two together. The last plank will sometimes be very narrow and fragile. As well, the long, angled cuts required for the last planks are easier to manage across the doubled width of two pieces.

THE STRIPPER'S ART

Prepare this double plank in advance by gluing the two planks together in the anticipated final curve. A simple way to pick up this curved shape is to use the edge of the bottom planks as a mold or to pick up the curve and bend it on the bench. Since the last plank must be installed with a square edge, plane off its beaded edge before bending and gluing the two planks together.

Glue the two planks together, and set them in place against the last plank you installed so that they are forced into the proper curved shape. (Or pick up the shape, and transfer it to the bench.)

This is temporary: don't glue them in or staple them down. To hold them in position while the glue sets, staple short pieces of planking onto the molds

Use dividers to transfer opening to double plank, *top left.* **Shape on plane,** *above,* **then glue,** *top right.*

to hold it in shape. After the glue sets, remove the double plank and set it aside until you are ready for it.

One last bit of preparation remains before installing the third from the last plank. Carefully remove the cove from this plank, producing a straight, square edge

that will butt cleanly against the double plank. Now install it just as you did the others.

FITTING THE LAST PLANK

Some things are not as hard as you think they might be. Picking up the shape of the last plank falls into this category.

Lay the double plank beside the opening, and draw a benchmark for reference somewhere near the middle of the plank. Use dividers to transfer the dimensions of the opening to the planks at intervals of an inch or so. Clamp the plank to your workbench, and use a batten to join the marks.

The long, angled cuts that are required for this final fitting can be difficult, because the wood

bends away from the plane. Try clamping the block plane in the vise and drawing the plank across the blade.

After planing the plank to shape, do the final fitting by working one end at a time, using benchmarks for reference.

Resist the urge to dry-fit this last piece more than you have to. It is hard to get out, and the long, fragile ends can break off. When the fit is good to the benchmark, glue the last plank in. You may have to reach underneath to support the planking as the piece is glued into position.

After the hull bottom is completely planked, the glue has to cure. The length of time required will depend on the glue you have

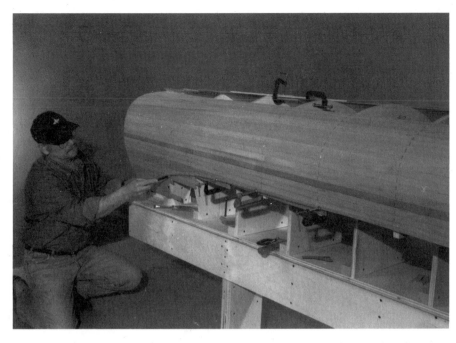

For a fair curve, clamp a batten amidships and bend toward end.

used. If you have not yet added short planks to fill in the bow and stern, this is a good time to do it.

You are now about a third of the way through the whole project—a perfect time to sit back in your moaning chair, congratulate yourself and dream about someday paddling this craft down a mist-shrouded lake.

CUTTING THE SHEER-LINE

The beauty of your canoe lies in its curves and its long, flowing lines, and any job that involves creating those lines is especially gratifying. Cutting the sheer-line is one of those tasks.

To mark the sheer-line, transfer its position from each of the station molds to the outside of the hull. To create a fair curve, clamp a batten amidships and bend it gently toward the ends, lining it up with your marks and clamping it as you go.

Using the batten as a guide, draw the sheer-line, then cut to the line with a sharp chisel. The approach is much the same as the one you used for cutting the centerline at the bottom of the hull, except that this time, you work from the ends toward the middle so that you cut across the grain as you proceed. Cut to the line, but don't worry too much about precision. You will eventually be setting

the gunwales about ⅛ inch below this line and trimming it off flush to achieve a nice, crisp joint.

ATTACHING THE OUTSIDE STEMS

Tools
drill
¼-inch chisel
sanding block
block plane/spokeshave
putty knife
glue brush
pencil
utility knife
straightedge
rasp

Materials
small amount of #403
    Microfibers and/or
    sanding dust
masking tape
wax for screws
1¼-inch #6 steel screws
    (about 6 per stem)
epoxy glue
lacquer thinner
flexible batten
sandpaper (#80)
whittled plugs
paraffin wax

Safety
gloves
ventilation
Review procedures for handling epoxy glue (see page 144).

The outside stems go on at this point so that when the hull is faired, they can be shaped into

the curves of the canoe. You'll find that the outside stem will sit quite neatly in place down near the sheer-line, especially if you have cut all the plank ends with care, but as it curves toward the keel-line, some of the wood planking will have to be chiseled away to make room for it. Even at the sheer-line, you will need to touch up the ends of the planks to create a better fit.

This part of the process involves three steps. First, the ends of the planking are trimmed. Then the end of the outside stem is tapered where it will be mortised into the hull. And finally, a mortise is cut into the planking at the top of the hull so that the tapered end of the stem will fit into its pocket. All three steps are completed at one end, then the procedure is repeated at the other.

Begin by placing the outside stem over top of the inside stem to examine the fit. The outside stem should be slightly wider than the leading edge it covers (the inside stem plus ends of planking).

The majority of the outside stem should sit right against the visible face of the inner stem. As you trim the ends of the planks, keep in mind that you want to create a surface which follows the leading edge of the inner stem and which also remains at a right angle to the centerline of the hull. In other words, it needs to be perfectly flat across the end.

To confirm the angle, lay a short straightedge across the stem. This will serve to exaggerate the angle. Choose a line that is at right angles to the centerline—for instance, the end of the strongback—and visually line up the straightedge. As you continue to trim the edges of the planking

Use straightedge to confirm angle.

down to the stem, you'll be glad that you took such care in trimming the planks to length.

PREPARING THE STEM

When you cut away planking to fit the outside and inside stems together, you don't want to make a hole right through the hull. To avoid this, cut an inch from the end of the stem that will eventu-

ally be faired into the hull bottom.

The outside stem should be tapered before it is installed so that less planking will have to be removed. There will be a point at which the inside stem plus the plank ends is the same width as the outside stem (7/8 inch)—usually where the stem profile begins to flatten at the keel-line. That is the spot where you begin to taper the stem. From that point to the keel end of the stem, taper the width of the outside stem gradually to 3/8 inch (the width of the brass band that will eventually cover the outside stems).

Shape the taper on the outside stem, then lay it in place on the hull, and trace its shape onto the planking. Remove the stem. With a sharp chisel, plane or spokeshave, trim the planks roughly to these lines so that the outside stem will sit closer to the inside stem.

Replace the stem. Have someone hold it in place, or, if you are working alone, tape it down with duct tape. Trace the lines again, this time with great care and precision, using a knife blade to project the shape onto the planking. Now remove the stem again, and go over the lines with a pencil.

To cut the mortise, make several passes with a utility knife, scoring the line deeper with each pass. Work from the middle of the boat toward the ends so that the blade will be led into the waste if the grain catches it. Cut down 1/8 inch or so, then stop, and working

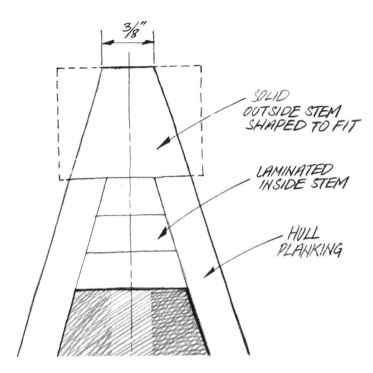

Shape the taper on the outside stem, trace this shape on the planking, then trim planks so that the outside stem sits snug to the inside stem.

in the same direction, use a narrow chisel to clear out the mortise.

Do it again—score with the knife, then clear out the wood with a chisel—until all the extra material is removed. The proper depth will be a flat-bottomed mortise that goes down to, but does not remove, the centerline on the inner stem.

GLUING THE STEMS TOGETHER

When the stem is tapered, the planks trimmed and the mortise cut, the outside stem is dry-fitted

to the inside stem. When the fit is as good as you can make it, the stems will be glued together with epoxy and clamped in place with a series of temporary wood screws.

Drill pilot holes right through the outside stems every 6 to 8 inches. Make the holes slightly larger than the 1¼-inch #6 wood screws you'll be using. (The screws should drop through the outside stem and only screw into the wood of the inside stem.) To be sure that the hole will be centered over the stem, mark and drill from the inside.

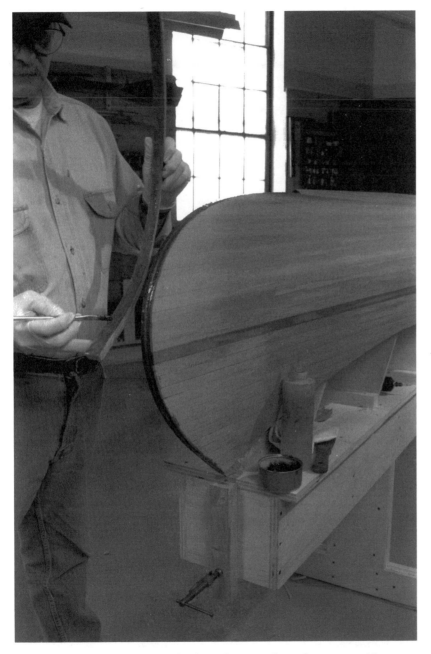

Saturate plank ends with unthickened epoxy, then glue on outside stem.

Later, when you install the screws, drill smaller pilot holes into the inside stems to guide the screws and to prevent the wood from splitting. To make sure these second pilot holes are the right depth—and don't extend through the inside stem—place a piece of masking tape on the drill bit as a guide.

Be careful not to overtighten the screws. It doesn't take much to strip the threads in the wood. The force created by the screw should not be expected to distort the stem enough to make up for a poor fit.

With the pieces snugged up tight to one another, do a close inspection of the fit. Small gaps between the stems are acceptable: they will fill easily with the thick glue that bonds them together.

If you find a sizable gap on both sides of the outside stem, however, it means there is a crown across the ends of the planks and inside stem. Correct this by cutting the ends of the planks back, but do not go past the surface of the stem. If there is a gap on one side and the fit is tight on the other, check the stem and shape it perpendicular to the centerline. In either case, make the necessary adjustments, but do not cut away any of the inside stem.

The outside stem will be glued to both the inside stem and the end grain of the hull planks. To get a good bond with the inside stem and the ends of the planks, the end grain must be saturated with unthickened but catalyzed epoxy. This is important to ensure a good mechanical bond between the stem and the ends of the planking. The thirsty end grain will absorb the glue and will starve the joint if not precoated.

Apply three or four coats of unthickened but catalyzed epoxy, brushing it on over a period of 5 to 10 minutes, until the end grain is saturated and remains shiny.

Now thicken up a shot of epoxy glue with cotton fibers such as #403 Microfibers, and add sanding dust for color. You can anticipate the color of the finished hull (after fiberglassing) by wetting the surface. If you are trying to color-match the glue to the planking, keep in mind that sanding dust will darken when it is mixed with epoxy and won't lighten again when the resin sets. If you are concerned about color-matching, mix up a trial batch first.

Make a mixture the consistency of peanut butter, stiff enough that it holds its shape when you pull the stir stick out of the can. Apply liberal amounts of glue to both surfaces. Use enough that the glue will squeeze out: it is a good indication that all the voids are filled.

Coat the screws well with wax so that the epoxy won't glue them permanently in place, then screw the stem down, being careful not to overtighten. It will take some time for the thick glue to squeeze out, so after all the screws are in, check to be sure that the stem is all the way down. Note: If a screw is removed for any reason, it must be carefully rewaxed before being driven in again.

Remove the excess epoxy with a putty knife, making sure that the crack is at least filled level or slightly above the surface. Any excess you fail to remove now will be difficult to get off later. If the

Remove excess epoxy.

epoxy is sagging out of a gap, use masking tape to mold it in place. Remove the tape after the glue has set.

When the glue has set, remove the screws. They usually come out easily if they've been waxed. Even with careful waxing, however, the glue may have squeezed

up into the pilot holes and seized the screws. If you are having trouble, try tapping the end of the screwdriver with a hammer as you twist.

Once the screws are out, clean any wax from the holes with a ⅛-inch drill bit, then whittle plugs and glue them into the holes.

SHAPING THE OUTSIDE STEM

The Redbird shown in the illustrations does not have a keel, but if your canoe calls for one, you have a choice now as to how you want to attach it. If you want the stem and keel to meet in a long-angled scarf joint, as shown in the illustration on page 82, cut this angle on the stem now. Then, before the hull is fiberglassed, cut a matching bevel on the keel in preparation for installation after the hull has been covered with fiberglass and the first coat of resin (see Installing the Keel, page 164).

Our first choice, however, is to fair the stem into the lines of the hull now, then taper the keel when you attach it. This method is relatively easy, is structurally sound and looks good.

Whether your hull includes a keel or not, the next task is to shape the end of each stem into a smooth curve that follows the stem and flows into the rocker of the bottom. Use a block plane or spokeshave and work slowly. Stand back often and check by looking at the hull in profile.

Angle the stem to take a keel, *left*, or fair it into the lines of the hull, *top*, shaping to a smooth curve, *right*.

Once you have established the shape of the stem in profile, mark the ⅜-inch width of the brass stem band in the center of the stem.

SHAPING THE SIDES OF THE STEMS

Now all that remains to do is to remove any wood that interferes with projecting the

lines of the planking out to the ⅜-inch leading edge of the stems. You still have to be careful, of course. Being overly aggressive on the hardwood stem could damage the adjacent softwood planking. This also rules out using a power sander as a shaping tool, since the planking will sand

Continued on page 140

The dust produced by machining parts and sanding the hull has potential health consequences that no one should ignore. Paying attention to a few simple, inexpensive precautions will ensure that the canoebuilding experience is as safe as it is satisfying.

The most important thing you'll need is a good mask. There is a simple rule for determining when to use an air filter. If what you are doing produces visible dust or a smell, then wear a mask to filter the particles before they reach your lungs. Keep in mind that even the lovely scent of cedar is a natural fungicide and is potentially unhealthy for humans in large doses.

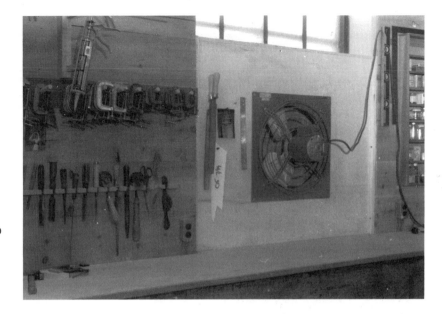

Many people are allergic to wood dust, and some will develop serious respiratory problems as a result of prolonged exposure. If you have a family history of asthma or respiratory allergies (even if you yourself have no symptoms) or if you have a history of lung inflammations or pneumonia, be especially cautious. Wear the best protective equipment you can. The absolute minimum requirement is a good disposable dust mask. An activated-charcoal filter mask is an even better idea for those at risk.

Even though you will be wearing a good filter mask, you should still provide effective cross-ventilation in your work area. Put a fan in the window and open the door, or sand outside in the breeze.

Eliminate the problem at its source by rigging up a good shop vacuum or dust collector, with the hose positioned close to where you are sanding. (Check the motor periodically for overheating, because not all vacuums are made for such continuous duty.)

Not only is wood dust a respiratory hazard; it can also be a skin irritant for some. It is wise, therefore, to wear work gloves, long sleeves and also a hat. (If you have any doubts about this, try wearing a hat for an hour of sanding, then look at how dirty it has become—that could be your hair and scalp.) Cover shelves and other hard-to-clean areas with plastic film to make cleanup easier.

When working around power tools, it is always a good idea to wear eye protection as well as ear protection. This is especially important when you are doing a job like sanding the hull, because it is not just the intensity of the noise but the duration that is hard on your hearing. (For other power-tool safety tips, see page 78.)

Finally, before you begin sanding the hull, find yourself something firm to stand on. You will need to work directly above the hull, so you need to have good balance and enough height for ample visibility. And be sure the light is adequate so that you can see what you're doing. ❯

Before beginning to sand, it is worth saying a few words specifically about some of the tools and materials you'll be using to fair the hull.

SANDPAPER

Buying cheap sandpaper is false economy. You'll use more of it, and the job will take longer.

Aluminum-oxide grit that is resin-bonded to a good-quality backing is suitable for sanding wood and will also sand epoxy. Silicone-carbide open-coat paper is even better for sanding epoxy and also works well for sanding varnish between coats. Under working conditions, silicone carbide will stay sharper longer, and the open coat will not plug up with sanding dust as quickly as cheaper alternatives will.

With production sandpapers, you'll need 80-grit for the first sanding and 120-grit for the finish sanding on the hull. (You'll need 220-grit to finish-sand the hardwood trim.)

We've noticed that with a good resin-bonded disc, the 120-grit sandpaper works well for both stages. If you are worried about the coarse sandpaper eating into the wood too aggressively, consider doing the whole job with a premium 120-grit sandpaper on a random orbital sander. You will go through more sanding discs, and it will be slower-going, but it will get the job done; and if this is your first boat, you may be grateful for the extra control.

Sandpaper is like any other cutting tool: it only works if it's sharp. When the grit is dull, it stops sanding and merely burnishes the wood, compressing the fibers. When you brush epoxy over a burnished surface, it is absorbed unevenly, creating a blotchy surface. So when the sandpaper stops cutting, change it.

A LONG BOARD

Also called a file board (commercially available as Speed File), a long board is a useful alternative to the power sander. It uses 2³/₄-by-14¹/₂-inch strips of sandpaper and, in the hands of anyone with a bit of energy, will produce a beautifully fair hull. The long board rides on the high points and distributes the pressure you apply to a long area of the hull as you slide it back and forth. This makes it next to impossible to create low spots with your sanding. The long boards are suitable for both the rough 80-grit sanding and the finer finish work with 120-grit sandpaper.

RANDOM ORBITAL SANDER

This tool represents a real step forward in canoebuilding technology. It works more efficiently than older-style half-sheet orbitals and quarter-sheet palm sanders. Being round, it fits well within the compound curves of canoe hulls, especially on the inside.

A light-duty 5-inch random orbital sander is a very affordable power tool and suitable for this project. Like the more expensive heavy-duty variable-speed machines, it comes equipped with one of two fastening systems for the sandpaper: a pressure-sensitive adhesive (PSA) or the so-called hook-and-loop (Velcro).

While the latter system is perhaps a little handier, the PSA is extremely flexible and allows you to cut your own sanding disc from a sheet of sandpaper and to attach it with a spray adhesive such as 3M Super 77 or Sprayway Disc Adhesive 66. With either spray, the disc can easily be removed while it is still hot from the friction of sanding.

SANDING PADS

The foam sanding pad on a random orbital sander is there to support the sandpaper and to help it conform to the contour of whatever is being sanded. The hard pad that comes with the sander is ideal for flat surfaces, but a variety of other pads are also available. A soft contour pad is recommended for this project, because it will conform to a sharper curve, making it superior for smoothing both the inside and the outside of the hull.

HAND SANDERS

A sanding block that takes either a quarter- or half-sheet of sandpaper will be handy for many of the upcoming shaping, smoothing and sanding jobs. You can buy one ready-made, or you can make it yourself by wrapping foam or cork on a rigid or flexible backing block. The dense foam that serves as packing for electronic equipment makes an excellent sanding block.

Cloth-backed, resin-bonded sanding belts also come in handy for shaping tight curves by hand and for getting into corners.

BLOCK PLANE AND SPOKESHAVE

Both are indispensable tools in canoebuilding. Not only can they save a lot of sanding, but using them can be one of the most pleasant parts of the process. And every time you peel off a shaving, think of the pile of dust you've avoided.

PAINT SCRAPER

A paint scraper with a sharpened blade can save you hours of sanding too. It will scrape off excess epoxy glue and also shapes wood well, removing a decent amount of material while still being easy to control. Think of it as a low-budget profile sander: it gets into corners, and you can file it to whatever shape you need. A traditional cabinet scraper will do the same job, of course, but a paint scraper has a handle that protects fingers from burning and knuckles from getting scraped.

BUILDER'S TIP: STAYING SHARP

For safety, control and predictable results in shaping the cedar hull, your tools must be razor-sharp. For instance, a dull plane will leave "chatter" marks, and a dull edge may pick up the wood grain.

It is worthwhile to take the time to put a proper edge on all your cutting tools. To do a good job on the wood, you should literally be able to shave the hair on your arm with the blades.

Learn how to sharpen the blade, and keep it sharp. The techniques are too varied and detailed to discuss here: whole books are written on the subject. Consult Sources, page 203, for suggested references.

Once the blade is sharp, rub a little paraffin wax on the sole of the plane to reduce friction. Then the only resistance you will feel will be the edge of the blade slicing through wood.

Filing the blade to a gentle arch will save you hours of sanding inside the hull. If the scraper has a replaceable blade with two edges, keep one straight for flat and outside curves and shape the other for inside curves.

Using the sharpened paint scraper involves a combination of cutting and scraping. The edge is filed like a plane blade, but the angle of attack is controlled by you rather than by the tool. Try different angles until you get a clean cut. If the scraper is "chattering," hold it diagonally to the grain.

You'll find the sharpened paint scraper ideal on hardwood, but it will also do a reasonable job on softwood if the blade is kept sharp. Because the metal in the blade is quite soft, the edge doesn't last long. As soon as you are no longer getting a decent shaving, stop and resharpen. ◗

Continued from page 136
considerably faster than the stem.

Use a block plane or spokeshave. (If you are concerned about damaging the hull, protect it with a layer of masking tape.) Check your progress with the sole of the plane or with the same sort of batten you used to shape the inside stems. Take care not to round off the stems or go past the ³⁄₈-inch line, and concentrate on producing crisp, clean lines.

As you approach the surface of the hull, finish up with a scraper and/or firm sanding block. These will provide more control when working with wood of different densities and wood grains running in different directions.

Finish with a firm sanding block using 80-grit sandpaper and long, even strokes.

Fairing the Hull Exterior

Tools
staple puller
putty knife
block plane
spokeshave
scraper
random orbital sander

sanding block
long board (optional)
vacuum cleaner
contour sanding pad (optional)

Materials
epoxy-based filler or plastic wood
lacquer thinner
sanding dust
sandpaper (#80, #120)

Safety
ventilation
gloves, hat, long sleeves
dust mask
eye and ear protection

At this point, the hull may look somewhat rough, what with the rows of staples and the occasional gap between planks, but it is also distinctly, delightfully canoelike. The next step will fully release that beautiful canoe shape from the flat glued planks.

Fairing the exterior involves five steps: shaping the hull, filling any voids between the planks, an initial sanding, raising the grain and a final sanding. At each step, you can accomplish your goal using a variety of tools and techniques. The choices you make will depend on the degree of finish you are satisfied with.

The choices in the Sanding Schedule box are listed in order from A, the most desirable, down to the least desirable. Following the choices that appear in bold type will produce a hull of excellent quality. You can be more of a

perfectionist than that, but you may not be happy with the results if you choose options below the one underlined.

STEP ONE: INITIAL SHAPING

Sharp tools and good materials will help immeasurably in this stage. Each of the narrow planks you installed is a flat surface which must be rounded into fair curves that roll smoothly from sheer to keel and flow toward the tapered ends of your craft.

Before you begin planing, all those staples have to be pulled. Because it is important not to bruise the wood or break the fibers while prying the staples loose, use a tack puller or an old screwdriver, bent at the end to provide leverage and padded with tape to protect the surface of the hull.

Start planing the hull at the ridge where the planks meet. The idea at this stage is simply to remove the high points, the edges of each strip. If possible, leave the centers of each plank (which are the low points) untouched. This way, no matter

Plane edges of planks, not centers.

Sanding Schedule

Options are listed in order of desireability. Following the choices in bold type will produce an excellent hull.

1. For the initial shaping of the hull, use
   A. plane with a block plane and/or spokeshave.
   B. scrape with a sharpened paint scraper.
   C. sand with 60-grit sandpaper.
2. Eliminate gaps between planks by
   A. filling with color-matched epoxy-based filler.
   B. filling with plastic wood, natural color.
3. For final shaping, use 80-grit sandpaper, and
   A. hand-sand with a file board.
   B. power-sand with a half-sheet orbital sander.
   C. power-sand with a random orbital sander.
   D. sand with dull paper.
4. To prepare for final finishing,
   A. raise the grain by dampening the wood surface with water.
   B. go directly from 80-grit to 120-grit sandpaper.
   C. stop sanding at the 80-grit stage (step 3).
5. For final smoothing, use 120-grit sandpaper, and
   A. hand-sand with a file board.
   B. power-sand with a random orbital sander.
   C. power-sand with half-sheet orbital sander (it can leave swirls).

where you are on the hull, you will be able to judge how much material you have removed and how much thickness remains.

If you are using a block plane or spokeshave for the first time, this is a good place to get a feel for these tools. Watch where the shavings exit from the blade:

Concentrate on one area at a time.

this shows where the cut is being made underneath the sole. Use the shaving as an indicator that the blade is centered on the ridge you are cutting.

Work one area at a time, concentrating on where the blade is and what it is doing. When this becomes a habit, the tool will seem like an extension of your hand and you'll be able to focus on the shape you are creating.

Watch and listen for slivers of wood being ripped out instead of being cleanly cut. Edge grain will be easier to work than will flat grain, which has to be worked in the right direction or the plane will tear out bits of planking. When that happens, reverse the direction of the tool so that it is

cutting cleanly across the grain.

On a strip-planked boat, grain will likely be running in both directions, making it difficult to always plane across the grain. You may find that even the sharpest plane or spokeshave, when worked on the diagonal, will tear out slivers. If this happens, try a firm sanding block with a fresh sheet of sharp sandpaper or experiment with a sharp scraper. Keep the edge of the scraper sharp, and experiment with both the angle of the blade against the work and the angle of the blade in relation to the direction of each stroke. If you are having difficulties with the blade chattering, work with the plane set at a greater diagonal to the grain.

STEP TWO: FILLING THE VOIDS

After the hull is planed, locate and fill any voids. This is not solely a matter of aesthetics. A gap be-

Fill gaps with tinted epoxy.

tween planks may later allow air to become trapped under the fiberglass, thus weakening the hull.

This is a good time for filling,

Sand the hull to a smooth curve, removing as little wood as possible.

because, having been over the hull once, you now have a better idea of what needs to be filled and the excess filler will be cleaned up with the aggressive 80-grit sanding that follows.

Mix catalyzed epoxy with a light fairing compound, such as Microlite from WEST SYSTEM™, and tint it for color using sanding dust, just as you did when gluing the outside stem. To achieve a good working texture, add fairing compound and sanding dust until the filler is the consistency of smooth peanut butter. (You may need to mix up different batches of filler to match the colors of various sections of the hull.)

Using a flexible metal putty knife, work the filler right down

into the bottom of each gap. If the filler is simply smeared over the surface, the gap will open up when the hull is sanded and you'll have to fill it again. Don't bother filling the staple holes. These will fill up nicely when you glass the hull.

Use your own judgment as to what needs to be filled, and don't use any more filler than is necessary. You'll just have to sand it off. Clean up excess material as you go, before it sets.

STEP THREE: FINAL SHAPING

Whether you choose to use a hand-sanding tool or a random orbital sander, the final step in shaping the hull is accomplished with relatively coarse, 80-grit sandpaper. The goal is to take off

Wet the hull to raise the wood grain before the final sanding.

as little wood as necessary and still arrive at a smoothly curving hull.

As in the first step, be sure to leave some of the original surface of each plank to serve as a reference. Once you sand into the flat of a plank, you won't be able to gauge how deeply you are sanding into the wood.

Work your way over the entire hull, completing one section at a time. Work from the keel down to the sheer in an area that is a comfortable, arm's-length size, about a 24-inch width. The staple marks are 12 inches apart, so it is easy to divide up the work surface.

When you've made your way around the entire hull, you should be finished. In other words, it shouldn't be necessary to go back over everything hunting for problem areas and touching up here and there, but check it anyway.

If you are using a power sander —and most of you will—be particularly careful wherever there is a distinct line—for instance, along the keel, around the sheer and especially at the stems. The soft pad on the bottom of the sander will fold around the hard edge and round it right off. It is a good idea to finish these areas with a firm sanding block.

STEP FOUR: RAISING THE GRAIN

Vacuum the entire hull, and prepare for one of the most gratifying moments thus far in the creation of your canoe. Dampen-

ing the surface of the hull shows you for the first time just how arrestingly beautiful your craft is going to be.

As you have planed and faired and sanded the hull, some of the soft fibers of the grain have been compressed below the surface of the wood. If you were to apply the epoxy coating now, those fibers would soak up extra finish and appear as a darker, roughened patch on the hull. Wetting the wood after the first sanding swells compressed fibers and lifts them back up. Then the final sanding will cut the fuzz.

Use a clean sponge or lint-free cloth and warm water to dampen the surface. (But don't wet it so much that there are puddles.) While the wood is still damp, look for spots of wood glue or epoxy filler that you may have missed with the sander and mark these problem areas (or remember them) so that you can deal with them after the surface has dried. If you don't clean away all the extra bits of glue, they will show as a lighter color when the hull is glassed.

STEP FIVE: FINAL SMOOTHING

With the grain raised and any rough spots identified, fine-sand the entire hull with 120-grit sandpaper. The purpose at this stage is to sand away the fuzz of the raised grain and to smooth the hull, removing the scratches left by the 80-grit sandpaper.

Once you get started, you won't have any of the original surface of the planking left with which to gauge your progress. Be system-

Close-up of raised fibers.

atic: keep moving smoothly over the hull, not lingering in any one area. You don't want to create hollows with the sander.

SHEATHING THE OUTSIDE OF THE HULL

Tools
2½- or 3-inch natural-bristle paintbrush
stir sticks
mixing containers
squeegee
scissors
utility knife
grunge cans (old cardboard frozen-juice containers)
rags

Materials
epoxy resin/hardener (about 2 gallons, total)
dispensing pumps
epoxy solvent
fiberglass cloth (4- or 6-ounce)
wet sandpaper for touching

up squeegee (#400)
dry sandpaper (#80)

Safety
mask and/or ventilation
waterless skin cleanser/hand
   cleaner
gloves/disposable sleeves

The secret to a clear coating is to control the film thickness of each layer of epoxy as it is applied. Think of it like making a mirror: the wood is the reflective coating, and the epoxy and cloth are the glass. The glass has to be clean and smooth and of a consistent thickness for the mirror to be perfect.

Consistency can't be achieved after the fact; the epoxy can't be applied haphazardly and then sanded back to an even thickness. Where epoxy is applied thickly, air will be trapped inside, appearing as a white blemish or streak. If this happens in the first coat, there is a good chance that air is trapped in the cloth or below it. You won't be able to remove it without cutting into the fiberglass, thus weakening the monocoque structure.

To get a consistent buildup of epoxy, you'll use a slightly different technique for each of the three coats. Each one accomplishes its own goal and is controlled by specific conditions.

On the outside of the hull, where durability and visibility are the primary considerations, you'll lay up one layer of cloth and three layers of epoxy. The first coat of epoxy bonds the fiberglass to the wood. The second coat fills in the weave and creates a level surface. The third coat buries the fabric, adding enough resin depth that you can sand the epoxy smooth without hitting cloth.

On the inside of the hull, you can omit the third coat of epoxy. The result is a surface that looks good but is less slippery—and about 90 percent of the sanding is eliminated (which amounts to a good day's work). You'll have to be extra careful with the squeegeeing of the first and second coats, however, to produce a surface of consistent texture.

TIMING

The first step in sheathing the hull is to assemble all the materials. The irreversible nature of this operation causes a certain amount of pressure even under ideal conditions. The process can't be put on hold while you run around looking for a likely grunge can.

Have everything tidied up and all nonessential equipment stored away. A clean, organized shop is safer, and there will be fewer distractions. It is best if all three coats of epoxy can be applied in one go, so if at all possible, set aside a block of time when you cannot be called away for anything short of a natural disaster.

Check the pot life and working time for the resin system you are using. Pot life is the length of time the resin remains liquid, which tells

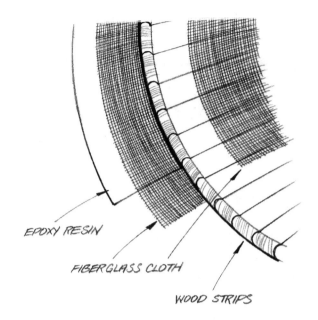

Fiberglass cloth and layers of epoxy resin sandwich the wooden hull.

you how long you have to get it out of the pot and onto the hull. Working time is the period during which you can still move it around and work it with a brush and squeegee.

At room temperature (70 degrees F), the WEST SYSTEM™ 105/207 resin has a pot life of about 15 minutes and a working time of about 40 minutes. Higher temperatures will accelerate the process and thus reduce your working time. Conversely, lower temperatures will retard the reaction and, as a result, increase the amount of time you have.

The pot life of resin can be extended by pouring the well-mixed epoxy into a flat pie plate or paint-roller pan. This helps dissipate the heat produced by the catalytic reaction so that the epoxy cures more slowly.

After the first coat is applied, the hull will be ready for a second coat in three to five hours, depending on the temperature and the resin system you're using. The resin should be firm enough to recoat but still green (uncured) enough that it will chemically bond with the next coat.

After about eight hours, a full chemical bond is no longer possible. The ability to bond chemically Continued on page 148

Cured epoxy is an inert solid and poses little health risk. As you sheathe your canoe, however, you will be handling epoxy in all its hazardous, uncured forms. It is wise not to be complacent about exposing yourself to this potentially health-threatening substance.

Gougeon Brothers Inc., maker of the epoxy system we use, publishes the WEST SYSTEM™ *Epoxy Safety Manual* (catalog number 000-574). You should acquire a copy at the time you purchase your materials and read and understand it before proceeding. If you use some other manufacturer's product, ask for its safety manual.

Epoxy is potentially both a contact and a respiratory hazard. Contact with the resin or the hardener or the uncured mixture can cause inflammation of the skin. Repeated contact can produce a longer-lasting dermatitis or even eczema or permanent sensitization. Once you are sensitized, an allergic reaction can be triggered by even tiny amounts of epoxy and the reactions can become increasingly severe.

Epoxy produces a vapor as it cures, but because epoxy products evaporate slowly, concentrations in the air will likely be low. The dust produced by sanding uncured epoxy is a much greater hazard than the fumes are. It can cause serious respiratory and allergic reactions.

The best way to prevent health problems is to limit exposure from the start. In short, avoid skin contact, protect your eyes, avoid breathing epoxy vapors and sanding dust, avoid inadvertently getting any in your mouth (from unwashed hands), keep your workshop clean, and dispose of spills and leftovers safely.

Provide your workshop with good ventilation to minimize respiratory hazards. Always use a dust mask—and, preferably, an activated-charcoal respirator—when sanding epoxy.

To protect yourself from skin contact when handling epoxy, wear gloves and a long-sleeved shirt or disposable sleeves (available from a body-shop supplier or your epoxy supplier). If you find gloves uncomfortable, sprinkle cornstarch or talcum powder inside to absorb the moisture. Barrier cream provides an added level of protection, especially on the bare skin above your gloves, but it can cause skin problems if used inside gloves.

If you get epoxy resin, hardener or mixed epoxy on your skin, wash it off immediately with a waterless skin cleanser. DO NOT use solvents to remove epoxy from your skin. Always wash thoroughly with soap and warm water after using epoxy, even if none is visible on your skin.

If you spill epoxy on your clothes, change them immediately. Use waterless skin cleanser to remove the spill. If the epoxy was not yet catalyzed and you can't lift the stain, you'll have to throw out the clothes. If the epoxy was already mixed, wait until it has set and cured, which can take up to 14 days.

Be sure to wash immediately any clothes exposed to the dust from sanding uncured epoxy. And wash them separately: you don't want residue contaminating other clothing.

A hat is a good idea. In addition to protecting your scalp, the hat will also protect your work surface when you start applying resins and, later, varnishes. Just as you don't want stuff falling into your hair, you also don't want your hair and perspiration falling onto your work.

Wear eye protection. If you wear plastic prescription glasses, protect them with safety glasses made to fit over standard spectacles. If a blob

of resin falls on a plastic lens, wipe it off with a dry rag. If epoxy gets in your eyes, immediately flush them with water under low pressure for 15 minutes and call a doctor.

While working with epoxy, neatness is a virtue. Avoid touching door handles, light switches, containers, et cetera, when you have epoxy residue on your gloves: you may touch these things later with bare hands. Lay cardboard on the floor around the perimeter of your area to catch drips. (Avoid plastic: it's slippery. And newspapers will stick to the floor.)

Clean up workshop spills with a scraper, collecting as much material as possible, then absorb the rest with paper towels. Use sand, clay or other inert absorbent materials to contain large spills. DO NOT use sawdust or other fine cellulose materials to absorb hardeners. And DO NOT dispose of hardener in trash containing sawdust or other fine cellulose materials: they can spontaneously combust.

Clean resin or mixed-epoxy residue with acetone, lacquer thinner, alcohol or a cleaning solution recommended by the epoxy manufacturer. Follow all the safety warnings on the solvent containers.

Safely dispose of resin, hardener and empty containers. Do not dispose of resin and hardener in a liquid state. Instead, mix waste resin and hardener together in small quantities, and let it cure to a non-hazardous inert solid. Place pots of mixed epoxy in a safe, ventilated area, away from people and combustible materials, and dispose of it only after it has completely cured and cooled.

If you develop irritated skin or any breathing difficulties whatsoever while using epoxy, stop immediately. If the symptoms persist or return, see a doctor. ❯

*Information in this section is adapted from the WEST SYSTEM™ *Epoxy Safety Manual* (catalog number 000-574), published by Gougeon Brothers Inc., Bay City, Michigan, 1996.

THE STRIPPER'S ART

Numerous *two-part epoxy systems* are available, but relatively few produce a strong, clear coating that is compatible with wood. The instructions below apply to WEST SYSTEM™ 105/207 epoxy. Other products will behave in roughly the same manner, but read the instructions for whatever system you buy and follow them closely.

If you plan to purchase an epoxy system not listed in Sources, page 201, find someone who has used the product and ask about the company's technical support and about the working time, cure time, smell, color/clarity, sandability and durability of the product. Whatever you buy, you'll need about 2 to 2½ gallons.

You can use either 4-ounce or 6-ounce *fiberglass cloth* to sheathe your canoe. The 4-ounce cloth is generally used for small, lightweight boats; if you use this, you can expect to exercise more care when paddling. One layer of 6-ounce cloth is standard. The hull will weigh a few more pounds, but the heavier cloth will provide greater strength and durability.

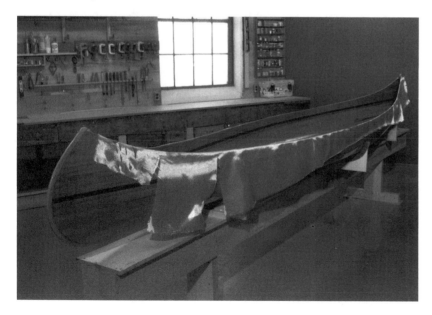

You'll need two pieces of fiberglass cloth (one to cover the inside and one for the outside). The inside piece should be the length of the hull, and the outside piece should be the hull length plus 12 inches. Fiberglass cloth comes in a maximum 60-inch width, which covers most hulls. If the 60-inch produces a lot of waste with your design, the cloth is also available in narrower widths. Measure around the hull at the center station, and choose cloth of an appropriate width.

When you buy fiberglass cloth, insist that it be rolled, not folded. A crease is virtually impossible to get rid of. You won't be able to make the glass lie down, and you could end up having to sand off the creased area and patch it. If the cloth can't be rolled, don't buy it.

Fiberglass cloth is finished with a coupling agent that ensures the cloth and resin will adhere well to one another. Different resins require different finishes. To be sure that yours is compatible with the epoxy you plan to use, buy the cloth where you buy the epoxy. Ask specifically about compatibility.

Most resin systems include a set of *mini-pumps* that dispense hardener and resin in the correct proportions for proper curing. The WEST SYSTEM™ pumps come with a volume/ratio tester that you should use to confirm the accuracy of the equipment. That way, if you encounter problems with curing, you will know that at least the ratios were correct.

Use natural-bristle *brushes*, 2½ to 3 inches wide. The bristles should be short and relatively thin so that you don't waste the epoxy that soaks into the brush. In most cases, the thicker and longer the bristles, the more expensive the brush, so let cost be your guide. Look for a cheap brush, but avoid the bottom-of-the-line "Chip" brushes with blond bristles. They shed too much. Dark-bristle brushes are a good idea, anyway: if they shed, you'll be able to find the bristle against the light-colored wood.

If, during a long lay-up, you feel the epoxy in the brush beginning to set, scrape out the excess resin and rinse the brush in solvent. Be sure to shake the brush completely dry before using it again. Between coats of resin, store the brush in a covered container of clean solvent.

Foam rollers may seem like a good substitute for brushes, but in fact, their effectiveness is limited to the final coats. Rollers don't work well at all for the first coat of epoxy, when you are trying to supply enough resin to penetrate the dry cloth and saturate the surface of the wood. For the second coat, the surface is rough, and a roller will cause the resin to foam, trapping air in the weave. For the third coat, some people appreciate the extra control over film thickness that you get with a roller. However, if you apply the third coat with a roller, you should plan to add a fourth coat as well.

Good *squeegees* are almost always available where you purchase epoxy and cloth. (The very best are produced for silk-screening.) These unimpressive-looking pieces of flexible plastic are essential to achieving a good finish on your hull and should be treated with great care. If the edge is nicked, repair it with 400-grit wet sandpaper.

Grunge cans are essential for this part of the process. Grunge is the excess resin picked up by each pass of the squeegee, and you need a way to get rid of it quickly and systematically. Frozen-juice cans work well. Cut a ¾-inch-long slit down from the top edge of the container. Each time you draw your squeegee through this slit, it will come away clean on both sides and the waste resin will collect in the can.

Note that as resin accumulates in your grunge can, it will begin to cure and give off heat. The more resin there is, the more heat it will produce. That heat will, in turn, speed up the reaction of the rest of the resin. The curing process thus accelerates, with the result that the grunge can become hot enough to burn you. What's more, the vapors are toxic. So as soon as you feel warmth through the sides of the grunge can, pour the waste resin into a disposal container that has a couple of inches of water in the bottom. The water will dissipate the heat.

Pay close attention to the *temperature* requirements of the product

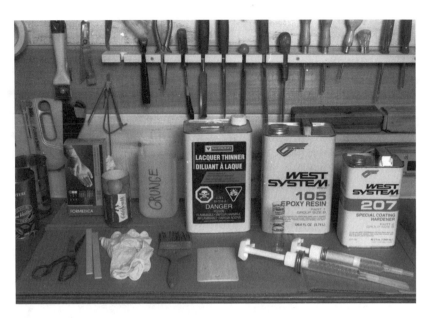

you use. The room as well as the hull and the epoxy itself must all be within the prescribed working temperature. In other words, you can't expect to arrive at a cold shop in the morning and start work as soon as the heater warms the air to room temperature. The epoxy and the hull surface will be much slower to warm to the same level.

When working at high temperatures, outgassing can be a problem. As the temperature of the hull rises, air within the wood expands, creating bubbles under the epoxy. Avoid working in direct sunlight. If it is possible, it is a good idea to begin reducing the temperature of the work space once resin is applied.

Epoxy manufacturers have come a long way in producing materials to accommodate fluctuating humidity and/or temperature. WEST SYSTEM™ 105/207 Special Coating Hardener takes care of many of the problems associated with high humidity or a cool environment. And WEST SYSTEM™ 105/209 Tropical Coating Hardener is available for extremely hot environments. Other epoxy systems have also addressed these problems, which can cause troubles with penetration and workability, with curing times and with moisture being absorbed into the resin and turning it milky. ◗

Continued from page 143
continues to reduce steadily over the next 14 days, the length of time it can take for the epoxy to fully cure. If the resin cures between coats, sand it by hand with 80- or 120-grit open-coat sandpaper to scratch it up so that there will be a strong mechanical bond with the next coat (instead of the chemical bond that is achieved with green resin).

The same timing will apply between the second and third coats.

MIXING THE EPOXY

Because of the short pot life, epoxy should be mixed in small batches. You need to maintain a wet edge at all times: you can't let the epoxy in one area set before you start on the adjacent area. It is practical, therefore, to get someone to help you with this stage of the process. As you apply one batch, the mixer can be preparing the next.

Mixing epoxy is a relatively simple job, but there is no room for error. If there is too much or too little hardener, the epoxy won't set, and that is a situation you want to avoid at all costs.

If used properly, the dispensing pumps eject resin and hardener in the proper ratios. To be sure, get in the habit of squirting the two liquids in equal shots: one resin, one hardener, two resin, two hardener, and so on. If you always start with the resin and stop after the hardener, there won't be any confusion.

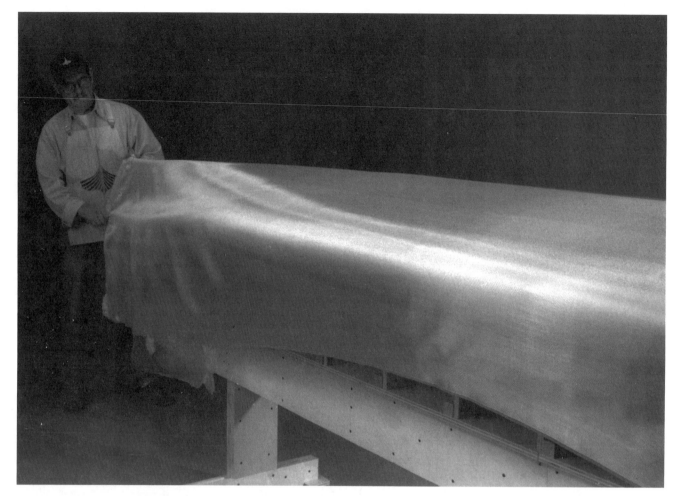

Drape fiberglass cloth over canoe, tugging ends to remove wrinkles.

We suggest the following batch sizes. For the first coat, brushed onto dry fabric, use four shots, or ½ cup, per batch. For the second coat, which fills in the weave, use two shots per batch. And for the third coat, which can be applied with either a brush or a roller, use three to four shots per batch.

Mix the resin and hardener in clean containers made of metal, plastic or wax-free paper. (Glass might break if you drop it, and foam may be dissolved by the solvent.) Stir the epoxy steadily for a full minute, scraping the sides of the container and reversing direction often.

If, as you are applying the epoxy, the container begins to heat up in your hand, discard the remaining epoxy. This is a signal that the epoxy has begun to thicken. It is important that the resin always be at a consistent viscosity; thicker resin will not soak into the surface of the wood or the glass fibers as freely as thinner, fresh resin will. This will show up as a lighter shade on the planking, and the glass fibers may be visible.

THE FIBERGLASS SHEATH

You have now reached a critical stage of construction. Most people who build their own canoes feel apprehensive before lay-up, because it allows no breaks. Once you start, there is no turning back, no starting over or slowing down. One of the most tense stages, it is also one of the most exhilarating, as you watch the colors of the wood brighten and sparkle under the wet resin.

To prepare the hull, wipe it down with epoxy solvent to provide a clean, dust-free base. Do not use paint thinner, because it leaves an oily residue.

Drape the fiberglass over the canoe with the help of a friend. Together, stretch it over the hull, and lower it into position. Since it is 60 inches wide and a foot longer than the canoe, the cloth should hang evenly below the sheer-line on both sides and extend a few inches past each stem.

Fiberglass cloth is fairly heavy, but it does have some give. Tug gently at the ends, and the wrinkles will disappear. Do not smooth it with your hands—you risk creating creases that way.

THE FIRST COAT

With the cloth draped over the hull, prepare to lay on the first coat of epoxy. This operation re-

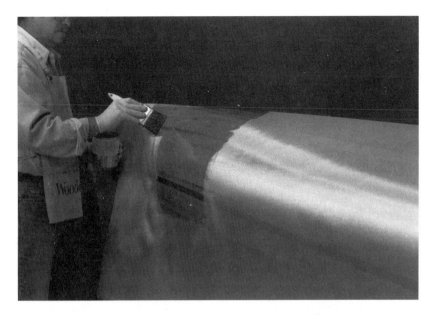

With a well-loaded brush, spread epoxy from wet to dry areas.

quires care, and it can feel intimidating, because it cannot easily be reversed. On the other hand, if you work methodically, you should have no trouble.

For the first coat, use the brush to transfer the epoxy resin from the can and spread it on the dry cloth. Do not use the bristles to try to force the resin into the weave. This will introduce air bubbles into the resin, and these may not come out when you squeegee. Instead, let the fabric absorb the resin at its own pace.

Keep your brush well loaded with resin. Work quickly and aggressively to spread the epoxy from wet to dry areas, but also keep your eye on the cloth you've already wetted. Add fresh resin to

areas that begin to look starved as the cloth and wood absorb it, but don't try to move a patch of resin of questionable age over to it.

Don't worry too much about making it look nice and neat at

Clean up runs and bubbles later.

this point. Runs and small bubbles will be cleaned up later with the squeegee.

Keep in mind that the surface of each plank will absorb the epoxy at a different rate—the dark heartwood will suck up more than the lighter-colored sapwood. Apply enough resin to ensure that there is more than enough for every plank. The cloth will wick the resin into the voids and also into the staple holes.

The main idea in wetting out the cloth is to work aggressively, keeping the resin as fresh as possible at the working edge so that the color will be consistent.

Mix up the first batch of epoxy, using four shots each of resin and hardener.

If you are wetting out the cloth by yourself, start 2 to 3 feet aft of the bow or the stern and apply the resin in that quarter first, working from keel to sheer and out toward the stem. Starting this way will serve to anchor the cloth so that you can then carry on toward the other end.

Wet the cloth right out to the stem, and let it project past the end of the hull. Move to the other side of the hull, and complete the stem section there as well.

Trim the wetted-out cloth back to within approximately an inch of the stems. (You will cut it cleanly later, after the epoxy firms up.) Don't trim the excess cloth hanging down the sides of the hull: it will soak up extra resin that would otherwise drip onto the floor.

After the stem section is wetted

out and trimmed, return to the first side and cover the next arm's length (about 3 feet) of hull, keel to sheer. From this point on, alternate sides every 3 feet or so, working both sides of the hull at once along the length of the canoe to the other stem. If you proceed in this manner, you will always be working a wet edge along the sides of the canoe and there will always be a wet edge along the keel-line of the hull as well.

This may seem like a lot of back and forth, one side to the other, but imagine what would happen if you wetted out one entire side first, then did the other half. By the time you started work on the second side, the epoxy along the keel-line would have started to set, creating an unsightly blemish and potential weakness right down the center of the hull.

In practice, you won't be applying resin nonstop to the entire hull. After 20 to 30 minutes, the first batch of epoxy you laid on will be ready to squeegee. Wherever you are in the process of brushing on epoxy (probably about halfway), you'll have to stop and go back to the first section of epoxy and remove the excess resin with the squeegee. From then on, you'll alternate between brushing fresh epoxy on the next dry area and going back to squeegee the area applied 20 minutes before.

It is important to give the epoxy in each area the same amount of time to soak in. To keep track

of this, canoebuilder and teacher Ron Frenette came up with an excellent system he calls "Time Tapes." As you finish applying resin to a section, stick a piece of masking tape on the strongback at the point where you stopped. Jot on the tape the time you finished plus 20 minutes, which is when you should return to that section to squeegee. If you have a mixer to help you, that person can look after the time tapes, reminding you when to put down the brush and pick up the squeegee.

After the resin is applied, the cloth in some areas will be floating in epoxy. The purpose of squeegeeing is to remove excess resin, leaving the cloth evenly saturated and lying flat on the surface of the hull.

Keep the squeegee angle low.

Squeegeeing may rightly be considered the trickiest technique in the canoebuilding process. It certainly governs what your boat will look like in the end. You have to do it correctly from the beginning—a warning that is not intended to intimidate but rather to make sure that you give it all the care and attention you can.

Most plastic squeegees have a slight curve along the edge. Hold the squeegee so that the corners turn up. (If you turn it over, the corners will dig in, scraping away too much resin.) Grip it in such a way that your thumb supports the bottom and your fingers spread out on top to control the pressure along the edge.

Pay close attention to the angle you hold the squeegee against the hull. Keep the angle low, with your thumb almost touching the hull. The steeper the angle, the more direct pressure there will be on the cloth, with the risk that you'll scrape too much resin out of the fibers. Be particularly conscious of the squeegee angle as you go around the turn of the bilge.

Pressure is as important as angle. Too little pressure, and you won't remove enough resin, leaving the cloth floating and the surface shiny. Too much pressure, and you'll squeegee too much resin out of the cloth, leaving the fiberglass coated and sealed but the fibers not completely filled. As a result, even after the second coat, the fibers may remain vis-

ible, especially in bright sunlight.

The best method is to squeegee a section down in stages, rather than trying to remove all the excess resin in one pass. Begin at the keel-line, and draw the squeegee down to the sheer with overlapping strokes. Work slowly enough

Clean squeegee in the grunge can.

that the resin can roll up in front of the squeegee. At the end of each pass, scrape the squeegee clean in the grunge can. Make repeated, overlapping passes of the squeegee on each section, picking up only as much resin as you can hold on the squeegee. At first, the overlaps will be considerable, but by the time a section is almost finished, you'll be making the pass with the full width of the squeegee.

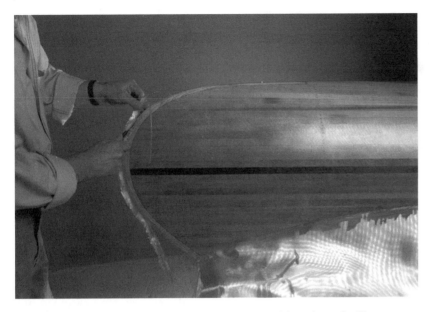

When epoxy is firm, trim fiberglass at stems with a sharp knife.

Squeegee on the second coat to fill the weave of the cloth, upper right.

Work gently over the section until all the vertical, shiny tracks are removed. You won't be able to get all of them, but try for as even a texture as possible without becoming obsessive and wasting a lot of time. (The rest of the hull will be waiting!) Squeegee technique will be even more important on the inside, where the texture

Strive for an even texture.

remains visible, so consider this stage a warm-up.

As you work out the last tracks, keep in mind that while you do want to see the texture of the cloth, you do not want to see the shimmery glisten of the fiberglass itself. If that happens, apply fresh resin to the section. (Don't use what is going into your grunge can.)

After about three hours' time, when the epoxy at the stems has firmed up enough, cut the fiberglass at the stems cleanly with a sharp knife. (If you try to cut it too soon, the cloth will move around and create problems with the setting resin. If you leave it longer than three hours, it merely becomes harder to cut.) Before you apply the second coat of epoxy,

tidy up the cut edge of the cloth with 120-grit sandpaper.

Note: If your design includes a keel, ideally it should be installed after the first coat of epoxy sets. (See page 164 for instructions.) After the keel is installed, continue with the second coat.

THE SECOND COAT

The purpose of the second coat of epoxy is to fill in the weave of the cloth and achieve a level surface. Don't try to build up the thickness of resin with this application. The surface is still so coarse that you can't brush on the resin without it foaming up, potentially trapping air at the bottom of the weave. Rather, you'll be floating it on, then using the

squeegee to force it to fill the weave as you remove the excess.

In general, the less time between coats, the better. For a true chemical bond, apply the second and third coats before the previous one has cured.

You'll be able to tell when to begin with the second coat if you keep your eye on the cloth at the stems. When you can cut it without resin sticking to the knife (about four hours), you can carry on with the next application of resin. We find, however, that the surface is somewhat easier to work if you wait until the hull can be lightly hand-sanded with 120-grit sandpaper. Depending on the resin system and the temperature of the workshop, the resin could be firm enough to sand in four to six hours.

Lightly hand-sand the surface to take off the tooth and make the surface easier to work on. (You'll also need slightly less resin to fill in the weave.) If it has been more than eight hours since you applied the first coat, you definitely need to sand the surface, since, with the epoxy curing that long, the bond between the coats will be mechanical rather than chemical.

For the second coat, use the brush to transfer the resin from the container to the hull. Because the brush will transfer more resin than you need to fill in the weave, brush resin only along the bottom third of the section, then use the squeegee to draw the resin up to the centerline.

Roughly spread each batch, concentrating on filling in the weave more than on making it look good. Then, after roughly spreading each batch, go over the section systematically, scraping off the excess and disposing of it in the grunge can. Using a steeper angle and slightly more pressure on the squeegee, work the resin aggressively enough that any air trapped in the weave is forced out.

Be sure you don't miss any spots. Listen to the squeegee: as it passes over a dry patch, you'll hear a harsher sound. Dry patches will also look dull. It can be hard to see bare spots, so check from all angles. Also be sure that the ends of the stems are coated evenly.

Paint on a thick, uniform third coat to bury the weave.

If you have trouble eradicating vertical lines, try finishing up by dry-brushing fore and aft (that is, horizontally instead of vertically).

THE THIRD COAT

The purpose of the third coat is to bury the weave of the cloth with enough epoxy resin that you can sand the surface smooth without cutting into the fibers. After the epoxy is applied, there will be no tangible texture, though you may still see a slight profile of the weave.

The third coat can be applied as soon as the surface is firm enough to work on. The less time between coats, the better: applying the third coat before the second one

has cured will result in a true chemical bond.

Because the hull now has a level surface, it is possible to brush (or roll) on the resin more aggressively with less risk of foaming. (If you do see bubbles forming, lighten up.) The goal is to apply a thick, uniform coat, and the way to gauge the amount of resin on the hull is by feel as much as by appearance.

Resin is applied at this stage with the familiar painting motion. The idea is to apply as much resin as you can get on in an even film thickness without having it run down the sides. Experience will help you find the balance between just right and too much.

Too much resin gives the brush

a mushy, skidding feel. Too little, and the brush has noticeably more resistance. Controlling by feel rather than sight may be more reliable, especially if the light isn't good. In practice, you'll probably find yourself using a combination of eye and touch.

Always brush from wet to dry to avoid overlapping thicknesses of resin. Use long strokes (an arm's length) to apply the resin horizontally, working in a vigorous but controlled back-and-forth motion. Then even out the consistency by brushing up and down and diagonally before finishing up with long, flowing horizontal strokes again. Hold the brush at a low angle, and draw the resin across the surface. We like to tell students to handle the brush as if it were an airplane gently touching down on a runway and then gently lifting off again.

There is a limit to how long you can play with the resin before it begins to set. You will know the time is up when the resin starts to pile up in front of your brush. When that happens, leave it alone. Anything you do from that point on can only make it worse.

The leveling agents in epoxy help the brush strokes to level; at the same time, however, they can also cause runs. Don't be overly concerned if there are only a few of them. They can be removed with a sharp cabinet scraper once the resin has cured.

Note: If there is a long delay after the third coat is applied and

BUILDING A CANOE CRADLE

You'll need to support the hull in an upright position so that you can sand, sheathe and epoxy the inside of the hull. There are a variety of ways of accomplishing this, so long as no hard edges dig into the hull and it is steady enough to withstand the considerable jostling that will occur during sanding.

For home canoebuilders producing only one boat, a fixed-height "horse" fitted with a carpet sling for the canoe is a good solution. Horses are easily and quickly built and can be used for display or storage. The ones we put together almost 20 years ago are still in use.

The basic horse can be built as shown in the illustration, though other configurations are equally acceptable. Adjust the height to suit yourself. The canoe sits upright in the sling for fairing, sheathing and sanding the interior. To work on the canoe in the inverted position, attach a 1-by-4-inch board across the top of the horse.

Take care when you are working vigorously on the inside of the hull that the horse does not get turned at such an angle that the wooden supports damage the epoxy, which could still be soft.

An excellent alternative is a fitted cradle mold, which is attached to the strongback. The advantage of the cradle mold shown on page 154 is that it keeps the hull from sliding around during sanding; it also supports the hull in the desired position for glassing.

Remove the hull and set it aside, then remove all the individual stations. Use the center station and a station from about a quarter of the way in from each end as the patterns for form-fitting cradles.

Trace the outline of these molds onto three pieces of plywood or particleboard on which you've drawn a centerline reference mark. Add another ⅜ inch to the station line to account for the plank thickness and padding (old carpet, foam pipe insulation or several thicknesses of cloth—anything that will cushion the epoxied hull without being slippery).

Cut out the forms, pad them, then attach them to the strongback in the same position as their corresponding station molds. Then set your hull into its cradle. ❯

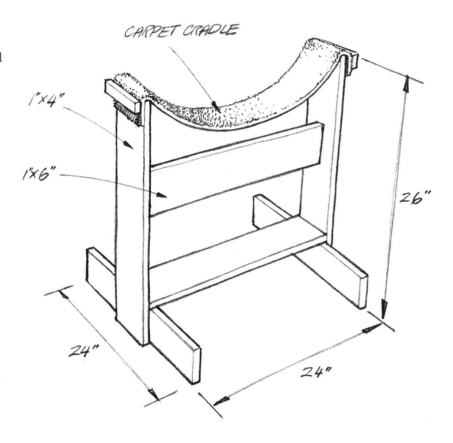

CARPET CRADLE

1"×4"

1"×6"

26"

24"

24"

MATERIALS LIST FOR ONE "CANOE HORSE"

12 to 14 linear feet 1-by-4-inch clear softwood
   (or ¾-inch plywood, milled to size)
Eighteen 1¼-inch #8 flathead screws
Four 2-inch #8 flathead screws
4-by-36-inch strip carpet or folded canvas
stabilizing blocks

A fitted cradle mold supports hull while inside is sanded and sheathed.

the epoxy has fully cured, sand the outside of the hull before lifting it off the molds (see Sanding the Epoxy, page 158). Held firmly on the strongback, the hull will rumble less as the outside is sanded. Remove the hull from the mold, then sheathe and sand the inside.

REMOVING THE HULL FROM THE MOLD

Raising your boat to its rightful upright position is one of the highlights of the canoebuilding process. That first glimpse will repay all your hard work and keep you going until the finished canoe slides into the water.

When the hull has cured sufficiently—at least overnight or longer, depending on the resin

system and the temperature of the work space—enlist a friend to help lift it off the strongback. Trim the fiberglass at the sheer-line, then remove the screws that you used to fix the bow and stern molds to the stems (see page 117).

If your canoe has a recurve stem profile, you will also have to unscrew the last full-width station mold and the stem mold from their blocks so that the assembly can be lifted up and slid toward the middle of the strongback as the hull is being lifted off.

The hull should lift off easily if the molds were taped or well waxed. Tap the side of the station molds to break them loose, if necessary. With one person at each stem, lift firmly and evenly. If the

hull still sticks, try to determine where and tap again at the adhering mold. This usually happens at the bow and stern sections.

If the hull still will not come off, unscrew the offending molds from their station blocks and lift the hull off with the molds still inside. You should have no trouble dislodging them once the canoe is upright.

Lay the canoe on the floor

Cradle attaches to strongback.

(cushioned on a piece of cardboard or a couple of sticks) while you position a cradle (see page 153), then move the canoe into its supported, upright position.

FAIRING THE INSIDE OF THE HULL

Tools
paint scraper
spokeshave
sanding block
5- or 6-inch random orbital sander
putty knife
vacuum cleaner

Materials
epoxy filler
sandpaper (#80, #120)

Safety
dust mask
safety goggles
ventilation

Shaping and smoothing the inside of the hull won't be as formidable as you might think. If you were diligent in wiping off the glue as you planked, this stage won't be onerous. It may be a little uncomfortable and frustrating to scrape and sand the awkward inside curves, but with the tricks we'll show you, the work will go quickly and the results will be well worth the effort.

If your canoe has a keel and if it was fastened with temporary steel screws (see page 164), remove them now. Fill these holes (and any other flaws) with filler made from epoxy glue and sanding dust. Be as neat as possible, and remember that the filler will not sand as easily as the wood.

The inside of the hull looks much like the outside once did: a series of narrow, flat strips waiting to be shaped into smooth curves. To do this, follow the same steps that were outlined for the hull exterior (see Sanding Schedule, page 140) but substitute a scraper for the block plane.

First, rough-shape the planks. When this is done, fill the voids, sand with 80-grit sandpaper, wet the wood to raise the grain, and sand the finish to final smoothness with 120-grit sandpaper. And the same caution applies: until the final sanding, be sure to leave untouched some of the original surface of each plank to serve as a gauge for how deeply you are sanding into the wood.

For the first step, you used a block plane on the outside of the hull, but on the inside, this tool will not prove very useful. Because of the concave surface of the hull interior, the corners of the plane sole will ride on the surface and the blade won't touch wood. You'll be able to work some of the flatter areas on the diagonal with a spokeshave, but for most of the roughing out of the inside of the hull, a shaped and sharpened paint scraper is the perfect tool.

Round the entire scraper blade with a file or a grinder so that the corners are swept back in a curve that will fit most of the shape inside the hull. In a tighter curve, you'll find it will work best to hold the blade on the diagonal to reduce the width and to keep the corners from digging into the planks.

Put a keen edge on the scraper blade, and be sure, as you pro-

Sharpen scraper blade with file.

ceed, to keep it sharp. Most paint-scraper blades are made of a mild steel that is soft enough to sharpen with a file. This means that it will also dull quickly. When the shavings no longer curl easily and it starts to make dust, touch up the edge.

Shape inside with paint scraper.

Try to do most of the first step with the scraper. Resist the temptation to get out your sander before the rough shaping is finished. Long experience has taught us that the paint-scraper technique produces the fastest results with the most control.

On the inside of the hull, the second step will be minimal and may perhaps be eliminated altogether. Check for any voids,

and fill them where necessary.

After the inside is shaped and any gaps filled, begin the third step: shaping the surface with a random orbital sander and 80-grit sandpaper. Because the scraper bruises the surface more than a plane, it is a good idea to dampen the surface with water to raise the fibers, letting it dry before sanding.

In the confined areas of the bow and stern, you will have to use sanding blocks and work by hand. In the tightest corners, belt-sander paper, which is stiffer and holds a curve better, will make the job a little easier. And for the hollow of the bilge, consider a bottle sander (see Builder's Tip).

When the inside of the hull has been completely sanded with 80-grit sandpaper, dampen the surface of the wood to raise the grain (step four) and allow it to dry before the final step of smoothing the surface with 120-grit sandpaper.

Vacuum out the inside, and wipe the surface with a rag dampened with lacquer thinner. This will pick up any remaining dust particles.

SHEATHING THE INSIDE OF THE HULL

For the most part, the tools, materials and techniques for fiberglassing the inside of the hull are the same as for the outside, and so are the safety considerations. Take a few moments to review the precautions recommended when handling epoxy (see page 144).

handling epoxy (see page 144).

BUILDER'S TIP: BOTTLE SANDER

A random orbital sander can sometimes create waves in the hollow of the bilge. An easy (and inexpensive) solution is to use a smooth-sided 500-mL plastic soft-drink bottle as a sanding block. Fill it with water to firm up the

sides and to give it some weight, then wrap the paper around it. It will sand the curve beautifully.

A few additional items should be considered when fiberglassing the inside of the hull. The cloth will have to be fitted to the inside stems: there is a trick to working with the cut edge of the fiberglass. You will most likely be applying two coats of resin instead of three, and in working the epoxy, you'll find yourself worrying about puddles instead of drips.

To begin, spread the cloth over the inside of the hull. Center it and cut it so that it ends about 4 inches short of each stem. There is no point in trying to overlap the cloth at the bow and stern: it simply won't go, and you'll waste a lot of time trying to do something that will leave a mess to clean up after the resin has set.

With a person at each end of the fabric, hold the corners, bring your hands together, and lower the cloth into the center of the hull. Fold the edges over the sides. If necessary, use clothes pegs to hold the cloth in place along the sheer, but leave enough slack that the cloth can fit snugly against the inside of the hull.

Starting in the middle and anchoring the cloth with one hand, smooth it up toward the sheer and outward toward the stems. At the bow and stern, tuck the cloth

Center the cloth, and cut so that it ends 4 inches short of stems.

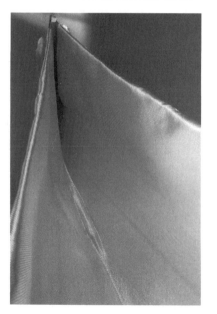

Tuck cloth on either side of stem.

down to each side of the stem and over the top. After the epoxy has been applied, you will cut the cloth and fit it up the sides of the stems.

Using the same system as for the outside, mix a batch of resin and hardener and apply it to the inside with a bristle brush. Work in the same sequence as you did on the outside. Don't worry about a finished appearance at this stage; just get the epoxy onto the hull. In the bow and stern sections, try not to get resin on the cloth that fits over the stem. (Dry cloth is easier to cut.)

In both the bow and the stern,

you will encounter problems with fibers of the cut cloth unraveling as you attempt to spread on the resin over the edge. To minimize this, stop applying resin about 2 inches short of the edge of the cloth. Wet out both sides, and fold the cloth back. Brush the resin onto the bare wood, then smooth the cloth back into place.

If the cloth still needs more

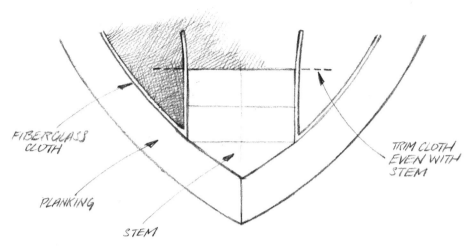

FIBERGLASS CLOTH

PLANKING

STEM

TRIM CLOTH EVEN WITH STEM

At the stems, stop applying resin 2 inches short of the cloth edge. Fold back cloth, brush resin onto wood, then smooth cloth in place. After squeegeeing, cut cloth with scissors and tuck in with squeegee. When resin is firm, trim cloth with sharp chisel and sand edges smooth.

Keep cloth at stems resin-free.

resin in this area, apply it with a sponging motion. Lay the brush on its side, and with gentle pressure, squeeze the resin out of the bristles. This is very effective for applying resin without disturbing the cloth. Laid flat, the brush fits neatly into the confined space. Don't apply too much pressure, though: first-time builders often lay too much resin in the ends on the inside, a place where it is very hard to clean up the excess.

Squeegee each section 20 to 30 minutes after it has been applied, using the same technique and the same timing as you did on the outside of the hull. After squeegeeing the end section, cut the cloth with scissors across the end of the stem and down the length

of the stem, then use the edge of the squeegee to tuck the cloth snugly into place.

Cut cloth along top of stem.

To produce a less slippery surface, you will need only two coats of resin inside the hull. To make this work, however, you should be extremely careful with squeegeeing the first and second coats. The texture of the weave has to be consistent to look good. After removing all the excess resin with the squeegee, use a dry brush, stroking in a fore-and-aft direction, to work out any remaining tracks in the epoxy.

As the resin cures, it will create heat. The outside of the hull is now completely sealed, so air can't escape. This means there will be

an increased chance of outgassing as air trapped under the resin expands. If you can, lower the temperature in the work area as soon as the inside lay-up is complete. This will slow down the air expansion. Keep an eye out for bubbles until the epoxy resin has firmed up. If they form, break them with the tip of a small glue brush or with the squeegee.

When the resin has set firmly, use a sharp chisel to trim away any cloth sticking up around the stems and sand the edges smooth. Lightly hand-sand the hull with 120-grit sandpaper to cut the tooth, then vacuum and clean the surface with a cloth dampened with lacquer thinner.

For the second coat, pour in a

Lightly hand-sand with 120-grit.

THE STRIPPER'S ART

Use a dry brush to erase shiny tracks from second coat.

puddle of resin, and spread it with the squeegee. After all the excess resin has been picked up, use a dry brush again to erase any shiny tracks in the resin. Use a brush to spread the second coat of resin over the stems. When the second (and last) coat has set, trim the cloth even with the sheer-line and sand off the sharp edge.

With two coats of resin, you will have a strong, lightweight finish with a nonslip texture to it. For an inside finish that is glossier and somewhat tougher (though heavier and more slippery), brush on a third coat of resin.

When the hull is fully cured—a process that can take up to 14 days—sand the inside to smooth the surface and prepare it for var-

nishing. If you applied only two coats of resin, a quick hand-sanding with 120-grit sandpaper will be enough. The object is simply to knock off the rough points without flattening the surface or cutting into the fiberglass.

Some brands of epoxy, especially when they cure at cold temperatures, leave behind a greasy residue called "amine blush." This comes to the surface during curing and is a by-product of the hardener. If amine blush isn't removed, it can compromise the bond between the epoxy and the varnish.

To remove amine blush, wash the hull with water fortified with ammonia, then rinse well with fresh water.

If you have applied three or more coats on the inside, follow the sanding procedure outlined below.

SANDING THE EPOXY

Tools
cabinet scraper
random orbital sander

Materials
open-coat silicone-carbide sandpaper (#80, #120)

Safety
gloves, disposable sleeves, hat
mask and ventilation
Before beginning, review the safety precautions recommended for sanding epoxy (page 144).

Sanding the epoxy is the step that produces a flawlessly smooth surface on your hull. It can be dirty and potentially hazardous, but there are ways to make it safe as well as relatively quick and comfortable.

Epoxy cures quickly to a sandable solid, but it may take more than two weeks at room temperature to cure completely. For this reason, you may want to go ahead with the inwales, decks and seats while waiting for the epoxy to cure.

In any case, don't begin sanding until you are sure the epoxy has fully cured. The biggest hazard associated with sanding epoxy is the toxicity of uncured epoxy dust, which can contain unreacted

hazardous components. Manufacturers advise builders NEVER to breathe the sanding dust from partially cured epoxy. Very serious health problems can result. When you inhale these dust particles, they become trapped in the mucous lining of the respiratory system, where they can cause severe respiratory irritation and/or allergies. If uncured epoxy dust settles on your skin, it can cause an allergic reaction or dermatitis.

You can sand the hull any time after the epoxy has cured and before you apply the varnish. If possible, wait for an opportunity to move the hull outside. Even though it isn't toxic, the dust from cured epoxy is extraordinarily fine and cleanup is bothersome. Even after cleaning the shop several times, we inevitably uncover little pockets of fine epoxy dust left over from sanding.

If you can't move the hull outside, use a window fan to create a good cross draft. Try to position yourself so that the dust is drawn away from you. To speed cleanup later, cover your workbench, machines, shelves, et cetera, with plastic film. When you clean the floor, vacuum rather than sweep, which tends to put the dust back into the air. If you must sweep, use sweeping compound to pick up the fine particles and to reduce billowing dust.

Even though you are sanding fully cured epoxy, you should still wear a dust mask or respirator

With sanding, epoxy changes from shiny to dull, from wavy to smooth.

and protective clothing or barrier cream. Don't eat or smoke while sanding. When you are finished for the day, wash all exposed body parts with soap and water, and wash your clothes too.

Sanding epoxy proceeds in two steps. Changes in the appearance of the hull will be visible as the epoxy is smoothed from a shiny, wavy surface to a smooth, dull one. These are a clue to where you

Cloth pattern shows with sanding.

are in the sanding process, and learning to recognize them will give you intelligent control over the process.

STEP ONE: ROUGH SANDING

When you begin this stage, the hull has a shiny epoxy surface. The profile of the weave is visible, and there are probably a few runs.

Sanding with 80-grit sandpaper will rough out the surface until only a few shiny spots remain. These serve as important references: once all the gloss is gone, you won't know how close you are to the cloth, because the color doesn't change again.

Begin by using a cabinet scraper to shave away any runs in the epoxy. If you try to sand these, the pad of the sander will follow the high spots and can cut right through the adjacent areas before the run has been worn away.

Once the runs have been cut level with the scraper, work your way over the hull with a random orbital sander using 80-grit sandpaper. Wherever you sand, the clear, shiny finish will become a whitened matte finish.

Because the epoxy follows the weave of the buried fiberglass, you will see the pattern of the cloth emerge as you begin to sand. The pattern will become more distinct as the sanding levels the epoxy.

Stop sanding when the gloss disappears: if you've laid on a proper thickness of epoxy, you will completely sand away that pattern before you reach the fiberglass itself.

When most of the gloss is gone, switch to 120-grit sandpaper and move on to the second step.

STEP TWO: FINE SANDING

As you begin the second step, the hull appears as a flat, even, white surface with a few shiny low spots. When you are done, all the gloss, as well as the scratches from the 80-grit sandpaper, will be gone.

At this point, you walk a fine line in sanding the epoxy. You want the surface as smooth as possible, but you don't want to cut into the cloth. As a general rule, when all the gloss has disappeared, leave that section alone and move on to another.

You will know when you've gone too far: the weave of the cloth becomes visible again. The pattern we've been eliminating with sanding was actually the space between the fibers. If you sand too deeply, you'll start to see the fibers themselves.

Cutting into the glass will make the fibers visible in bright sunlight after varnishing. If more fiber is sanded away, the integrity of the structure may be compromised. You can correct this problem by mixing up a fresh batch of epoxy and spreading it over the sanded area, but feathering the new epoxy into the old is tricky. It is far better to avoid the situation altogether by watching the surface very closely as you sand.

After the sanding, except for an ultraviolet-blocking coat of varnish, which will be applied after the gunwales and decks are in place, the hull is finished. Rushton used to sell canoes at this stage of completion as "shells" so that paddlers could install the trim to their own satisfaction. That pleasure will be all yours.

TROUBLESHOOTING

The following chart details some of the most common problems encountered in the woodstrip/epoxy construction method, their symptoms and causes. Read the chart before beginning to build: prevention is a lot easier than fixing a botched job.

SYMPTOM	CAUSE	PREVENTION/CURE
Strongback twists out of square.	Wet wood drying.	Place weights on the feet. Construct box beam of plywood or particleboard.
One entire mold too small (obvious during fairing).	Improper tracing or cutting out of mold. Faulty pattern.	Slide mold toward closest end until it fairs in smoothly.
Wood strips crack or break during ripping.	Poor-quality wood with checks, shakes, cross grain.	Dispose of defective strips; splice strips during planking process.
Planking springs out of alignment on mold.	Square edge planks with butt joints. Too much compound bend. Poorly machined bead and cove.	Staple between stations. Drive ½" #4 screw and washer into mold. Try using stapleless jigs, as described on page 128.
Planks break in compound bends.	Cross grain. Too much tension.	Find strip with straighter grain. Position first plank parallel to waterline.
Gaps between planking.	Improper fit; planks breaking or chipping along edges.	Fill with epoxy glue/sanding dust filler.
Planks "shingle."	Bead and cove not centered; inaccurate stem bevel.	Machine planking with precision. Stop planking until problem solved.
Runs in epoxy.	Inconsistent or too much resin.	Control film thickness of each coat; sand or scrape off if cured.

SYMPTOM	CAUSE	PREVENTION/CURE
Cloth shifts during lay-up.	Excessive working of resin.	Work resin gently with sponging motion of brush. Work from wet to dry. Pull cloth from end of hull to remove wrinkles.
Cloth lifts off hull as resin curing.	Air expanding under partially cured resin/ glass, lifting cloth before it can escape. Excess cloth hanging in such a way that cloth pulls away at edges.	Break bubble. Trim cloth.
Uneven resin coat.	Improper squeegeeing/brushing or missed portions.	Sand to even thickness, but do not damage cloth; if fewer than three coats remain after sanding, apply another coat.
Weave of cloth visible after final coat.	Incomplete wetting out of cloth due to cold or partially set-up resin. Cloth starved by squeegeeing too hard or insufficient resin.	Warm ingredients to room temperature before mixing; use fresh, small batches. Less pressure on squeegee; more resin on first coat.
Epoxy cloudy as it cures.	Air introduced by overworking resin. Air trapped in resin-starved cloth. Resin too thick (low temperature). Resin too thick (started to set). Moisture contamination.	Use proper application and squeegee technique. Use proper wetting-out or squeegee technique. Warm ingredients; maintain proper humidity. Use fresh batches; squeegee before resin sets. Live with it; paint it. If cloudy in only one spot, let cure, then treat as repair.
White spots in glassed surface.	Glue/filler residue prevents absorption of resin into wood fibers.	Prevent by proper sanding; live with it, or treat as repair.
Finish clouds after curing.	Ultraviolet deterioration.	Prevent by keeping hull out of sun between lay-up and varnishing.
Fiberglassed hull looks blotchy; dark and light patches in wood.	Incomplete sanding of planking.	Prevent by wetting down to raise grain and preview problems. Fine-sand before lay-up. No cure, only prevention.

CHAPTER 9

CHARACTER DEVELOPMENT

Installing the Trim

IT HAS LONG BEEN AN AXIOM OF MINE THAT THE LITTLE
THINGS ARE INFINITELY THE MOST IMPORTANT.

—*Sherlock Holmes*
Copper Beeches

An untrimmed hull, while not an unattractive shape, is badly in need of rigidity and structure in a few key places. It is stable at the stems and below the waterline, but its untrimmed flanks near the sheer edge need some additional support—gunwales to stiffen it from stem to stem, and thwarts, seats and decks to tie it all together.

The sequence for attaching most of the trim is not carved in stone, but the inwales are always installed first to provide basic bow-to-stern support. The center thwart is fixed temporarily to establish the proper midship width. Then the decks are fastened, followed by the outwales. The seats are also fitted temporarily (either before or after the outwales

and decks), because they have to be removed while the inside of the hull is varnished.

As you read through the chapter, there may seem to be a formidable amount of measuring, clamping and double-checking. But experienced boatbuilders—and some of you may be working on a second or third canoe and know this from your own experience—will agree that there is no such thing as being too careful. Working well into the wee hours with a portable television or a blasting stereo for company can lead to painful mistakes if your concentration is broken long enough to glue an inwale on backwards.

Epoxy joints, as the saying goes, are forever. Mistakes are correctable, but only after hours of chiseling. If you devote the careful attention to detail you've exercised up till now, you should be able to avoid them completely.

The following tools and materials include everything necessary to install all the trim, including the keel, inwales, outwales, decks, seats and thwarts.

Tools
string line (if keel)
dozuki saw (hacksaw, in a pinch)
coping saw

straightedge
sliding bevel-square
12 C-clamps (2-inch or larger)
glue brush

drill/driver
screwdriver
block plane
sharp pencil
ruler/tape measure
router/roundover bit (optional)
countersink/counterbore
plug cutter (optional)

Materials
epoxy glue
epoxy solvent
½-inch #4 noncorrosive flathead
   wood screws (inwales and keel)
1½-inch (1¼-inch if plugged)
   #8 noncorrosive flathead wood
   screws (outwales)
sandpaper (#80, #120, #220)
2-inch carriage bolts or machine
   screws (thwarts)
4-to-6-inch carriage bolts or
   machine screws (seats)

spacer blocks (seats)
2 finishing nails (keel)

Safety
gloves
ventilation
Review safety precautions
for working with epoxy (see
page 144).

INSTALLING THE KEEL

The Redbird we've been building is a keelless design. However,
your plans may include a keel,
which was machined from a
length of hardwood at the same
time as the other trim details
(see page 82).

Ideally, the keel should be installed long before those other
details, just after the first coat of
epoxy is applied to the outside of
the hull. In that way, subsequent
coats of epoxy can cover and protect it. Because time is limited between epoxy coats, the keel should
be dry-fitted right after you finish
sanding the hull.

Begin by cutting the machined
keel to length—long enough to be
fastened into both stems. Then cut
a taper on either end so that it will
merge smoothly with the stems.

Because the top of the keel has
already been shaped to take a
brass stem band ³⁄₈ inch wide (see
page 82), cut the taper from the ⁷⁄₈-
inch base. As you fair the keel into
the profile of the stems, a small
amount of material will be removed from the top of the keel as
well. This should require adjusting

the bevel to preserve the necessary
³⁄₈-inch width.

Measure back 16 inches from
each end of the keel, and draw a
taper from this point to the ends,
rising from the wide, flat hull side
of the keel to within ¹⁄₈ inch of the
shaped ³⁄₈-inch edge. Cut away the
wedge of extra material on a table
saw or band saw, or simply plane
it down to the taper line.

Position the keel over the centerline on the bottom of the hull,
and make any necessary final adjustments in shaping. This process
is largely a matter of judgment
and depends on the particular
design of your canoe. The purpose
is to create a smooth flow of line
from the keel into each stem.

ATTACHING THE KEEL

Installing the keel is a two-
person job. Have your helper hold
it firmly in position while you
predrill and fasten a ¹⁄₂-inch #4
wood screw and washer through
each end of the keel into the
stems. Then remove the screws
and keel, and proceed with the
fiberglass and first coat of epoxy.

The keel can be attached as
soon as the first coat of resin
has lost its tackiness and is firm
enough to work on. It can also be
installed after lay-up is complete,
but doing the job after the first
coat will save applying epoxy to
the keel separately later on.

Spread epoxy glue liberally on
the underside of the keel, reposition it on the hull, and wax and

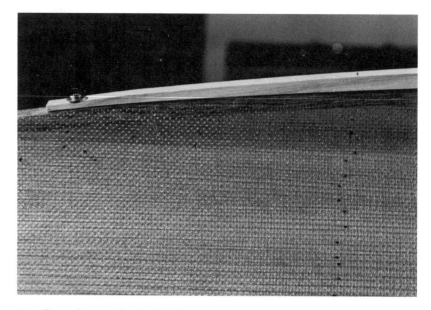

Dry-fit and taper the keel. After the first coat of epoxy, fasten in place.

replace the screws you predrilled
into the stems.

Predrill and fasten a long finishing nail into the middle of the keel
near each end. Stretch a string line
between the two nails. With your
helper positioning the keel directly
under the taut string line, crouch
under the canoe and predrill
through the hull into the keel,
using the planking seam as your
guide. Mark the depth on the drill
with a piece of masking tape so
that you don't drill right through
the keel itself.

Starting in the center and working out toward each stem, drive a
¹⁄₂-inch #4 screw between each
station while your helper holds
the keel in position and checks
for straightness. It helps to begin

by fastening between every second mold, allowing the keel to
straighten itself. Use permanent
brass screws, and set them flush
with the wood. Or use waxed steel
screws, which are temporary and
will be removed later.

Scrape off the excess glue, making sure that the glue joint is full,
then clean up the keel with epoxy
solvent. Sight down the length of
the keel. If minor waves are appar-
ent, set a block of wood beside the
keel and tap it gently into position.

Apply the second coat of epoxy,
brushing it over the hull and keel
but leaving the keel ends bare
around the screws, where they join
the stems. By the time the second
coat is firm, the glue on the keel
will be set. If you used temporary

Spread glue on underside of keel. Fasten to hull with screws between every second mold, letting the keel straighten itself. Clean excess glue and sight down the keel, *top*. Remove minor waves by setting a block of wood beside the keel and tapping it gently into position, *above*.

screws to fasten the keel to the outside stems, they can be removed now. Plug the holes with little pieces of wood, whittled to fit and dipped in epoxy. When the plugs are set, cut them off flush.

Complete the taper so that it feathers into the hull. Dress each keel-stem joint to a feather edge with a plane or spokeshave. Apply the third coat of epoxy over the entire hull, leaving no bare spots this time. Remember to touch up the dressed ends of the keel with a second coat of epoxy later, when laying up the inside.

If there isn't enough time to fasten the keel between the first and second coats, leave it until the lay-up is complete and the hull is sanded. It is more important to get the three coats of epoxy on in succession so that there is a good chemical bond.

If you wait until lay-up is complete, you still attach it as described. Then lay a strip of masking tape on the hull flush to each side of the keel. Brush a coat of epoxy over the keel. While the epoxy is still fresh, remove the tape and let the epoxy sag gently into the crevice between the hull and keel. When the epoxy is tacky, retape and apply a second coat.

INWALES

By the time you come to install the inwales, you will already have made several decisions about the shape and style of the material you will be working with (see Material Matters, page 76). The scuppers will have been laid out with the seat supports and center thwart in mind, so be sure that you position the inwales on the correct side of the hull.

Also, if the inwales are to be tapered, this should be done as part of the preparation, before the final fitting. Note that the taper goes down to half the width of the inside face of the inside stem.

The inwales will be installed one at a time. After the first is fitted, glued and screwed in place, the same process will be repeated on the other side.

FITTING THE INWALES

The rough inwales are machined a little longer than the hull. Since you can't determine their correct length by fitting them down into position, more precise methods of measuring must be used.

Begin by clamping the center point of an inwale to one side of the hull amidships, lining it up over the middle row of staple holes. The ends of the inwales will be hooked behind the stems and will hang over the ends of the canoe.

Measure from the inside of the stem back along the inside edge of the hull about 24 inches, or to a point where you can get the inwale down flush to the top of the hull. Transfer this point from the hull to the inwale, and measure back along the top outside edge of

Find a point common to the edge of hull and inwale.

the inwale the 24 inches to establish the exact point where the inwale should end. From this point, it is easy to pick up the angles and, using a sharp pencil, to trace out your cut lines.

After fitting the other end, make a benchmark between the hull and the inwale at the

With a sharp pencil, mark the angle of the inwale at the stem.

centerline to use as a guide for repositioning the inwale after applying the glue.

GLUING THE INWALES

Install the inwales one at a time. Apply thickened epoxy to the inner surface of the inwale, then clamp it back in place. Before you clamp, line up the benchmarks and position the top of the inwale below the unfinished top edge of the hull, low enough that there will be a crisp joint between the hull and the gunwale. Unless there is an obvious twist or kink in the wood, let the inwale find a fair curve.

The inwales follow the sheerline of the canoe from bow to stern, so the more your design

swoops up at the stems, the more difficult it will be to bend the inwales to shape. Starting amidships, work toward the ends, clamping every 8 to 10 inches as you go. (The spacing will depend on how many clamps you have.)

If the inwale resists a hard, fast bend at the stem, draw the end up by clamping it to a board laid across the stem. This will give the clamp something firm to draw against. There is a limit, however, to how far a 3/4-by-7/8-inch inwale can be bent before breaking. If the bend is quick or extreme, it will have to be steam-bent (see Builder's Tip, facing page).

If you don't have enough clamps for the entire inwale or if you want to get to the other side,

Clamp glued inwale often, *top*. Draw inwale up to a board laid across the stem, *above*.

predrill from the hull into the inwale every 6 to 10 inches. Fasten with 1/2-inch #4 noncorrosive flathead screws drawn in flush with the hull. Wipe off any excess glue, and clean up with epoxy solvent.

With the first inwale glued

BUILDER'S TIP: STEAM-BENDING THE GUNWALES

The more recurve there is to the bow and stern, the more difficult it will be to bend the inwales to the shape of the hull. The alternative, in this case, is to steambend the wood.

To make the bending forms, cut the shape of the curved sheerline from a piece of 2-by-6 about 6 feet long, as shown above. Determine where the bend will begin by measuring from stem to stem along the edge of the hull, and mark the gunwale before steaming. Note: The

point for the inwale will be to the inside face of the stem, while the outwale will extend to the end of the hull.

Steam-bend the inwale using the method on page 111. When the inwale is pliable enough, clamp it to the template and allow to dry. Dry-fit the steamed end of the inwale, and measure carefully, using benchmarks to establish the point at which the bend begins at the other end.

After gluing the inwale in place, plane the hull edge smooth and flush.

and either clamped or screwed in place, repeat the procedure with the other one.

When the glue has set, remove the clamps and plane the hull flush with the top of the inwale. Lightly mark the screw positions on the top of the inwale with a pencil so that you will not hit them with the outwale screws.

CENTER THWART

The center thwart or a temporary spacer should be clamped into position immediately after the inwales are installed to establish the correct width at the center of the canoe.

Cut the center thwart to length according to the width of the hull specified in the plans. If the canoe

has plumb sides, the cut will be square. If the sides are tumblehome or flared, cut the angle on the ends of the thwart to fit the curve of the hull.

Cut the angle of the thwarts to fit.

Spread the sides of the hull, and fit the thwart, clamping it temporarily into position under the inwales. This will ensure that the

CHARACTER DEVELOPMENT

Scribe the sides of the fitted deck to match the sheer-line, *right*. Secure the deck in the gluing jig, *above*. Shape to the scribed line.

Refit the shaped deck, and sand it smooth with 120-grit sandpaper.

canoe is the proper width, and it should be kept in this position while the decks are fitted and the seats hung. The thwart is not attached permanently until the trim is complete so that it can be positioned at the proper balance point for portaging.

DECKS

Once the inwales are in place on the hull, trace out a template for your decks and proceed to glue them up according to the instructions for machining decks on page 87. The rough deck should be somewhat larger than necessary so that you have room for fitting. If

your material is ⅞ to 1 inch thick, in most cases, there will be enough wood to shape a crown.

FITTING THE DECKS

Center the deck on the hull, with the top facing down. From inside the canoe, trace the exact outline of the inwales onto the deck. (This works because the deck will sit between the inwales.) Then turn the deck right side up, and position it exactly where it

will sit, with the lines you just drew matched to the gunwales. To project the angle of the inwale onto the end of the deck, use a ruler or a short batten.

Cut the deck to the lines. Then use a sharp block plane to dress down the edge to a tight fit. Test the fit repeatedly so that you produce the required rolling bevel.

Now dry-fit the deck, predrilling through the hull and inwale into the edge of the decking. Fasten with 1½-inch #8 noncorrosive wood screws, putting the first screw at the wide end to stabilize the deck position. Continue toward the stem, fastening three or four screws on each side to secure the deck without gaps. If you are going to shape the top of the deck

or if it has a crown, place the screw at an angle that will accommodate the anticipated shape.

If the sheer-line rises toward the stems, a flat deck will have to be shaped to match this curve. Fit and fasten the deck flush to the top of the inwales, both at its widest point and at the stem, as shown, then scribe the sides of the deck with an awl or a knife guided along the curving top of the inwale.

Remove the deck and secure it in the gluing jig (see page 86) to shape it. Using a spokeshave, block plane and cabinet scraper, shape the deck down to the scribed line, giving its top surface a pleasing crown or camber. After the deck is shaped, refit it,

With tape in place, brush glue on mating surfaces of deck and inwales.

making any final adjustments. Then sand it smooth, working up to 120-grit sandpaper.

GLUING THE DECKS

When both decks are dry-fitted to your satisfaction, remove them. Then prepare a batch of thickened epoxy glue. Brush it on the mating

Mold tape to cover glued join.

surfaces of the deck and inwale, then screw the deck firmly in place. Wipe off any excess glue squeezed out on top, and clean up the joints with epoxy solvent. Repeat the same procedure with the other deck.

To keep glue from dripping into the boat and to hold glue in a less-than-perfect joint, run half the width of masking tape along the

bottom of the inwale. After fastening the deck in place, reach under and mold the overhanging edge of tape over the join. Peel off the tape after the glue has set.

If your deck has a coaming, it was dry-fitted to the deck at the time the piece was machined, and removed while the deck was being fitted between the inwales. Now that the deck is installed, the feathered coaming can be glued and screwed firmly back in place. If the coaming is designed to overlap the gunwales, wait until after the outwales are installed to fit and glue it permanently in place.

With both decks installed, round off the inside edges of the inwales with a plane and 80-grit sandpaper or with a router with a $\frac{1}{4}$-inch roundover bit.

OUTWALES

There are three options for attaching the outwales. If you own enough clamps, you can simply glue the outwales in place and draw them tight to the hull with clamps set approximately every 10 inches, between the scuppers and not at the deck. When the glue has set, remove the clamps.

If you don't have lots of clamps, you can use $1\frac{1}{2}$-inch #8 stainless-steel or silicone-bronze screws and set the heads flush with the wood. Or you can use $1\frac{1}{4}$-inch #8 screws, counterbore the holes and cover the screw heads with wooden plugs. This third option takes a little more time, but it seals

169

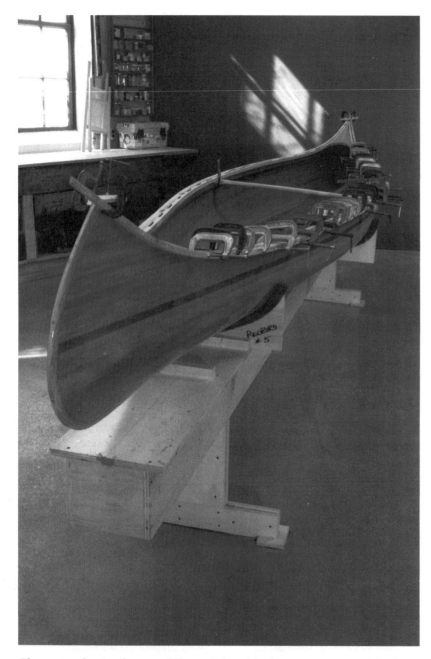

Glue outwales in place, and draw tight with clamps set every 10 inches.

the fastener inside the wood and adds a nice nautical touch. For a cheap trick that looks sharp, cut the plugs from wood of a contrasting color.

For any of these options, start amidships, and clamp one outwale to the outside of the hull, making sure it extends slightly past both stems. Mark the true end, then make benchmarks at the middle and remove the outwale. Taper the ends about the same as you did on the inwale. Round over the outside edge.

Mix a batch of thickened epoxy, and apply it to the outwale. Then clamp the outwale back into position. Note the position of the deck and inwale screws so that you can avoid hitting them. Arrange the outwale screws in a logical pattern, taking into account the seats and thwarts still to come and fitting them between the scuppers. Aim for a spacing of 6 to 10 inches.

Place a clamp as close as possible to the screw-hole position, then drill through the outwale and the hull into the inwale. (Position the handle of the clamp inside so that it isn't in the way of the drill and driver.) Draw the outwale tight to the hull, and fasten with screws long enough to extend half or three-quarters of the way into the inwale.

You should see a little glue squeeze out with the clamping and screwing. Be careful not to split the outwale by overtightening the screw. Wipe off excess

glue, and clean up with solvent. Fasten the other outwale in the same manner.

When gluing in a plug, line up the grain in the plug with the grain

Tap plug just enough to seat it.

of the outwale so that the woods blend when the plug is cut off. Tap the plug just enough to seat it, but don't break the fibers of the wood. When the glue is set, trim the plug with a very sharp chisel until it is flush with the outwale. Shave it a little at a time until you are sure which way the grain is running and to ensure that the wood doesn't split below the surface.

The permanent trim has now all been installed. (The seats and thwarts have to be removable so that the canoe can be varnished,

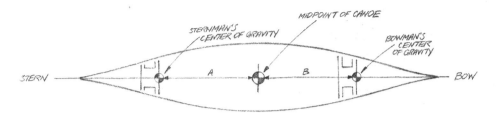

STERNMAN'S WEIGHT X A EQUALS BOWMAN'S WEIGHT X B

Calculate seat positions with this formula if two paddlers of very different weights will be regularly using the canoe.

SEATS

The seats in a canoe are normally hung from the inwales, rather than fastened to the hull, so that the canoe can flex and absorb stress evenly. Before you install them, you need to decide how high they will be and where they will be positioned within the canoe.

For safety and stability, the seats should be high enough that you can easily get your feet out from under them. On the other hand, they must be as low as possible to keep the center of gravity low, since this has a major influence on how stable a canoe will be. A space of 9½ to 10½ inches under the seat is a good average.

Unless you have strong opinions about the matter, locate the seats as indicated in your plans. Paddlers and conditions change, so abiding by a theoretical average is probably a good idea. Adjusting the trim to changing conditions is part of the seamanship of paddling.

If you are an experienced paddler who wants to customize your craft, or if this is your second canoebuilding effort and you want to improve on the last hull, position the seats with the following principles in mind.

Placing the seats close to the ends, where the width is narrow, makes for easier paddling and maximum steering leverage. The trade-offs are that it reduces the stability of the craft unless it is loaded, and there is less room for feet and knees. Placing the seats

now and in the future.) As a finishing touch, round off any rough edges on the decks and gunwales with a router or plane and 80-grit sandpaper, then sand it all thoroughly with 120-grit. Wet the wood to raise the fibers, let it dry, then finish-sand with 220-grit.

Use a seat jig with sliding measuring sticks to position seats.

closer to the center gives a canoe more lift in the ends and provides bow paddlers with more legroom.

HANGING THE SEATS

Two devices quickly made from scrap lumber will greatly simplify seat installation. The seat jig is a plank or piece of plywood that, when set on its edge, holds the seats steady at the correct height from the bottom of the canoe while they are being fitted and hung. The sliding measuring stick is simply two lengths of wood that are extended or shortened to measure the distance between the sides of the hull.

To be on the safe side, fit the bow seat first; if there is a problem, the seat can be recut for the shorter stern seat.

Put the seat in position. Clamp a 1-by-2-inch board across the inwales on the stem side of the seat. Remove the seat, and measure each inwale from the stem to the seat to confirm that the seat is positioned squarely between the gunwales. Clamp the jig to the midpoint of this bar to hold it plumb along the keel-line. (The 1-by-2 is notched so that the clamp securing it does not interfere.)

Because the canoe widens as it approaches amidships, the back members of the bow seat frame will be longer than those at the front. Also, if the side of the canoe has tumblehome, the seat will have to be wider than the measurement at the gunwales.

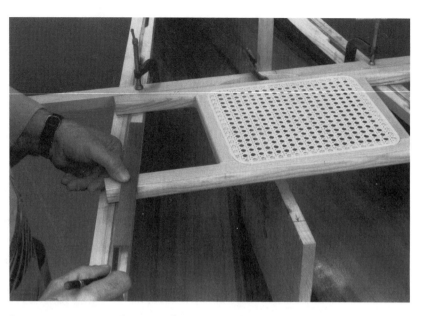

Set seat over gunwales to pick up top and side angles.

To determine the dimensions accurately, set the sliding measuring stick on the front edge of the seat jig, then expand it to touch the hull sides and clamp. Transfer this measurement to the front edge of the seat frame. Repeat for the back member of the seat.

For a reliable measurement, the measuring sticks must be in exactly the same position that will be occupied by the seat frame. When finding the centerline of the seat frame, go by the seat rather than the arm. (There is no guarantee that the arm will be the same length.)

Now that you know the length of the seat frame, you need to pick up the angle in both directions. To do this, lay the seat frame in position across the gunwales, flush to the 1-by-2 and directly over the jig. Lay a straightedge over the cutting marks, and mark an angle parallel to that of the outwale. Because of the curving side of the hull, joining the marks from front to back won't work.

To pick up the bevel, place the sliding bevel-gauge on the seat-frame arm so that it extends down the side of the hull to the level at which the seat will be installed. (This will work best if done before the outwales are installed.)

Cut the seat frame to length at the proper angles, then set it in place on the seat jig. Be sure that it is level side to side; check it against the plank lines. Cut and fit the spacer blocks or dowels between the seat frame and the inwales.

Drill a loose hole through the center of each spacer, then set the spacers in place and drill a hole through the inwale to fit the bolt snugly. Let the bit move through the spacer hole to mark the top of the seat frame. Remove the spacers, and drill holes slightly larger than the bolts through the frames at these marks. (The holes need to be large, because the wood will swell around the bolt over time, locking it in place so firmly that taking it off can damage the inwales.) Sand off any rough edges.

Assemble the seat frames and spacers, and fasten them together with $^3/_{16}$-inch noncorrosive carriage bolts or machine screws. If carriage bolts are used, the dome-shaped heads will sit on top of the inwale. If machine screws (flathead stove bolts) are used, they should be either countersunk flush or counterbored and plugged.

If plugs are used, set the heads of the bolts in thickened epoxy so that they will not turn below the plugs when the seats are removed for occasional varnishings. After assembling the seats, cut the bolts off at the nut and file any sharp edges.

This process is repeated for the stern seat, except that the jig's position will be reversed.

THWARTS

Structurally, a canoe up to 18 feet needs only one thwart, positioned in the center. An extra

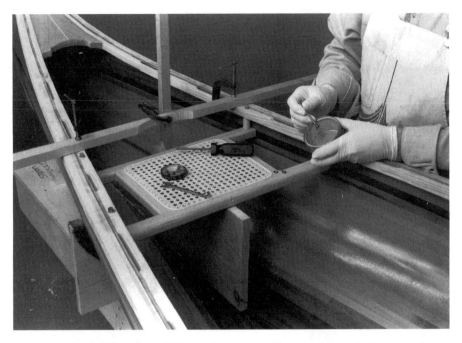

bond for the varnish and also to limit the absorption of varnish into the wood.

Use a sealer that is compatible with the varnish you are using. Alternatively, you can seal the wood with the varnish itself, thinned to 50 percent.

Once the bare wood has been sealed, the varnish will build at the same rate as on the epoxy-coated surfaces.

Set the bolt heads in thickened epoxy so they won't turn below the plugs.

thwart installed aft of the center thwart is common in canoes over 16 feet, but its position is for convenience rather than for balance.

All thwarts are through-bolted to the inwales in the same manner as the seats. With the center thwart clamped temporarily in position, install any remaining thwarts.

After everything is installed on the canoe, find the balance point and fix the center thwart permanently. With a person on either side, pick up the canoe, centering your fingers under the thwart. Move the thwart back and forth until the stern is just slightly heavier than the bow. (This will be important when it comes to portaging.)

Note: The thwarts on many traditional pleasure canoes were positioned 10 to 12 inches aft of the center—great for solo paddling in the kneeling position or with a backrest and a double-blade paddle.

Drill through the inwale into the thwart, and bolt them together, using two bolts on either side. Treat bolt heads the same as those for the seats.

SEALING THE TRIM

All the bare wood trim parts must be sealed before the canoe is varnished. The purpose of the sealer is to penetrate the wood to provide a deep mechanical

Varnish Room

CHAPTER 10

FINAL DETAILS

Adding the Finishing Touches

THE CREATION OF BEAUTY IS MORE SATISFYING AND JOYOUS THAN MERE POSSESSION.

—John Gardner

Many years ago, I relocated my boat shop to a long-vacant old building in the village of Bancroft, Ontario. It was midwinter, and I was pressed to complete a client's Redbird canoe. The hull was built and trimmed; it needed only a few coats of varnish to be ready for delivery.

Worried about the dust that had accumulated in the building during years of disuse, I painstakingly vacuumed and vacuumed again, sucking the dust from the floors, walls and windows. I let the shop settle for a day or two, mindful that even a vacuum leaves a residue of particles hanging in the air.

Confident that the workplace was clean, I fired up the woodstove and set to work. As the temperature rose to a varnish-drying norm, hundreds of dormant flies began to stir, kicking themselves awake and swarming with delight to the toastiest spot in the room—the unvacuumed ceiling.

It was as the third coat of varnish was drying that I noticed the rain of dust drifting down. Since thin coats of varnish are all-important and must be perfect to maintain a canoe's freshly built beauty, I resolutely sanded off the hull and started over again.

This cautionary tale serves as a reminder that, just as an athlete within sight of the finish line can't slack off, so, too, must a canoe-builder pay close attention, even after the most demanding work has been done.

VARNISHING

Tools
1½-to-3-inch foam or natural-bristle brush (preferably badger-hair)
tack cloth
clean cloths

Materials
varnish
solvent
sandpaper (#220)
disposable paint filter

Safety
ventilation
dust mask

While most first-time builders view rocks and deadheads as the sworn enemies of their lustrous new hulls, it is, in fact, the sun that can do the most damage to a new woodstrip/epoxy canoe. Curiously, in spite of epoxy's tough surface, it takes a coating of varnish to prevent ultraviolet rays from breaking down the resin and turning it milky. Varnish also protects the bare trim from water damage while accentuating the highlights of the wood grain.

The hull is varnished with the seats and thwarts removed so that you can reach the hull interior without obstruction. And if the decks are very long, the hull interior and deck undersides should be varnished before they are installed. (Each of the seats and thwarts is reinstalled only after a thorough varnishing.)

The secret to a lasting varnish job is good equipment and generous doses of care and patience. Your work area must be clean, warm and dry and as dust-free as possible.

Your work area must also be well ventilated. Fumes are a significant hazard with this part of the process, so have a good cross draft as well as a supply of fresh air. Airflow should be steady but not so brisk that it stirs up dust. In a basement shop, draw air from the house and exhaust it to the outside so that fumes won't invade the living area. If you are sensitive to solvents, wear a charcoal-filter respirator.

I use a badger-hair brush to apply varnish, but good results are also possible with other natural-bristle or foam brushes. Use a 1-inch brush for the trim and a 2-to-3-inch brush for the hull and deck.

Even an expensive bristle brush will shed a little when it is new. Before beginning, spin the handle between your hands and remove any loose bristles. Although foam brushes don't shed and they are cheap, available and disposable, you may go through a lot of them. Because varnish doesn't build up as fast with a foam brush, consider applying an extra coat. Use a disposable paint filter to strain the varnish before brushing it on (even from a newly opened can).

A good varnish job depends on three things: preparation, prepara-

tion and preparation. If it has been a while since the epoxy surface was sanded, run over the hull with 220-grit sandpaper to clean the surface and then avoid touching the surface with your hands, which can leave an oily residue.

Give the shop a good cleanup, using a sweeping compound to pick up and hold the fine dust that otherwise is swept into the air. Wet down the floor, if possible, to keep down the dust, raise humidity and reduce the static electricity that will draw dust particles out of the air onto your hull.

Vacuum the boat, blowing out screw holes and tight corners, then wipe it down with a water-dampened rag. Just before you apply the finish, go over the hull carefully with a tack cloth to pick up any tiny particles that have settled while you prepared the varnish.

The final finish is the sum of all the buildup coats that preceded it, so apply each coat of varnish as if it were the last. The job is easier if you plan ahead, breaking the surface into manageable sections and masking the break line to avoid an overlap of varnish between sections and at sharp corners.

Varnish has a short working time, so complete a section, then move on to the next. Once the surface has begun to skin over, reworking will only make it that much worse. Use ½- and 1-inch masking tape to mask off the sections, and peel it off as soon as the varnish is applied so that

Varnish inside, paying attention to undersides of decks and gunwales.

it will flow out, leaving a soft edge.

Varnish the inside of the canoe, the gunwales and the deck first. Cover one half of the hull at a time, dividing it down the keel-line. Do not neglect the crevices up under the decks or the undersides of the gunwales. Mask under the outwales all around the canoe, as shown, to demarcate the line between varnishing the inside and the outside.

The seats and thwarts (which have been removed) should be varnished at the same time and with the same number of coats as the inside of the hull and the trim.

The technique for applying varnish is the same as for applying

the third coat of epoxy (see page 152). Soak your brush with varnish, and quickly spread it over an arm's-length section, holding the brush firmly at a high enough angle to push and spread the varnish evenly over the entire area. A firm yet aggressive stroke intro-

Apply at least three exterior coats.

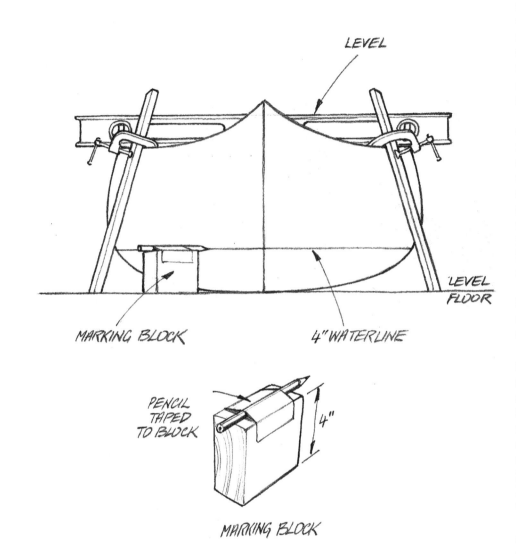

LEVEL

LEVEL FLOOR

MARKING BLOCK

4" WATERLINE

PENCIL TAPED TO BLOCK

4"

MARKING BLOCK

Keeping a straight edge while painting the underside of a canoe is difficult. On a level floor, clamp "feet" to each gunwale amidships, adjusting them until the canoe is level. Then tape a pencil to a 4-inch block of wood, and trace around the canoe, marking the waterline.

duces less air and spreads the varnish better than a choppy, slapping motion. After spreading the varnish in a fore-and-aft direction, work the surface on both diagonals to blend the parallel strokes together.

Next, work the section in a careful, systematic pattern to make sure the varnish is smooth and of consistent thickness. Draw the brush back and forth, making a full, long stroke that both lands and lifts off gently. As you move on to the next section, work from wet to dry, being conscious not to build up a double thickness of varnish where the sections meet.

If the brush starts to fill up with bubbles, scrape the grunge into a clean can. The scraped varnish can be strained and reused later.

Let the first coat dry completely, following the manufacturer's instructions. Then sand the entire surface lightly but thoroughly with 220-grit sandpaper. Vacuum up the dust, and clean the area with sweeping compound. Pick up any remaining dust on the canoe surface with a water-dampened rag. Before applying the second coat, wipe down with a tack cloth.

Apply the second coat, let it dry, then sand again with 220-grit sandpaper or fine steel wool. Clean the surface, and brush on a third coat.

When the inside is dry, turn the canoe over and varnish the exterior of the hull. Three coats are adequate, but of course, the more

coats you apply, the tougher the shield—if you have six coats of varnish and a scratch gouges three, the hull is still well protected. I apply nine coats of varnish to the vintage mahogany runabouts that I restore, but five or six are probably the maximum justifiable on a woodstrip canoe. The trade-off you make for protection is weight: each coat adds at least an extra pound.

One diligent builder brushed on five or six thin coats and then, after a final sanding, paid an autobody shop to spray on a flawless finish coat. As he admits, "It is hard not to get carried away when building these canoes."

PAINTING

For greater abrasion resistance, the outside of the hull can be painted to the gunwales or just to the waterline.

Prepare the surface exactly as you would for varnishing. Select a marine linear polyurethane (LP) paint designed for use over epoxy. The two-part LP systems are light-, salt- and abrasion-resistant and bond extremely well to a cured resin surface. Apply two coats (following the manufacturer's instructions), and sand between coats.

It may be difficult to bring yourself to cover the wood, even though you want the added resistance of paint. You can have the best of both by painting just to the 4-inch waterline so that the underside of the hull is protected while the canoe above water is still obviously a woodstrip.

To mark the waterline, set the canoe on a level floor, right side up. Stabilize it by clamping a stick to the outwales at amidships on either side, checking that the hull is perfectly level. Make up a marking block (as illustrated), and run it around the boat so that the waterline is evenly traced.

Mark the bottom of this line with masking tape, and varnish the topsides. Avoid a hard edge by removing the tape just as the varnish begins to set, retaping for each of the second and third coats.

When the varnishing is complete, tape at the waterline so that the paint will slightly overlap the varnish. Apply two coats, sanding and cleaning the surface between coats. Remove the tape before each coat is dry.

GRAPHITE FINISH

Graphite is a very fine black powder that, mixed with epoxy resin, produces a slippery, highly abrasion-resistant finish. The tough, low-friction surface is ideal for whitewater and wilderness canoes. WEST SYSTEM™ 406 Colodial Silica added to WEST SYSTEM™ 423 graphite powder will produce a rock-hard finish.

Prepare the hull as you would for painting to the waterline. Varnish the topsides first, then invert the hull and tape at the waterline so that the graphite will overlap the varnish slightly.

Mix a batch of epoxy, adding up to 25 percent graphite powder and 5 percent Colodial Silica. Brush or roll it on carefully, because it has a determined tendency to run. When the graphite coat is rubbery, cut along the edge of the tape with a razor blade or sharp knife and peel it off. Do not remove the tape while the coat is runny, but do not wait until it is rock-hard.

To achieve an even black matte finish, rub down the entire surface with very fine steel wool. It will come out as smooth as silk and as tough as steel.

STEM BAND

Tools
drill/⅛-inch bit
countersink
file

Materials
½-inch #4 brass flathead wood
    screws
½-inch #4 steel screws
bedding compound
brass stem band
painter ring (optional)

The stem band may seem superfluous, but it will save a great deal of wear and tear on the leading edge of your canoe. After one season in the water, the stem band will inevitably be scuffed and scratched, proof that it has been protecting your varnish job.

This metal strip normally covers the full length of the stem. If there is a keel, it is advisable to

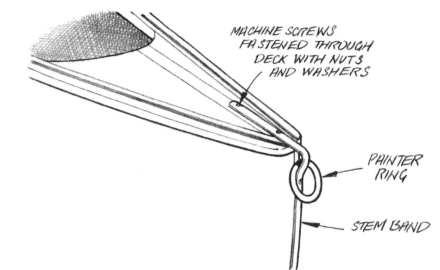

The leading edge of a canoe sustains the most wear and tear—protect it with a brass stem band fastened along the stem and keel.

continue the band along its full length, stem to stem. On one wooden canoe that I restored, the unprotected keel was worn down ¼ inch below the banded stem.

Drill and countersink the center of the metal band at 5-inch intervals with a ⅛-inch bit, then place it on the stem. Use care in bending the metal, as it will want to break first at the drilled holes.

The stem band is screwed in place with ½-inch #4 brass screws. Brass screw heads are notorious for twisting off under pressure, but you can avoid this by first twisting in a ½-inch #4 steel screw to cut the threads in the wood. Remove the steel, and screw in the brass

with a little silicone sealer or bedding compound on its tip. Be sure to countersink the head flush so that it will not catch and rip out the screw. File down any rough edges.

Continue around the stem and keel until the band is firmly in place. The metal should extend a couple of inches over the stems onto the deck.

If you want a painter ring for tying lines onto, you can fasten the band with a raised eyelet to take the ring (as shown, above). For more support, fasten the band at the end with machine screws that extend through the deck, secured with nuts and washers on the

The end result: a boat as lovely on the water as in the imagination.

underside. Alternatively, drive the last screw ½ inch from the end of the band, and use an available fitting to attach the painter (see Sources, page 201).

For an even more finished look, you can mortise or countersink the end of the brass band right into the wood of the stem where it curves to the bottom of the hull.

As a final finishing touch, have a small brass plate engraved with the name of the boat, the date of first launching and the name of the builder. You now richly deserve this bit of recognition.

CHAPTER 11

CLASSIC CARE

A Guide to Maintenance & Repair

FRAILEST OF ALL CRAFTS IN WHICH FRAIL MAN EVER SET FORTH UPON THE WATERS OF THE WORLD, THE CANOE IS YET THE ONE NEAREST PERFECTION.

—Marlow Shaw

Store the canoe where it is dry, level and supported on a padded rack.

"The first thing to find out about a boat is her age," wrote Charles Hallock in the 1877 *The Sportsman's Gazeteer and General Guide*. "Five years is about as old as is desirable under ordinary circumstances, as boats (as they are built nowadays) begin to get old when they pass this age." Some canoes built in Hallock's day are still in active service today, long past their predicted prime. They have survived partly because of the way they were built but mostly because they have been intelligently used, properly stored and carefully maintained.

Woodstrip/epoxy construction eliminates many of the traditional problems associated with wood, but your canoe still requires maintenance.

Mostly, it demands good common sense—storing it so that moisture does not contaminate the non-epoxied trim, transporting it carefully and keeping the varnish intact. You may need to repair the scratches and scrapes that are an inevitable part of paddling, but since you built this craft, no repair is beyond your skills.

STORAGE

For a long life, this canoe should be stored with the same respect for the work that went into shaping those fair curves. Keep it dry, keep it level, and keep any weight off it. Store the boat indoors during the winter, if possible, slung from the boathouse rafters or supported on a cradle. More than one owner of a woodstrip/epoxy canoe admits that his pride and joy spends the frozen months in a place of honor in the house, to be admired over the winter like a piece of fine furniture. But if outdoor storage is unavoidable, at least be sure that the canoe is covered and protected against

Use a three-point system to tie the canoe to front and back bumpers.

Winch canoe to racks with stevedore's knots. Pad ropes to protect finish.

the weight of heavy snow and falling trees.

In summer, always store the canoe out of the sun. If you are going to cover it with a tarp, be sure there is adequate air circulation around the hull to eliminate any heat or moisture buildup. And if you leave it outside, tie the canoe down so that it does not blow away.

Each time the canoe is removed from the water, rinse any sand out of the inside and wipe it down with a chamois inside and out. Store the canoe upside down, making sure no water is lying inside the decks.

It is best to build a permanent rack on the wall of the garage or boathouse, padding it to preserve the gunwale finish, but if you must leave it overturned on the ground, set spacers under each stem and under the gunwales to keep the canoe away from ground moisture that could damage the trim.

CAR-TOPPING

The monocoque hull is much tougher than most people think, but bouncing off a car onto an asphalt highway at 60 miles per hour is an unnecessary test of endurance. Learning proper "car-topping" techniques will not only prevent such disasters but save the finish on your canoe from minor abrasions caused by rubbing ropes.

Fasten roof racks securely to the vehicle, padding them with carpet to protect the gunwales. Tie the canoe to both racks using stevedore's knots to winch the boat tightly against them.

Fasten the canoe to the front and back bumpers of the car in a three-point system that has ropes running from each end of the canoe to both sides of each bumper. The lines should be tight and should angle toward the midsection of the canoe, tied to the scuppers or thwarts, to counteract wind force at the front and braking force at the back, as well as to minimize the effect of crosswinds.

ROUTINE MAINTENANCE

The three to four coats of varnish you applied have a life span of at least three years on the outside and four to five years on the inside under average conditions, but the longevity of your boat will be extended considerably, with less effort, if you inspect it regularly. Check the bottom of the hull for scratches, and the gunwales for wear from car racks or rubbing paddles. Be sure that the screws in the stem band and the nuts on the seats and thwarts are tight.

The frequency of maintenance will depend on the amount of use and the amount of exposure that the canoe is subjected to. Touch up scratches as soon as they appear: when the finish starts to look scruffy from patching, re-varnish the hull.

The old varnish need not be

stripped off to revive the canoe's finish. Lightly wet-sand the hull and trim with 220-grit sandpaper to smooth the surface, removing the seats and thwarts to sand the inside. Clean off the hull with a solvent, wipe with a tack cloth, and apply fresh varnish using the same brand.

CARE IN THE WATER

Having built the canoe, you will undoubtedly have an acute interest in how it is used.

For some, the creative process fosters an overprotectiveness toward their craft: "It is so beautiful that I have not yet launched it," reports one builder.

For others, it is a release: "Building a canoe sets you free to really use it, knowing that if you do some damage, you can fix it."

As a paddler, you can put complete confidence in the boat you have built. A woodstrip/epoxy canoe will withstand as much hard use as a canoe built with any other construction technique—maybe more.

Anything will sustain damage when taken out of the medium in which it was designed to function. Avoid rocks and floating obstructions when possible. Be careful when hauling the canoe up on the beach, and do not step into the hull unless it is resting on its cushion of water.

Ultimately, because scratches on the surface, deep cuts and even holes are easily repaired, the care

you take in the water depends on your willingness to deal with the consequences of abuse.

REPAIR

Sand off stain and revarnish.

Very few of the hundreds of Bear Mountain canoes built to date have ever sustained more than superficial damage, despite rigorous use. The construction method, combined with the stiffening dome effect of good hull design (i.e., shallow arch, moderate rocker, slight tumblehome), makes these canoes capable of absorbing and distributing incredible stress.

My most challenging repair was the result of an out-of-water accident. A spanking-new canoe, stoutly crated and en route to its new owner, was crushed in a boxcar by two tons of heavy equipment. The crate, a sturdy 1-by-2-inch frame covered with ³⁄₈-inch particleboard, looked as if it had exploded, but the canoe's hull was intact, with only two cracks in the resin. The maple deck was split on one side: the glue joint held, but the hardwood fibers gave way and

the #8 stainless-steel screws were torn in half. Even so, this canoe was so successfully restored that it is difficult to imagine any stress that could push a woodstrip/epoxy canoe past the point of repair.

LOOSE SCREWS

If a screw is ripped out of the stem band, first plug the hole with a little piece of cedar dipped in epoxy glue. When you twist in a new screw, the fibers of the cedar will spread with the screw action, sealing out moisture.

SCRATCHES IN THE VARNISH

Minor surface wear most often appears on the outside of the hull bottom from bumping rocks, on the inside hull from the abrasive action of sand and sharp-edged gear and on the gunwales from paddles and unpadded car racks.

On the hull, clean the scratches, and flow in a little varnish with a fine brush. On the gunwales, if the varnish is worn down to bare wood, repair the damage as soon as possible. If the wood has turned gray with exposure, sand down to

Minor surface wear.

a fresh color, wet the wood to raise the fibers and fine-sand again.

To restore discolored wood to its natural hue, swab with a concentrated solution of oxalic acid. Varnish with a product compatible with the original, building in layers.

SCRATCHES IN THE SHEATHING

A very sharp rock under considerable force might gouge a deep scratch into the resin, down to the glass but not the wood. To repair a resin scratch, sand the epoxy (using 80-grit sandpaper) about 1 inch in all directions around the damage, feathering out gradually.

Sand deep scratches, then patch.

Do not sand deep enough to expose the wood. Protect the varnish on the rest of the canoe by masking off the area to be patched before you start to sand.

Cut a patch of fiberglass to cover the scratch, overlapping the feathered edge of the old cloth. Brush epoxy on the sanded surface, lay in the patch, and wet it out with a little more resin.

For a smooth one-coat finish,

Clean superficial scratches well, and flow in varnish with a fine brush.

Deep scratches to the wood core require a cloth patch and fresh epoxy.

lay a piece of waxed paper over the repair, and squeegee, working out from the center to remove excess air and resin. Let the patch cure, then peel off the waxed paper. If you have been feathering and squeegeeing carefully, the patch will be smooth and at the same level and density as the original sheath. If not, feather the edges, and brush on another coat of resin.

Sand the cured epoxy, and build up the varnish over the patch to match the hull. For an invisible repair, sand the entire hull lightly, and brush on a coat of varnish.

SCRATCHES TO WOOD CORE

Begin as above, but sand down to the wood. Remove any loose fibers, then fill the scratch with epoxy filler. Be sure to use fine sanding dust that is a lighter color than the planking so that they will match when set up.

Sand level with 80-grit sandpaper, wet down, and fine-sand with 120-grit. If you neglect the wetting and second sanding, the patch will show up darker than the original planking. Proceed as above, laying in cloth, epoxy, then varnish.

DAMAGE FROM A BLOW

A blow from a rounded object may cause a slight dimple or dent that you can feel with your hand along the outside of the hull. If there are no other signs, there is likely no damage needing repair.

If the sheath goes white in one spot, it indicates that the cloth stretched slightly inside the resin. If the surface of the varnish is intact, the epoxy layer itself is probably unharmed and the glass unbroken. The hull is still waterproof, and repairs can wait until the end of the season; then restore as described above.

The blow may crack the glass and resin, especially along the grain of the wood on the side of the hull opposite the blow, as damage is more likely to occur where the hull lets go in tension than where it is hit. If a crack is discovered, treat as a scratch in the sheathing.

After a violent blow to the hull, if there are no obvious breaks in the sheath, check for separation within the wood strips, the weakest link in the monocoque structure. The fibers themselves may shear apart when the hull layers are stretched out of alignment.

Press on the spot and tap it. If there is movement, if it feels spongy or if you hear a dulling of the normal wood resonance, the area needs repair. If the sheath is still watertight, there is no rush, though the process becomes complicated if moisture seeps in.

To repair the wood without disturbing the sheath, drill a 1/8-inch hole into the high side of the damaged spot and mask off the area. With a syringe, squirt heated resin into the void. Warm the hull with a hot-air gun so that the resin will be as runny as possible, seeping into all the cracks. When cured, sand smooth and varnish.

If the blow breaks the resin and glass and cracks a plank, sand down to the wood. Take out any loose fibers, and try to fit the plank back together. If it can still be forced into position, spread the break, coat all surfaces with

To repair delamination, sand back to wood and patch fiberglass.

epoxy glue and press the plank back into shape. Secure the strip into position with duct tape. It is important to retain the curvature of the original core.

If the break is at a difficult point and the repair wants to pop out, tie ropes around the hull and force wedges between the ropes and the glued plank to hold it firm as

it sets. When the epoxy has cured, sand the wood smooth, wet to raise the fibers and sand again. Finish as for a scratch.

Even though it is almost inconceivable that a hull could be so badly damaged that the wood itself becomes irreparable, it would still be readily fixable. First, you remove the damaged section so that there is only sound wood around the perimeter of the hole. (Avoid the temptation to cut out a square or a rectangle, and aim for a more irregular shape that will produce a stronger bond and be less obvious.)

Feather the edges of the fiberglass and epoxy in preparation for patching, then take several wooden strips and begin planking over top of the hole on the outside of the hull (being careful to align the edges of the new planking with that of the rest of the hull), extending these new strips well over the hole onto the solid hull. After gluing enough repair strips together to cover the hole, tape the oversize patch to the hull and let the glue dry.

Once the glue has dried, you have the basis of a patch that, while bigger than the actual puncture, has been constructed to take the same curve as the hull. To give this custom patch extra strength, add some fiberglass cloth and one coat of epoxy to it and allow to dry. When it has set, trace the shape of the hole from inside the hull so that you can remove the patch from the hull and cut it to shape.

Then set the patch into the hole.

Sand and lay up the patch on the inside, extending the glass over the cut edges. On the outside, lay a strip of cloth around the perimeter of the patch to bond the repair to the original hull. Continue building up the epoxy to the same thickness and density as the original, and finish as above.

If you are unable to find matching wood strips for the repair (you may wish to save a few pieces from the original batch for just such an unlikely occasion), make the best of a bad situation by cutting the damage out in a design shape and fill it with contrasting wood. It may look as if you did the inlay as an artistic fillip.

CHAPTER 12

DIFFERENT STROKES

Making Your Own Paddle

EVERY MAN MUST PADDLE HIS OWN CANOE.

—*Idiom*

The saying quoted above is, not surprisingly, Canadian in origin. It stems, many believe, from a remark made by "Indian" in the novel *The Settlers in Canada: Written for Young People*, published in 1844 by Captain Frederick Marryat, a sea captain and a wildly popular writer of the day. The full quote, for the record, is: "Now, I think that it much better that, as we all go along together, that every man paddle his own canoe. That my thought."

Wise words. Paddling one's own canoe has come to reflect the essence of personal responsibility. The inspiration for the idiom bears this out. Little satisfies, empowers or indicates one's place in the world as much as sitting in the stern of a canoe and paddling quietly through water, which brings you so close to the sunfish and the lily pads and the great blue herons that you understand how intimately you are part of the living whole.

The experience becomes even more satisfying, of course, when the boat is of your own making. If the paddle, too, is not only in your hand but of it, the experience comes close to being complete.

Paddle-making requires a minimum of skill and equipment and creates a minimum of mess. In many ways, it makes sense to carve the paddle first, then build the boat, since some of the basic tools and techniques used in boatbuilding are used here too. You'll get to know how to use cutting tools and shaping tools, such as the block plane, spokeshave and cabinet scraper. You'll become proficient in maintaining a keen edge on your tools, and you'll get a feel for how wood responds to shaping.

If you have already built a boat, carving a paddle will seem a breeze, a relaxing weekend project. And unlike the canoe, which most people store out of sight in the boathouse or garage, you can keep the paddle close by, displayed in the house or the office as a reminder of the satisfaction that comes from making things with your own hands.

Although it is a relatively simple project, there is lots of room for creative license as you design a paddle specifically for your body and for your canoeing needs. Aside from the fun and satisfaction that comes from making your own paddle, there are economic benefits as well. For the price of a handmade paddle, you can buy a good piece of wood, a block plane and a spokeshave and make it yourself, getting exactly what you want in the bargain.

The necessary tools and materials are listed below. The basic technique assumes that the carver has access to a power jigsaw or a band saw, as well as a plane, spokeshave and scraper.

Tools
jigsaw or band saw
Two 3-inch clamps
clamp pads
bench vise (optional)
cabinet scrapers (or shaped
    paint scraper)
smoothing plane (optional)
block plane
spokeshave
sandpaper (#80, #120, #220)

MAKING A PATTERN FROM AN EXISTING PADDLE

Once you have found a paddle with the shape and features you are looking for, use it to prepare a pattern. As well as reproducing the design features you like, you will be able to adjust the size, combine blade and grip styles and smooth out any irregularities in the original.

The material for the pattern can be any thin solid wood: plywood, hardboard, poster board or heavy paper. Choose something that cuts accurately and is stiff enough to hold its shape for tracing. Paper is easier to cut, but wood will be a permanent reference, and you will be able to clean up a less-than-perfect cut with a sanding block.

Begin your pattern by drawing a centerline slightly longer than the paddle. Before tracing the shape, lay out the shaft with a straightedge, as well as the parameters of the blade you have decided on. Place the paddle on the pattern, and center it by eye. If the width is being adjusted, move the paddle around until one side is where you want it, then trace. Use a flexible batten to fair the line.

You could stop right here and cut out half the pattern, since the shape will be traced onto the paddle blank from one side of the pattern only (thereby assuring that the paddle will be symmetrical).

If you are curious and want to see what the whole paddle will look like, transfer the shape to the other side of the centerline as well. To do this, draw reference lines perpendicular to the centerline. The lines should be close enough together that the points plotted on these lines will reproduce the shape when a batten is bent around them. Obviously, they would be closer together at the grip than along a gentle curve on the side of the blade.

Use dividers or a ruler to transfer the distances across the centerline. Or, if you want to keep it simple, try a tick strip. This most ancient of measuring devices is a reliable means of transferring measurements. To pick up the distance from the centerline, lay a piece of paper or wood along the perpendicular line and make a tick mark for the centerline and one for the edge of the paddle shape. After all the points are plotted by whatever method, join the points with a batten to complete the pattern. ❯

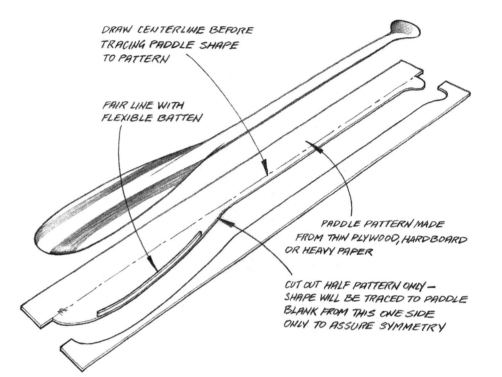

DRAW CENTERLINE BEFORE TRACING PADDLE SHAPE TO PATTERN

FAIR LINE WITH FLEXIBLE BATTEN

PADDLE PATTERN MADE FROM THIN PLYWOOD, HARDBOARD OR HEAVY PAPER

CUT OUT HALF PATTERN ONLY — SHAPE WILL BE TRACED TO PADDLE BLANK FROM THIS ONE SIDE ONLY TO ASSURE SYMMETRY

Paddles can have a variety of blade shapes, shaft lengths and grip styles.

varnish brush
screw eye or hook

Materials
wood plank (minimum 1¼ inches
    thick by 6 inches wide)
varnish

Safety
Review the precautions for shaping wood (page 137) and
for varnishing (page 176).

PADDLE DESIGN

Experts offer a range of opinions about the ideal size and blade shape of a paddle. You may have ideas of your own, or you may know the folk wisdom that a paddle should be long enough to reach from the floor to somewhere between the chin and nose.

Such guidelines can be helpful, but keep in mind that the shape of the blade as well as the length and width of the shaft and the style of the grip all depend on variables such as the style of hull you are paddling and where and how you prefer to sit (or kneel). For instance, solo paddling typically requires a shorter paddle than tandem paddling with a person at both bow and stern.

The style of the paddle also depends on where you intend to go. Paddles designed for shallow water and for whitewater, for example, usually require laminated blades to achieve the extra width and durability required for those conditions.

Ultimately, the size and style of your paddle should be determined by your own particular needs and preferences. To simplify the matter, most first-time carvers opt for either the beaver-tail or the otter-tail style, because both designs can be carved from a single plank of dimensional lumber.

However, you don't have to feel limited to these two choices. The best way to decide what you are going to carve is to try out several existing paddles and then reproduce what works best for you (see Making a Pattern From an Existing Paddle, facing page). It is always important to have confidence in the design you choose before you invest the time and effort.

Don't worry if you are a novice: the style of the paddle has little to do with the skill required to make it. Carving techniques are pretty much the same no matter what the paddle shape. For more experienced woodworkers, skill level will come into play in the way details are developed.

CHOOSING THE WOOD

Some canoebuilders, outfitters and sport or paddle specialty shops occasionally sell a paddle "blank" already cut from a suitable piece of wood. In this case, all that remains to be done is the shaping and smoothing.

If, however, you prefer to start from scratch, you'll need to find a suitable clear board. From the wide variety of woods that are available, choose your species for

Laminating a Paddle Blank

If you are unable to locate a suitable ⁵⁄₄-inch (1¼-inch) board, two or more pieces can be glued together with epoxy glue to make up the blank. There are several ways of increasing the thickness and width that will make the best of available material.

The simplest method (top) is to glue two ⁵⁄₈-inch-thick planks together. This puts the glue line in the middle, where it won't show and there is no chance of the glue line emerging as the paddle is shaped.

It may be simpler to begin with a dressed ¾-inch board, cut to shape and built up by gluing small pieces on both sides where needed (middle). This will require a ¼-inch strip on both sides of the shaft and little blocks to fill out the grip. This approach will use up some of the offcuts, save some planing on the blade and allow you to combine wood for color and to engineer the performance of the paddle.

Or take contrasting color one step further (bottom). Begin with a 1¼-by-1¼-inch shaft that runs the full length of the paddle, and glue the blade and grip up from as many pieces as you like. By making the shaft from two pieces of ⁵⁄₈ inch by 1¼ inches, a straight shaft can be made from two curved pieces by clamping up with the curves working against each other.

You can engineer the responsiveness of the shaft through the choice of materials and the way they are combined. Save weight by combining softwood (cedar, basswood, pine) in the middle with hardwood (ash, oak, cherry) pieces on the outside for strength and stiffness. Or make a more flexible shaft by placing the hardwood in the middle and the less dense softwood on the outside.

One disadvantage of a laminated paddle is the problem of shaping. The grain will always be going in the opposite direction somewhere, and this will make it impossible to cut gracefully in either direction without tearing out splinters. All you can do is keep your tools sharp and switch to the scraper before final shaping. The scraper does a good job of working against the grain without tearing out slivers and gets the surface to a point easily finished with a sanding block. (This also works for wild grain such as fiddleback or bird's-eye maple.) ◗

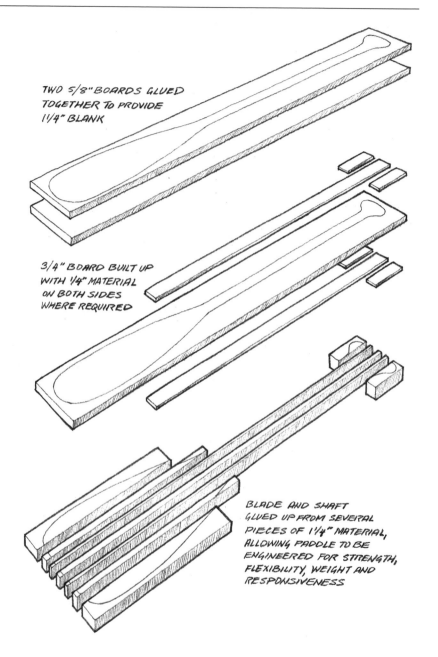

TWO 5/8" BOARDS GLUED TOGETHER TO PROVIDE 1 1/4" BLANK

3/4" BOARD BUILT UP WITH 1/4" MATERIAL ON BOTH SIDES WHERE REQUIRED

BLADE AND SHAFT GLUED UP FROM SEVERAL PIECES OF 1 1/4" MATERIAL, ALLOWING PADDLE TO BE ENGINEERED FOR STRENGTH, FLEXIBILITY, WEIGHT AND RESPONSIVENESS

its beauty and workability as well as for durability, fiber strength and weight. Cherry, ash and soft maple

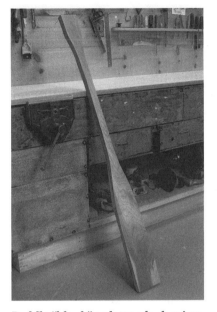

Paddle "blank" only needs shaping.

are the most suitable, but poplar, basswood, cedar and mahogany of various kinds will also work.

In general, hardwoods are strong and heavy. To reduce weight and increase flexibility, hardwood can be thinned down to a ⅛-inch blade without sacrificing strength. The trade-off is that hardwoods are more difficult to shape with hand tools. A cabinet scraper does a fairly good job of smoothing a hardwood, even one with a wild grain.

Softwoods are easier to work with hand tools, especially if the grain is straight, but these species

Lay the pattern on the board to check for grain direction and knots.

generally lack the durability and fiber strength of the hardwoods.

You'll need an air- or kiln-dried board 1¼ inches thick and at least 6 inches wide, depending on the blade pattern you've picked. As you make your selection, try to visualize the paddle that might be buried in that piece of wood.

Have your pattern (or the paddle you intend to reproduce) with

you when you buy your wood. Lay the pattern on the board, and look closely at the direction of the grain and where the knots and defects are. Look for grain that runs straight along the entire length of what will be the shaft. If the grain runs off at an angle or runs across the shaft, there is a good chance the paddle will break under a load.

Knots will cause problems at

the edge of the blade or anywhere on the shaft except perhaps in the grip, and even then, you can only have knots in the grip or in the center area of the blade if those knots are good and tight. Knots produce a swirling grain that radiates outward and can make shaping by hand a challenge.

If you can find only narrow, thin or poor-quality wood, all is not lost. It is possible to laminate wood together to create your paddle blank. Laminating also allows you to combine the natural properties of hardwoods and softwoods, creating your own personal ideal balance of weight, flexibility and durability (see Laminating a Paddle Blank, page 190).

GETTING READY

You don't need a fully equipped workshop to make a paddle. A workbench provides a good working surface, but a sturdy table is just as good. All you need is some place to clamp the paddle blank so that it won't move around as you work. A vise is handy for some cuts, but it is not essential.

Steps in Making a Paddle

- Mark paddle shape on wood plank.
- Cut to shape and clean up profile.
- Draw reference line on edge of paddle blank.
- Taper one face of blade from the shaft end to the tip.
- Shape from centerline (thickest) to ¼-inch reference line at blade edge.
- Refine blade shape.
- Sand blade with #80-grit sandpaper.
- Repeat for other face of blade.
- Shape the grip.
- Shape the shaft.
- Finish-sand entire paddle.
- Finish wood with varnish or oil.

You'll need a jigsaw or a band saw to cut out the paddle blank according to your pattern. The blank is then roughly shaped. Several tools can be used for this stage of shaping. Walter Walker roughs out the blade freehand on a band saw. If you are experienced with a band saw, you can do this too, provided you use extreme caution and care.

Old-time production paddlemakers used a table saw to roughly shape the blade. This skirts the far side of safety and is not recommended. An electric plane, on the other hand, is fast, relatively safe and not too hard to control on this sort of shape.

Hand tools work extremely well and are satisfying to use as well as efficient. Use your largest, sharpest plane: the weight of it adds momentum, pushing the blade through the wood as it takes a thick bite. The long sole is intended to keep the cut straight, but that is of secondary importance at this initial shaping, since the real goal is to remove material as quickly as possible.

The block plane or spokeshave is the most common tool for the casual paddle-maker. Of the two, the block plane is preferable for rough-shaping the blade. It offers the best control, taking bites small enough that the process doesn't get away from you. Also, the sole of the plane helps to keep waves out of the work. Wax the sole with paraffin so that you feel the blade

Before tracing the pattern (foreground), draw a centerline on the wood.

cutting the wood rather than the drag created by friction between the two surfaces.

The spokeshave will be used to fine-tune the shape, adding the slight concave hollows on either side of the blade.

Edge tools work most safely and efficiently when they are kept sharp. This will be especially true if you are working with a hardwood or a difficult grain (such as the end grain of the handgrip). Your tools will perform like an extension of your hands if they are maintained properly and the cutting edge is kept razor-sharp.

Chattering of the plane or spokeshave can be a sign to stop and check the edge of the tool. It may be time to resharpen, although

chattering can also be caused by working the grain in the wrong direction or by a lot of friction of the sole against the work surface.

MARKING OUT THE PADDLE

With the wood plank resting on a stable work surface, lay the pattern in position so that all the decisions you made about grain direction and knots are taken into account. Make the best of the wood you've chosen, checking the back as well for defects within the paddle outline.

Begin by marking a centerline on the wood at what will be the grip end of the paddle and again at the tip of the blade. Use a straightedge to connect these lines, then line up the centerline

Correct irregularities in paddle blank with spokeshave or block plane.

Use tri-square set to draw thickness centerline all around paddle edge.

of the pattern over the centerline drawn on the wood, and tape the pattern in place.

Trace one half of the paddle, then flip the pattern over and trace the same profile on the opposite side of the centerline, producing a perfectly symmetrical outline. (Use carbon paper, as described on page 94, or cut out the whole pattern, not just half.)

CUTTING THE PADDLE BLANK

Use a band saw or a jigsaw to cut the paddle blank to shape. The more accurately you can do this, the less hand shaping will be required to clean up the profile.

Cut to the outside of the line,

trying to split the line so that half remains as a reference. You will have better control with a sharp blade; a dull one will wander and burn the wood. If using a jigsaw to make the cut, be sure the cut remains at right angles to the wood.

After cutting, hold the blank up to the light and check the profile. This outside edge will become a reference for the entire shaping process, so if there are any irregularities, correct them now with a spokeshave and/or block plane.

MARKING REFERENCE LINES

When the profile is clean and accurate, use a marking gauge or a tri-square set to half the thickness

of the blank and draw a thickness centerline all the way around the edge of the paddle. Use a ballpoint pen to make a dark impression in the wood.

After establishing the thickness centerline, draw two more lines around the blade, one on either side of the centerline, parallel to it and $\frac{1}{8}$ inch away, as shown. These two lines define the $\frac{1}{4}$-inch leading edge of the blade. The center of the blade will be shaped to this $\frac{1}{4}$-inch edge.

If, despite your best efforts, it turns out that the plank has a twist to it, lay the paddle blank flat on the table with a weight on the shaft to hold this part steady. Find a block equal to half the thickness of the blank at the shaft. Hold the

tip of a ballpoint pen to the edge of the block, and guide it around the perimeter of the blade, drawing an accurate centerline.

Draw the side profile of the grip.

At the opposite end of the board, draw the side profile of the grip, as shown.

Now transfer the centerline on the top face of the paddle to the back side. Use a square to project the line across the thickness of the blank at both ends, then use a straightedge to connect the marks.

Mark the profile of the shaft where it tapers and then curves out again to form the grip. This is easiest if you simply mark where the taper begins and ends and then connect the marks by eye.

THE SHAPING SCHEDULE

If you consider the process as a series of defined steps, you'll see that there is no magic to shaping a symmetrical, balanced paddle.

The order of the steps is determined by the need to securely hold the paddle without damaging it. During the shaping of the blade and grip, the paddle can be clamped at the shaft, which is a square stock, easily protected with clamping pads.

Since it involves removing the most material, the blade is shaped first and the grip is shaped next. The shaft, which requires the least shaping, is done last.

ROUGHING OUT THE BLADE SHAPE

The blade is shaped one face at a time, and on each face, one half at a time. The object is to reach a shape that is repeatable from one half to the other and then to the back side too.

In general, the wood has to be roughly tapered from its full thickness at the centerline to the ¼-inch edge all around the blade.

Clamp the paddle at the shaft while the blade is shaped.

Accomplishing this involves removing all the wood that interferes with a straightedge laid from the centerline to the edge line.

Once the shape is roughed out using the straightedge as a guide, the final shape is refined by eye and by feel. The principle here is to remove as much wood as pos-sible without compromising the necessary strength of the paddle.

To keep the paddle blank from moving around during the roughing-out process, use a C-clamp or short bar clamp to hold the shaft securely to the bench. Position the blank so that it lies parallel to and flush with the edge of the table or workbench. If you are working with softwood, protect the shaft with a clamp pad.

To begin the roughing out, taper the blade from its full thickness where it meets the shaft to the top line drawn on the edge of the blank. The object is to remove a large amount of material in a safe but fairly aggressive manner.

To accommodate the direction of the grain, work the plane from the end of the shaft toward the tip of the blade. Begin by making short passes over the area where most of the material is to be removed. This will set up the desired angle early on in the shaping process.

Once this angle is set up, it is a simple matter of bringing the cut straight down, stopping when you have shaped down to the reference line at the edge. If one end is taken down before the other, there is a good chance you will go past the line when other areas are being shaped. Check your progress from time to time with a straightedge, laying it from the centerline to the edge.

Redraw the centerline on

Begin by tapering the length of the blade from shaft to tip with a block plane, *top*, then redraw the centerline, *above*.

the blade. (It was carved away when the blade was tapered.) Now shape the blade from the center-line out to the ¼-inch mark all around the blade edge.

The blade will be flat at the

tip, with the shape changing to a slight V-shape where it becomes the shaft. As you work to create this shape, check for a straight line from reference line to reference line with the side of the plane or with a short straightedge.

When one face of the blade has been worked, turn it over and repeat the process on the other side. Support the shaped face of the blade with a soft wood block or wedge so that it doesn't bend down as the top surface is worked. You don't want to damage the surface or break the blade you've just worked hard to shape.

REFINING THE BLADE SHAPE

This step involves freehand shaping that removes material past the reference lines. The object is to remove any remaining super-

Shape from centerline to paddle edge, *top*, checking the angle with a straightedge, *middle*. Turn over and shape other side.

With spokeshave or scraper, refine blade shape, creating center spine.

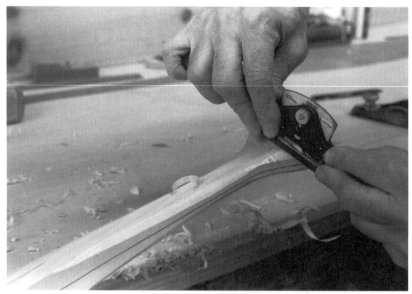

With shaft clamped securely, shape grip using spokeshave.

ficial wood, as well as to create design details, if desired.

If you want to leave some wood to add strength and stiffness to the paddle, create a slight "spine" down the middle of the blade. The shape of the shaft is carried into the blade and gradually feathers to nothing before reaching the tip.

The area between the centerline and the edge of the blade will be concave. This is shaped with a spokeshave, working at a diagonal out from the centerline. Hold the spokeshave at a skewed angle to reduce the width of the blade presented to the wood. This will allow the straight blade to work in the concave shape.

If a more distinct ridge is desired, work past the spokeshave's

concave shape with a combination of gouge, round rasp, scraper and sanding block.

For a lightweight hardwood paddle, you can reduce the ¼-inch thickness around the edge to about ⅛ inch. Use your judgment as to how thin to make the wood. This will depend on the strength of the species, the person who will be using the paddle, the desired flexibility of the paddle, and so on.

After shaping the blade to your satisfaction with cutting tools, remove any cutting marks by going over the surface with a sharpened cabinet scraper, then finish with 80-grit sandpaper on a firm sanding block. There is no point in fine-sanding beyond 80-grit at this

stage: the surface will be subjected to quite a bit of handling before shaping is complete.

SHAPING THE GRIP

Clamp the shaft of the paddle blank so that the grip hangs over the end of the table or workbench.

Shape the profiles of the grip first (as seen from the side and the top). It will be easy to see the shape if the corners are sharp. When you are sure that the grip is symmetrical, round the corners by eye and by feel.

Use a spokeshave for this job. Be aware of changing directions in the grain. If the tool is sharp but is not cutting the wood cleanly, it is working against the grain somewhat, so change direction.

A round rasp is handy for doing the final shaping of the grip after the bulk of the material has been removed with the spokeshave.

As the final step in shaping the grip, sand with 80-grit sandpaper.

SHAPING THE SHAFT

At this point, clamping gets awkward, because all of the paddle except for the shaft has been carefully shaped and sanded. As a result, the clamp has to be fixed to a finished part of the paddle. To keep from marring the finish, generously pad all clamping points on the grip and blade.

Secure the paddle with clamps at the edge of your bench or in a vise. If you use a vise, you will probably need some clamps as

Pad and clamp blade in vise before shaping shaft with block plane.

For paddles, boiled linseed oil is an alternative to varnish.

To shape shaft, draw reference lines dividing square into octagon.

well. Place the blade of the paddle in the vise, then clamp supports underneath it so that it won't split when you push down on the shaft with your plane. Be sure to pad the jaws of the vise and the clamps so that you don't crush the wood fibers of the finished areas. And never clamp right at the very tip of the paddle if you can avoid it.

Before beginning to shape the shaft, work out the measurements to transform the square shaft into a rounded shaft. Draw reference lines that will divide the square into an octagon, as shown.

Shape to these lines. The block plane is the tool of choice for this job. A plane will keep the shaft straight; it will be difficult to prevent waves if a spokeshave is used.

Dress off the corners of the octagonal shaft by eye to produce a 16-sided shaft. Then move from the 16-sided shape to a round or an oval, shaping by eye.

Take up your spokeshave to blend the shaft into both the handgrip area and the blade. Work out remaining irregularities using the spokeshave and sandpaper.

Finally, remove the tool marks using sandpaper, beginning with a back-and-forth shoe-shining motion and progressing to sandpaper wrapped around the shaft to produce a fine, smooth finish.

FINISH-SANDING THE PADDLE

Dampen the surface of the wood with warm water to raise any crushed fibers or dents in

it. Sand with 120-grit sandpaper until smooth. It is a good idea to use a firm block when finish-sanding the blade.

Consider repeating this step, dampening the wood and sanding a second time, if the surface has been abused or if your paddle is made of a wood such as cherry or mahogany. Sand with 180-grit or 220-grit sandpaper in the direction of the grain.

VARNISHING THE PADDLE

Like any wood that will be exposed to both water and sunlight, a paddle must be well protected. Most paddles are varnished, using the same routine as was followed to finish the trim on the canoe (see pages 175 to 177).

Install a small eye hook at the top of the grip so that you can hang the paddle while it is drying.

Instead of varnish, you might consider oiling the shaft with boiled linseed oil or teak oil: according to some paddlers, oil reduces blisters.

True satisfaction: paddling your own canoe with a hand-carved paddle.

PLANS

CANOE PLANS

Bear Mountain Boat Shop
P.O. Box 191
Peterborough, ON K9J 6Y8
(705) 740-0470
(877) 392-8880 (toll-free)
www.bearmountainboats.com

The Canoe and Paddle Store/
Loon Canoes
Moenchstrasse 22A
70191 Stuttgart
Germany
(711) 256-9365

Databoat International
1917 West 4th Avenue
Suite 23
Vancouver, BC V6J 1M7
(800) 782-7218
www.databoat.com

Feather Canoes
1705 Andrea Place
Sarasota, FL 34235
(941) 355-6736

Hironori Nagase
813 Higashi-Inbe
Matsue, 6900036
Japan
81-852-33-2673

M.U.H. Von Der Linden GmbH
WeftstraBe 12-14
D-46483 Wesel/Rhein
Germany
281-22046

WEST SYSTEM™ Norge As
Gjerdrumsvei 12
Oslo, 0486
Norway
22-23-3500

WoodenBoat Store
P.O. Box 78
Brooklin, ME 04616
(800) 273-7447

CANOE SAILS AND SAIL PLANS

Addiction Sailmakers
1 Merrill Crest Drive
Madison, WI 53705
(608) 233-3223
Sails and plans for traditional and
contemporary canoes. Watch for
Todd Bradshaw's book on canoe
sail rigs published by WoodenBoat
Books—everything you need to
know about outfitting a canoe for
sailing, with dynamic illustrations.

Balogh Sail Designs
2188 Laconia Road
Red Oak, VA 23964
(804) 735-8262

GENERAL SUPPLIERS

The following are sources for
canoe materials, accessories, kits
and advice:

Ace Hardware/Shell Lumber
2733 SW 27th Avenue
Coconut Grove, FL 33133
(305) 856-6401
(800) 621-6391

Bear Mountain Boat Shop
P.O. Box 191
Peterborough, ON K9J 6Y8
(705) 740-0470
(877) 392-8880 (toll-free)
www.bearmountainboats.com

Canadian Canoes
7885 Tranmere Drive
Unit #27
Mississauga, ON L5S 1V8
(905) 676-1998
www.canadiancanoes.com

Clark Craft
16 Aqua Lane
Tonawanda, NY 14150
(716) 873-2640

Duck Flat Wooden Boats
230 Flinders Street
Adelaide, 5251
South Australia
88-232-2344

Feather Canoes
1705 Andrea Place
Sarasota, FL 34235
(941) 355-6736

Glen-L Marine
9152 Rosecran Avenue
P.O. Box 1804
Bellflower, CA 90707-1804
(562) 630-6258
www.glen-l.com

Monaghan Lumber Specialties
2129 Davis Road
Peterborough, ON K9J 8G0
(705) 742-9353
www.monaghanlumber.com

Newfound Woodworks
RFD. #2, 67 Danforth Brook Road
Box 850
Bristol, NH 03222
(603) 744-6872
www.newfound.com

Noahs Marine Supplies
54 Six Point Road
Toronto, ON M8Z 2X2
(416) 232-0522
Fax: (800) 894-1783
www.noahsmarine.com

Wooden Canoe Heritage Association
P.O. Box 226
Blue Mountain Lake, NY 12812
www.wcha.org
The Wooden Canoe Heritage Association is a good source of information on canoebuilders/suppliers in your local area. A directory is available online or by mail.

MATERIALS & TOOLS

WOOD

Anchor Hardwoods Inc.
P.O. Box 3577
Wilmington, NC 28406
(910) 392-9888
Fax: (910) 392-9078
www@anchor.wilmington.net

Great Northern Craft
Ian Magrath
Suite #433
1641 Lonsdale Avenue
North Vancouver, BC V7M 2J5
(604) 886-8052

M.L. Condon Company Ltd.
250 Ferris Avenue
White Plains, NY 10603
(914) 946-4111

Edensaw Woods Ltd.
211 Seton Road
Port Townsend, WA 98368
(800) 745-3336
Henderico BV
Groningen, Holland
050 541 3200

Wermlandia Kanoter
Algarden 5
Arvika, S-671-92
Sweden
http://home.bip.net/wermlandia

EPOXY RESIN & FIBERGLASS CLOTH

WEST SYSTEM™ Epoxy and
Episize cloth
For a dealer in your area, contact:
Gougeon Brothers Inc. (USA)
100 Patterson Avenue, P.O. Box 908
Bay City, MI 48707-0908
(517) 684-7286
www.westsystem.com

MAS-Phoenix Resins (USA)
1501 Sherman Avenue
Pennsauken, NJ 08110-0518
(888) 627-3769
www.masepoxies.com

Payne Distributors Inc. (Canada)
1173 North Service Road West
Unit D1
Oakville, ON L6M 2V9
(800) 668-8223

Payne's Marine Supply Inc. (Canada)
1856 Quadra Street
Victoria, BC V8T 4B9
(250) 382-7722

System Three Resins Inc. (USA)
Box 70426
Seattle, WA 98107
(206) 782-7976
www.systemthree.com

Wessex Resins and Adhesives Ltd.
(Europe, Africa and the Middle East
distributors of WEST SYSTEM™)
Cupernham House,
Cupernham Lane
Romsey, Hampshire, S051 7LF
England
44-1-794-521-111
www.wessex-resins.com

FASTENERS

Jamestown Distributors
Box 348
Jamestown, RI 02835
(800) 423-0030
Fax: (800) 423-0542
www.jamestowndistributors.com

Majestic Fasteners
Box 193
Morris Plains, NJ 07950

CANING SUPPLIES

W.H. Kilby & Co. Ltd.
1840 Davenport Road
Toronto, ON M6N 1B7
(800) 267-5732

H.H. Perkins
10 S. Bradley Road
Woodbridge, CT 06525
(203) 389-9501

SEATS, THWARTS, PADDLES & ACCESSORIES

Cooke Custom Sewing
7290 Stagecoach Trail
Lino Lakes, MN 55014-1899
(651) 784-8777
Canoe covers.

Essex Industries
Pelfisher Road
Mineville, NY 12956
(518) 942-6671
Seats, yokes, backrests, motor mounts, rowing rigs.

Gray Owl Paddles
62 Cowansview Road
Cambridge, ON N1R 7N3
(519) 622-0001
Fax: (519) 622-0723
Laminated and solid-wood paddles.

Mitchell Paddles, Inc.
RD-2, Box 922
Canaan, NH 03741
(603) 523-7004
Fax: (603) 523-7363
Laminated wood single-blade and
bent-shaft paddles.

The Boundary Waters Catalog
Piragis Northwoods Company
105 North Central Avenue
Ely, MN 55731
(800) 223-6565
www.piragis.com
One of the most interesting mail-
order sources of canoeing gear,
books, et cetera, that we have seen.

Sawyer Paddles and Oars
299 Rogue River Parkway
Talent, OR 97540
(541) 535-3606
Laminated wood double- and
single-blade paddles.

Under Cover
P.O. Box 609
Hyannis, MA 02601
Canoe and kayak covers.

TOOL CATALOGS

CMT
310 Mears Boulevard
Oldsmar, FL 34677
(800) 531-5559

Highland Hardware
1045 N. Highland Avenue NE
Atlanta, GA 30306
(800) 241-6748

House of Tools
#100 Mayfield Common NW
Edmonton, AB T5P 4B3
(800) 661-3987
mailorder@houseoftools.com

Japan Woodworker
1731 Clement Avenue
Alameda, CA 94501
(800) 241-6748

Klingspors Sanding Catalogue
Box 3737
Hickory, NC 28603-3737
(800) 228-0000
www.sandingcatalog.com

Lee Valley Tools Ltd.
1090 Morrison Drive
P.O. Box 6295, Stn. J
Ottawa, ON K2H 1C2
(800) 267-8761
www.leevalley.com
Bead-and-cove router bits.

Lee Valley Tools Ltd.
P.O. Box 1780
12 East River Street
Ogdensburg, NY 13669-6780
(800) 267-8735
www.leevalley.com

MLCS
Box 4053
Rydal, PA 19046
(800) 533-9298
www.mlcswoodworking.com

Woodcraft
Box 1686
Parkersburg, WV 26102-1686
(800) 225-1153

Woodworker's Supply
1108 North Glenn Road
Casper, WY 82601
(800) 645-9292

CANOEBUILDING COURSES

Bear Mountain Boat Shop
Box 191
Peterborough, ON K9J 6Y8
(705) 740-0470
(877) 392-8880 (toll-free)
www.bearmountainboats.com

White River Artisans School
2519 Denton Ferry Road
Cotter, AR 72626
(870) 430-5437
www.mtncom.com/artisans

WoodenBoat School
P.O. Box 78
Brooklin, ME 04616
(800) 273-7447
www.woodenboat.com

REFERENCES

HISTORY

*The Old Town Canoe Company:
Our First 100 Years*
by Susan T. Audette
Tillbury House Publishers
Gardiner, ME, 1998

*The Story of the Chestnut Canoe:
150 Years of Canadian Canoe
Building*
by Kenneth Solway
Nimbus Publishing
Halifax, NS, 1997

*Boats and Boating in the
Adirondacks*
by Hallie E. Bond
The Adirondack Museum/
Syracuse University Press, 1995

The Canoe
by Kenneth G. Roberts and
Phillip Shackleton
MacMillan of Canada,
Gage Publishing
Toronto, 1983.

*Fire in the Bones: Bill Mason and
the Candian Canoeing Tradition*
by James Raffan
Harper Collins Publishers Ltd.
Toronto, 1996

*Bark, Skin and Cedar: Exploring
the Canoe in Canadian Experience*
by James Raffan
Harper Collins Publishers Ltd.
Toronto, 1999

*Canoeing North Into the
Unknown: A Record of River
Travel 1874-1974*
by Bruce Hodgins and
Gwyneth Hoyle
Natural Heritage/Natural
History Inc.
Toronto, 1994

*Canexus: The Canoe in
Canadian Culture*
edited by James Raffan and
Bert Horwood
Betelgeuse Books
Toronto,1988

The Canoe in Canadian Cultures
edited by John Jennings, Bruce
Hodgins and Doreen Small
Natural Heritage/Natural
History Inc.
Toronto, 1999

*Idleness, Water and a Canoe:
Reflections on Paddling*
by Jamie Benidickson
University of Toronto Press, 1997

*The Great Canadian Canoe:
History, Plans and Secrets*
by Ted Moores and Robbie Sprules
Boston Mills Press, Erin, 2000

DESIGN

Understanding Boat Designs
by Edward Brewer and Jim Betts
International Marine
Camden, ME, 1980

Yacht Design Explained
by Steve Killing and Douglas Hunter
W.W. Norton & Company
New York, 1998

LOFTING

"Lofting Demystified"
by Greg Rössel
WoodenBoat Magazine
Part 1: Number 110, p. 66
Part 2: Number 111, p. 35
Easy-to-follow instructions with
some great tricks and shortcuts.
Rössel, a master boatbuilder and
teacher, presents this complicated
process as a straightforward system,
without the mystery generally associated with the subject.

Lofting
by Alan Vaitses
Republished by WoodenBoat Books,
Brooklin, ME, 1999
Devoted strictly to the subject of
lofting, Vaitses' very readable text
covers several different hull forms.

"Taking the Lines Off a Boat"
by Barry Thomas with Clark Posten
and Bret Laurent
WoodenBoat Magazine, Number
115, November/December 1993

"On Teaching the Lapstrake Way"
by Simon Watts
WoodenBoat Magazine, Number 115,
November/December 1993

BOATBUILDING

American Small Sailing Craft
by Howard Chapelle
W.W. Norton & Company
New York, 1951
Extensive, detailed instructions for
backyard builders, including 100
plans for sailboats under 40 feet.

Boatbuilding
by Howard Chapelle
W.W. Norton & Company
New York, 1941
Complete handbook of wooden-
boat construction.

Boats, Oars and Rowing
by R.D. Culler
International Marine
Camden, ME
Includes plans for a double-paddle
canoe, sprit-rigging and oar-making.

Building Classic Small Craft
by John Gardner
International Marine
Camden, ME, 1977
Inspiration for builders interested in
the best of small boats of the past.

Building Small Boats
by Greg Rössel
WoodenBoat Books
Brooklin, ME, 1998
Traditional construction for boats
under 25 feet. Good source of information for lofting.

Building a Strip Canoe
by Gil Gilpatrick
DeLorme Publishers
Yarmouth, ME, 1979
Instructions for woodstrip/polyester
resin canoes, including plans for
five models.

Featherweight Boatbuilding
by Henry "Mac" McCarthy
WoodenBoat Books
Brooklin, ME, 1996

*The Gougeon Brothers on Boat
Construction*
Gougeon Brothers, Inc.
Bay City, MI, 1979
Describes the WEST SYSTEM™
of cold-molding in wood.

Kayakcraft
by Ted Moores
WoodenBoat Books
Brooklin, ME, 1999
Fine woodstrip kayak construction,
featuring kayaks designed by
Steve Killing.

*The Stripper's Guide to Canoe
Building*
by David Hazen
Tamal Vista
Larkspur, CA, 1982
One of the first woodstrip/
polyester resin construction man-
uals. Includes plans for several
canoes and kayaks.

SHARPENING

The Complete Guide to Sharpening
by Leonard Lee
Taunton Press, 1995

Sharpening: The Complete Guide
by Jim Kingshott
Distributed by International
Marine Catalog
Camden, ME

FINISHING

*Brightwork: The Art of
Finishing Wood*
by Rebecca J. Wittman
International Marine/McGraw-Hill
Camden, ME

PADDLE-MAKING

The Art of Paddle Carving
Video and plans
Bear Mountain Boat Shop
P.O. Box 191
Peterborough, ON K9J 6Y8
(705) 740-0470
(877) 392-8880 (toll-free)
www.bearmountainboats.com

Building the Maine Guide Canoe
by Jerry Stelmok
International Marine
Camden, ME, 1980
Discusses paddle-making
techniques for single blade.

Sensible Cruising Designs
by L. Francis Herreshoff
International Marine
Camden, ME, 1973
Includes Herreshoff double-blade
paddle design.

SAILING

Building the Maine Guide Canoe
by Jerry Stelmok
International Marine
Camden, ME, 1980
Chapter devoted to rigging a
canoe for sail.

*Sail Your Canoe: How to add sails
to your canoe*
by John Bull
Leicesterer, UK
Cordee, 1989
Project-oriented, with drawings,
measurements, blueprints, et cetera.

POLING

The Basic Essentials of Canoe Poling
by Harry Rock
ICS Books
Merrillville, IN, 1992

MAGAZINES

Boat Design Quarterly
The Woodenboat Store
Box 78
Brooklin, ME 04616

Canoe and Kayak Magazine
10526 NE 68th Street
Box 3146
Kirkland, WA 98083
www.canoekayak.com

Epoxyworks
Gougeon Brothers Inc.
P.O. Box 908
Bay City, MI 48707-0908
www.westsystem.com

Kanawa
P.O. Box 398
446 Main Street W.
Merrickville, ON K0G 1N0
(613) 269-2910
(888) 252-6292
www.crca.ca

River
P.O. Box 1068
Bozeman, MT 59771
(406) 582-5440
www.rivermag.com

Voyageur Magazine
92 Leuty Avenue
Toronto, ON M4E 2R4
(416) 693-5676

WoodenBoat Magazine
P.O. Box 78
Brooklin, ME 04616
(800) 273-7447
www.woodenboat.com

The Whole Paddler's Catalog
edited by Zip Kellogg
International Marine/Ragged
Mountain Press
Camden, Maine, 1997
Sources and commentary on a
wide variety of subjects relating
to paddle sports.

CANOE MUSEUMS

Adirondack Museum
Blue Mountain Lake
New York 12812

Canadian Canoe Museum
910 Monaghan Road
Box 1664
Peterborough, ON K9J 7S4
(705) 748-9153
www.canoemuseum.net

Lake Champlain Maritime Museum
R.R.#3
P.O. Box 4092
Vergennes, VT 05491
(802) 475-2022
www.lcmm.org

The Mariners Museum
Newport News, VA 23606-3759
(757) 596-2222

Mystic Seaport
47 Greenmanville Avenue
P.O. Box 6000
Mystic, CT 06355-0990
(860) 572-0711
www.mysticseaport.org

Peterborough Centennial Museum
and Archives
300 Hunter Street E.
P.O. Box 143
Peterborough, ON K9J 6Y5
(705) 743-5180
www.kawartha.net/~jleonard/
home.htm

Thousand Islands Shipyard Museum
750 Mary Street
Clayton, NY 13624

CANOE ASSOCIATIONS

Canadian Canoe Association
1600 James Naismith Drive, #709
Gloucester, ON K1B 5N4

The Traditional Small Craft
Association
P.O. Box 350
Mystic, CT 06355

Wooden Canoe Heritage Association
P.O. Box 226
Blue Mountain Lake, NY 12812
www.wcha.org

ACKNOWLEDGMENTS

OUR FIRST THANK YOU GOES TO THE MANY BUILDERS OF BEAR MOUNTAIN Boat Shop canoe kits and to the countless backyard boatbuilders whose enthusiasm and persistence inspired the original writing of this book, as well as the second edition.

We appreciate the assistance of the many experts who took an interest in this project and gave us the benefit of their expertise, especially the late Dr. Donald Cameron, canoe historian; the late John Gardner, former Associate Curator of Small Craft at Mystic Seaport; Kirk Whipper and the Kanawa Canoe Museum; Jan Gougeon, one of the developers of the WEST SYSTEM™; the late Bill Mason, author, film-maker and paddler par excellence; the descendants of Daniel Herald, Walter Dean, Thomas Gordon and John Stephenson; amateur builders M.E. Walker and Richard Barlow; veteran canoebuilder Walter Walker; Fred Johnston of the Canadian Canoe Association; and the librarians and archivists who patiently assisted us in our searches.

We are especially grateful to Merilyn Simonds for her assistance in revising the original text; Tracy Read for her skillful editorial direction; Charlotte DuChene for thorough and precise copy-editing; and Ulrike Bender for the elegant redesign.

—Ted Moores

(Unless indicated below, all other photography is © Jennifer Moores and Ted Moores.)

The Bettman Archive, Inc., pages 19, 23, 26
Courtesy Ken Brown, page 15
Centennial Museum, Peterborough, Ontario, pages 174, 180
Michael Cullen, page 207
George Douglas/ Courtesy Kathy Hooke, pages 6, 12
Jim Merrithew, pages 24, 38, 60, 71, 87, 89, 145, 164, 165, 198
Miller Services Ltd., page 16
The Public Archives of Canada, page 20

TED MOORES OPERATES THE BEAR Mountain Boat Shop in the Lakefield/Peterborough area of Ontario with his partner Joan Barrett. In 1972, Ted pioneered the wood-strip/epoxy boatbuilding system for canoes and, since then, has promoted the fine art of wooden-canoe and kayak construction. During the past 25 years, the company has built or restored hundreds of mahogany runabouts, vintage canoes and small water-craft from elegant one-off designs to the fastest C4 and C15 sprint racing canoes on the water. Today, the Bear Mountain Boat Shop specializes in providing quality professional instructions and plans for the casual canoe- and kayak-maker. Ted and Joan are active volunteers for the Canadian Canoe Museum in Peterborough, where they have developed a woodworking and restoration shop and where they continue to document and study the collection. Ted teaches kayak- and canoebuilding classes throughout North America. He is also author of *Kayak-Craft* and, with Robbie Sprules, of *Canoe Barons*, a survey of the key players during the heyday of wooden-canoe manufacturing.